Vital Records of Three Burned Counties

Births, Marriages, and Deaths
of
King and Queen
King William
and
New Kent Counties
Virginia

1680-1860

Therese A. Fisher

HERITAGE BOOKS
2006

HERITAGE BOOKS
AN IMPRINT OF HERITAGE BOOKS, INC.

Books, CDs, and more—Worldwide

For our listing of thousands of titles see our website
at
www.HeritageBooks.com

Published 2006 by
HERITAGE BOOKS, INC.
Publishing Division
65 East Main Street
Westminster, Maryland 21157-5026

International Standard Book Number: 978-0-7884-0336-2

TABLE OF CONTENTS

ABBREVIATIONS USED IN THIS BOOK

CVR COLONIAL VIRGINIA REGISTER compiled by William G. & Mary N.Stanard.
C&P CAVALIERS AND PIONEERS by Nell Marion Nugent
KWH OLD KING WILLIAM HOMES AND FAMILIES by Peyton Neale Clark published 1966 by Regional Publishing Co, Baltimore,MD
KWC KING WILLIAM COUNTY, VA by Elizabeth Ryland 1955 Dietz Press, Richmond, VA
ONKH OLD NEW KENT HOMES
KQC KING AND QUEEN COUNTY, VIRGINIA by Rev. Alfred Bagby originally published in 1908 by Neale Publ.Co. NY
IR Individual Record. Indicates that the information was supplied by an unpublished source.
CTR Charles Talley Marriage register. A minister that covered the area of Hanover, Henrico, King & Queen, King William & New Kent Counties. The register contains marriages recorded by him between 1822-1839. Copies of the register can be found at the Virginia State Library File # 20805.
ML Marriage License. These are the marriage licenses that the minister stated existed at the time of the marriage. Unless otherwise noted, these no longer exist. The county that issued the license follows the abbreviation.
VG Virginia Gazette Colonial newspaper that included the areas of King and Queen, King William & New Kent, among other areas of Virginia. Microfilm copies can be found at the Virginia State Library, Richmond, Va among other Virginia Libraries.
BF Beverly Fleet compiler and author who produced VIRGINIA COLONIAL ABSTRACTS.
VMHB Virginia Magazine of History & Biography
FB Family Bible, many copies of which can be found at either the VA Historical Society or State Archives
BKQCHS Bulletin of the King and Queen County Historical Society copies can be found in the Virginiana Room of the Central Rappahannock Regional Library, Fredericksburg, VA
GN Genealogical Notes from various families. Reliablity of the information in these notes varies from good to fabrication. Most notes can be found in the Virginia State Library and Archives under the last name of the family. In some cases, the GN is followed by the file #
KWD King William County Deed book followed by the book number and page number. Only a few survived the fire.
RA Richmond Argus newspaper
RCC Richmond Commercial Compiler newspaper. This can be found at the Virginia State Library on microfilm.
RCA Richmond Christian Advocate religious newspaper
RE Richmond Enquirer newspaper published in Richmond, VA
RH Religious Herald newspaper

v

RW   Richmond Whig newspaper
VIC   Virginia Independant Chronicle newspaper
VCA   VA COLONIAL ABSTRACTS by Beverley Fleet
VCS   Virginia Conference Sentinel religious newspaper
VHS   Notes located in the files of the Virginia Historical
        Society, Richmond, VA
VBHS   Virginia Baptist Historical Society located at the
        University of Richmond, Richmond, VA
MVG   Magazine of Virginia Genealogy published quarterly
        by the Virginia Genealogical Society. Materials
        have generally been extracted from other sources.
VSA   Virginia State Archives Record followed by the
        microfilm or manuscript number, when available. These
        can be found at the Virginia State Archives, Richmond
VCA   Virginia Christian Advocate newspaper
SAR   Sons of the American Revolution genealogies. These are
        extremely well documented genealogies. Considered
        reliable source of information.
SPPR   St.Peter's Parish Register,New Kent Co.,VA originally
        published by the National Society of Colonial Dames of
        America, Richmond 1905
SMP   Stratton Major Parish Register transcribed by
        C.G.Chamberlayne published by the VA State Library
SMPR   St, Martin's Parish Register. Published.
KQMR   King & Queen Marriage Register available on microfilm
        at the Virginia State Archives, Richmond, VA
KQBP   King and Queen Birth Register available on microfilm
        at the Virginia State Archives, Richmond, VA
MBC   Mattaponi Baptist Church minutes published
EHR   papers of Elizabeth H. Ryland stored and available
        at the Virginia Historical Society, Richmond
WA   Weekly Advertiser weekly newspaper printed in
        Fredericksburg. Microfilmed copies at Central
        Rappahannock Regional Library, Fredericksburg, VA.
CCPR   Christ Church Parish Register, Middlesex County,VA
BP   Blisland Parish Register for New Kent and James City
        Counties. Published.
NKMR   New Kent Marriage Register
KK1   KITH & KIN: VOL.1 compiled by N.M.Barham & M.R.Barham
        1992
KK2   KITH & KIN: VOL.2 compiled by N.M.Barham & M.R.Barham
        1993

bap   baptised (used when that is the only date available)
b.d.   birth date
d.d.   death date
DOM   Date of Marriage
POC   Person of Color
FPOC   Free Person of Color
POR   Place of Residence when residence is stated or when the
        person in stated as being "of" a place.
POB   Place of Birth
POM   Place of Marriage

POD Place of Death
Dr. could mean a physician or a PhD. Usually meant
     physician.
d/o daughter of
s/o son of
w/o wife of
wi/o widow of
gs/o grandson of
br/o brother of
s   single (this just means single at the time of marriage)
S   single (this just means single at the time of marriage)
p.m. previously married; used when the bride was listed as
     "Mrs" or "widow" or there was some indication that a
     previous marriage existed.
(dec) deceased
[sic] this shows the exact spelling or name or term used in
     the original record, no matter how weird it seemed to
     me.

INTRODUCTION

A note about the sources:
As any experienced genealogist will testify, sources come in a wide variety of reliabilities. The sources used for this book are no exception. While I have attempted to use the best sources available, considering the counties involved, the best sources may not fit the definition of a reliable source in any other county.

For example, Beverly Fleet's papers and the VIRGINIA COLONIAL ABSTRACTS which provided a great deal of information on these burned counties, relied heavily in part on the papers of Elizabeth H. Ryland, who also wrote KING WILLIAM COUNTY. While there is much to admire in Fleet's and Ryland's works and while they provide information not available from other sources, there appears to be some speculation in some of their data. While I did not include that which was blatantly speculative, I did include some marginal entries that are possible speculation. In the editing process, I eliminated many of the entries that were speculation; if those entries were later proved using another source, I left the more objective source as the sole entry. In some cases, where one source stated the name or date one way and a secondary source stated it another, I included both entries. My advice to the researcher in such cases is to consult the original sources for each entry and then weigh the evidence to determine which entry is correct.

There are instances where a compiler made a typo (unbelievable as that may seem) and another compiler had the correct entry.

Occasionally, in what appears to be a subjective source, as in a family history or county history, there will be several sources of data, such as family bibles or letters, that may correct what appears to be a more reliable document such as a newspaper notice. While this may sound more complicated and involved then the casual genealogist wants, the search for truth should outweigh a quick and easy solution. That is why I included the sources for each entry. While many of these sources are not easily accessible to the average researcher (that's why a book like this is helpful), it is possible to use them.

It will be extremely helpful to the
researcher to consult the original work for a
second reason. Most sources contained a great
deal more information then I included in this
book. Sometimes the information was not included
because it did not fit the parameters of this work
in date or location. Frequently, there were
marriage relationships stated (with maiden name
and parents) but no dates or places. The
elimination of such information was determined by
the format of the book. Sometimes there were
family stories that helped to flesh out the bare
bones names and dates. I got to know some of your
ancestors quite well as I read about their
personalities and activities. This is another
reason I carefully documented where each vital
record activity was recorded.

    The data compiled from the vestry book of
Blisland Parish and Stratton Major Parish are
different in format from most of the other data.
I calculated death dates based on the last mention
of the person as alive in the vestry books and the
first mention of the person as deceased, thus the
entry "d.d. between ____ and ____". When a person
was stated as "buried by..." it means that the
vestry book contained an entry in which some
member of the parish had provided services,
supplies or financing for the named person's
burial. This was not done for all parishioners.
It appears almost exclusively for those
parishioners who were being helped financially by
the parish vestry. These burial entries reflect a
death that occurred in the past year since people
were not fond of leaving their dead lying around
for long periods of time. The vestry met annually
(more or less) and the vestry records reflect the
expenses that occurred in the parish from the time
of the last vestry meeting. In my compilation,
where I use the phrase "d.d. by.." in relation to
the vestry records, I used the first date where
the person was mentioned as deceased. This
sometimes took the form of the person's child
being mentioned as cared for by another and the
parent being named as deceased. There were other
children of the parish named in the vestry records
as being cared for by others than the parents, but
if the parent is not mentioned as deceased, these
children were not included. This is another
excellent reason to consult the original source.
There is so much more information available on
family members other than the ones mentioned in
this book.

While researching early colonial Virginia church records it is helpful to realize that there was a change in the calendar.

In England, Ireland, Wales and the British American colonies the Gregorian calendar was adopted in place of the previously used Julian calendar effective in September 1752. The Ecclesiastical system of beginning the year on 25 March and ending the following 24 March was changed effective 1 January 1752 in favor of the historical system that is in use today of beginning the year on 1 January and ending it on 31 December. Consequently, before the change to the new system dates occurring between 1 January and 24 March are double dates. For example, the date 1 January 1732 under the old system would be 1 January 1732/33 under the new system and would be recorded as 1 January 1732/33 or 1732/3.

The idea of having a marriage register for a burned county that predates the "Recent Unpleasantness" in 1861-65 may seem incredible, but is true in the case of King & Queen County. It appears that the court clerk attempted to recreate the marriage licenses from 1853-65. Without being present at the presumed re-creation, I could only guess at what sources were used. Knowing court clerks to be sticklers for accuracy (usually), we can assume he used reliable sources.

In this area of the Peninsula, as in some of the older Tidewater and Northern Neck areas, some family histories are very much wrapped up with the history of their homes and estates. The older, land owning families maintained large land holdings as long as they financially could do so. These land holdings became a way of identifying the family. If the family you are researching is named as one of the land owning families of these counties, it would do you well to consult one of the House History books mentioned in the abbreviations. It is probable you will find considerable additional information on your family.

The material available for a burned county is neither copious nor complete. I put together sources that were admittedly not the best in all cases but were all that I could find. Comparisons of the names included here with any census of King & Queen, King William and/or New Kent Counties will show the wide gaps that exist in the

materials available. However, my viewpoint is
that something is better than nothing. By
initiating this recreation of records, I hope to
encourage others to continue the research on these
valuable counties and fill in the gaps that exist.

HISTORY

New Kent County, Virginia is considered a
burned county, as are King William and King and
Queen because their records suffered considerable
damage at some point in their history from fire.
In the case of New Kent this occurred twice. Once
in the 1790's which totally destroyed all the
colonial records in the keeping of the courts and
secondly in 1871 which made a considerable dent in
the records that were created after the first
fire.

The records of King and Queen County were
destroyed in the second raid of General Kilpatrick
10 March 1864 when his men burned the courthouse
and the clerk's office. Previously, in 1828, they
were destroyed in a courthouse fire.

King William is considered a burned county
because of the extensive record damage that
occurred in a fire at the county clerk's office on
17 Jan 1885. Since all that was saved were a few
old deed books, any marriage, birth or death
records must come from other sources. As in the
case of King & Queen, it appears the court clerk
made an attempt to recreate some of the births of
King William County in a Register of Births which
can be found on microfilm at the Virginia State
Archives in Richmond.

While all three of these counties have been
pivotal in the formation of many other counties as
well as being the county of origination for
countless families in Virginia, Tennessee,
Kentucky and points west, I am not going to try to
give abbreviated histories of them. There is too
much history to include in such a short space. I
recommend reading one of the county histories
mentioned in the list of abbreviations to get a
picture of how each county grew and contributed to
Virginia history.

Useful data to know while researching your
family is that New Kent county was formed in

November 1654 from the northwest part of York
county. King and Queen County was formed, along
with Hanover County, from New Kent. Many of the
county's earliest settlers came from Kent County,
England, thus the name "New Kent". King & Queen
was formed in 1691. In 1702 King William was
created from King & Queen. King and Queen helped
to form Spotsylvania and Caroline Counties in 1721
and 1728. Kentucky, Tennessee and West Virginia
were settled in their earliest days by people from
King & Queen County. Their migration to the lands
west of the Appalachians occurred around the time
of the Revolution. While we cannot say that the
earliest settlers of' these states were exclusively
from this county, King & Queen played a
significant enough role in the settlement that it
is worthwhile to look among these records if your
ancestor settled in the states west of the
mountains during or immediately after the
Revolution. Of course, you should also keep in
mind that military land grants were given for the
same areas, regardless of where the land grant
petitioner lived.

According to Milton Rubincam, the only
newspapers published in Virginia until 1780 were
those that issued out of Williamsburg. Richmond
soon followed as well as Norfolk and
Charlottesville. Religious newspapers were also
widely read in Virginia. The Virginia State
Library and the Virginia Genealogical Society have
both published indexes and abstracts of obituaries
and marriage notices for some of the religious
newspapers as well as some of the Richmond
newspapers. Of course, the "Virginia Gazette"
(1736-1780) has been indexed by Cappon & Duff.
Robert Hodge has indexed "The Virginia Herald"
(1786-1836) and "The Weekly Advertiser" both
published in Fredericksburg and both of which
contain information from surrounding counties.

While newspapers do not contain information
on every inhabitant of the counties, they do
provide data on the better known individuals and
some of the middle class families.

This particular collection of records has
been the most demanding project that I have
undertaken so far. I readily admit that it is not
perfect. I am certain that there are omissions,
even from among the materials that are available.
There are probably typographical errors in spite
of repeated editing. For those who delight in

finding fault with anything that comes into print,
I suggest that you attempt the same project before
you become too critical.

MINISTERS AND THEIR RELIGIONS

Information related to the religious leaders of King & Queen County was taken from the HISTORY OF KING & QUEEN COUNTY by Rev. Alfred Bagby originally published in 1908. The earliest names were taken from the vestry minutes of Stratton Major Church.

Information related to ministers from New Kent County was taken from the vestry minutes of Blisland Parish and St. Peter's Parish.

Baptists

The years following the names denote the first year of their ministry in King & Queen.

John Waller 1771
Iveson Lewis 1775 Exol Church
Robert Ware Lower King & Queen
Yonger Pitts 1774 Upper King & Queen
Theodrick Noel 1780 Upper King & Queen
Robert B. Semple 1790 Bruington
James Healy 1807 Poroporone
William Todd 1804 or 5 Lower King & Queen.
   He became the minister at Mattaponi in 1828
Andrew Broaddus 1827 Upper King & Queen
Richard Claybrook 1832- 1834 Bruington
Eli Ball 1834 Bruington
William Southwood 1840 Bruington
T.W.Snydor 1841 Bruington
R. Hugh Bagby 1842 Bruington
Alfred Bagby 1853 Bruington
William S. Ryland 1853 Bruington
George F. Bagby 1858 Bruington
John Spencer until 1842 Poroporone
Thomas B. Evans Olivet for 33 years
W.B.Todd
Isaac Digges
Andrew Broaddus Jr. during 1860 Upper King & Queen
Church
J.W.Ryland
W.A.Street
F.B.Beale
O.D.Loving
Alexander Fleet

Disciples of Christ

R.B.Templeton   1831
Temple Walker   1831
Thomas Henley   1832
James C. Roy at the death of P.B.Pendleton

Methodists

Stephen Roswell 1790
Harry B. Cowles 1800 Shepherd's
Samuel Gerrard   Richard Bennett
Lewis Skidmore   RichardMitchell
Hezekiah McLelland   Thomas Durham
John Hersey   William Davis
Rufus Ledbetter   John W. White
Samuel T. Moorman   John P. Gregory
William H. Starr   James McDonald
Thomas S. Campbell   James W. Lewis
Moses Brock   Robert Michaels
George W. Nolley   William E.Grant
Edward Cannon   Richard Hope
Richard Corbin   Isaac M. Arnold
David Fisher   James E. Joyner
Thomas Crowder   Gervis M.Keesee
Abram Penn   Joseph H. Davis
Hezekiah P. Mitchell   Joseph Lear
Thomas M. Beckham   Stephen W.Jones
George M. Wright   Thomas H.Briggs
Josiah D. Hank   John Bayley
Charles E. Watts   John B. Laurens
William E. Evans   B.H. Johnson
Benjamin C. Spiller   Charles H.Boggs
William W. Lear   Joseph Griffith
William A. Crocker   William H.Starr
John T. Payne   John G. Rowe
Joseph W. Shackelford
John William Shackleford
Robert E. Barrett

Episcopal

The years following their names denote the first mention in parish records.

Daniel Taylor 1721 Blisland Parish
David Mossom 1729 Blisland Parish
    also minister at St.Peter's Parish in New Kent 1727 to 1767
William LeNeve 1729 Blisland Parish
Chicheley Thacker 1730 Blisland Parish
Price Davies 1763 Blisland Parish
John Skaife 1729 Stratton Major Parish
John Reade 1736 Stratton Major Parish
Bartholomew Yates 1743 Stratton Major Parish
Robert Yates 1743 Stratton Major Parish
William Robinson 1744 Stratton Major Parish
William Dunlap 1768 Straton Major Parish
John Dixon 1773 Stratton Major Parish
Arthur Hamilton 1778 Stratton Major Parish
William Sellake 1683 or 4 St. Peter's Parish
John Carr 1684 St. Peter's Parish
John Ball 1686 St. Peter's Parish
John Page 1687 St. Peter's Parish
James Slater 1688 St. Peter's Parish
Rev. Williams 1689 St. Peter's Parish
John Gordon 1690 St. Peter's Parish
Jacob Ware 1690 St. Peter's Parish
Rev. Monroe 1696 St. Peter's Parish
Nicholas Moreau 1696 St. Peter's Parish
James Bowker 1698 St. Peter's Parish
Richard Squire 1703 St. Peter's Parish
William Williams 1703 St. Peter's Parish
Daniel Taylor 1707 St. Peter's Parish
Samuel Grey 1708 St. Peter's Parish
Benjamin Goodwin 1709 St. Peter's Parish
William Brodie 1710 St. Peter's Parish
Thomas Sharp 1720 St. Peter's Parish
Rev. Bromscale 1720 St. Peter's Parish
Zacarias Brooks 1721 St. Peter's Parish
Francis Fountain 1722 St. Peter's Parish
Rev. Forbess 1722 St. Peter's Parish
Henry Collings 1722 St. Peter's Parish
John Lang 1725 St. Peter's Parish
David Mossom 1727 St. Peter's Parish
Patrick Henry 1740 St. Peter's Parish

XVII

_____, Cipieo POC owned by Mr.Ebenezer Adams d.d.
31 Oct 1719; SPPR
_____, Hannah mulatto owned by Richard Apperson
d.d. 20 Feb 1726/7; SPPR
_____, John POC owned by William Clopton bap 25 Jun
1710 SPPR
_____, Moll POC owned by William Adams d.d. 30 Nov
1719; SPPR
_____, Nan POC owned by Ebenezer Adams d.d. 8 Sep
1725; SPPR
_____, Peg POC owned by David Clarkson b.d. 1
__ber, 1706 SPPR
_____, Phillis POC owned by Richard Cottorel Jr.
b.d. 10 Feb 1708/9 SPPR
_____, Aivranara (?) s/o Dorothy POC owned by
Samuel S. Gresham b.d. May 1853; KQBR
_____, Anastasia d/o Courtney POC owned by Samuel
S. Gresham b.d. Jul 1853: KQBR
_____, Bebdana POC owned by Capt. Joseph Foster
b.d. 20 Aug 1686 SPPR
_____, Beck POC owned by Jon Lightfoot b.d.8 Sep
1694; SPPR
_____, Betty POC owned by Mr. Whitlock b.d. 3 May
1710; SPPR
_____, Billy POC owned by Charles Fleming b.d. 12
Jun 1704 SPPR
_____, Daniel POC owned by William Bassett b.d. 18
May 1716 SPPR
_____, Davy POC owned by Thomas Butts b.d. 24 Apr
1715 SPPR
_____, Dick POC owned by Thomas Butts b.d. 1 Mar
1714 SPPR
_____, Doll POC owned by Capt. Joseph Foster b.d.
20 Oct 1692 SPPR
_____, Doll POC owned by David Clarkson b.d. 28
Jun 1706 SPPR
_____, Doris POC owned by Major Field b.d. 23 Mar
1705/06 SPPR
_____, Francis POC owned by William Clopton b.d. 5
Aug 1703 SPPR
_____, Frank POC owned by Mr. Whitlock b.d. 4 Mar
1712; SPPR
_____, Hagar POC owned by John Bacon b.d. 14 Jun
1711 SPPR
_____, Hanna POC owned by John Lewis at Chemokins
b.d.6 Nov 1689 ;SPPR
_____, Isack POC owned by Gedeon Macon b.d. 28 Jan
1697; SPPR
_____, Jack POC owned by John Lightfoot b.d 1 Feb
1686/7; SPPR
_____, Jack POC owned by Jos. Joy b.d.1 May 1712;
SPPR
_____, Jack POC owned by Richard Allen b.d Apr
1704 SPPR

1

_____, Jack POC owned by Richard Littlepage b.d.
26 Nov 1686; SPPR
_____, James molatto POC owned by Richard Allen
b.d. 3 Oct 1704 SPPR
_____, Jenne POC owned by Capt. Joseph Foster b.d.
30 Jan 1683/4 SPPR
_____, Jenny POC owned by John Googer b.d. 20 Feb
170_ SPPR
_____, Jenny POC owned by Jon Lightfoot b.d.3 Jul
1692; SPPR
_____, Jessie POC owned by Jos. Joy b.d. Feb 171_;
SPPR
_____, John mulatto owned by Major John Custis
b.d. 18 Mar 1709 SPPR
_____, Judith POC owned by William Clopton b.d. 26
Jan 1715 SPPR
_____, Kit POC owned by John Bacon b.d. 13 Jun
1713 SPPR
_____, Liddia POC owned by Gedeon Macon b.d. 1 Apr
1701; SPPR
_____, Matthew POC owned by Jon Lightfoot b.d.25
Mar 1680; SPPR
_____, Merrea POC owned by Gedeon Macon b.d. Jan
1695; SPPR
_____, Moll mulatto owned by Capt. Nicholas
Meriwether b.d. 2 Nov 1699; SPPR
_____, Moll POC owned by Gedeon Macon b.d. 6 Nov
1695; SPPR
_____, Moll POC owned by John Whitlock b.d. 2 Jul
1715; SPPR
_____, Moll POC owned by Madam Field bap 170_ SPPR
_____, Nan POC owned by Gedeon Macon b.d. Jul
1692; SPPR
_____, Nanc POC owned by William Clopton 29 Apr
1704 SPPR
_____, Nane POC owned by Capt. Joseph Foster b.d.
28 Apr 168_ SPPR
_____, Patty POC owned by John Custis b.d. 18 Mar
1709 SPPR
_____, Phil molatto POC owned by Richard Allen
b.d. 15 Aug 1698 SPPR
_____, Phill POC owned by Gedeon Macon b.d. 16 Jan
1696; SPPR
_____, Phill POC owned by John Lewis at Chemokins
b.d. Jun 1689; SPPR
_____, Presh POC owned by Charles Winfrey b.d. Sep
1710; SPPR
_____, Robert s/o Caroline POC owned by Lewis C.
Hart b.d. Aug 1853 POB King & Queen; KQBR
_____, Robin POC owned by Charles Fleming b.d. 12
Jun 1704 (see _____, Billy) SPPR
_____, Sara POC owned by Capt. Joseph Foster b.d.
20 Feb 1684/5 SPPR

_____, Sarah POC owned by Gedeon Macon Sep 1698; SPPR

_____, Sarah POC owned by Gedeon Macon b.d. 29 Jan 1681; SPPR

_____, Sarah POC owned by John Googer b.d. 8 May 1705 SPPR

_____, Sue POC owned by Charles Winfrey b.d. 20 Sep 1713; SPPR

_____, Sue POC owned by John Aldridge b.d. Apr 1716 SPPR

_____, Tom s/o Juliett POC owned by Elizabeth Hundley (reported by Joseph T. Hundley legatee & son of E. Hundley) b.d. Oct 1853 POB King & Queen; KQBR

_____, Tresana POC owned by Gedeon Macon b.d. 24 Dec 1701; SPPR

_____, Will POC owned by Capt. Joseph Foster b.d 1 Sep 1697 SPPR

_____, Will POC owned by Gedeon Macon b.d. 2 Feb 1683; SPPR

_____, Will POC owned by Gedeon Macon b.d. 25 Nov 1700; SPPR

_____, Will POC owned by John Lightfoot b.d. 20 Aug 1690; SPPR

_____, Will POC owned by Stephen Crump b.d. 12 Jan 1715; SPPR

_____, Alonso s/o Jane POC owned by James W. Gaines b.d. Apr 1853; KQBR

_____, Ann POC owned by Joseph Eubank (James M. Davis who reported the birth hired 1853) b.d. Aug 1853 d.d. Aug 1853 (born dead); KQBR

_____, Anna d/o Elizabeth POC owned by John W. Watkins POB King & Queen b.d. 18 Mar 1853; KQBR

_____, Barbary d/o Catharine owned by William Boulware b.d. Apr 1853 POB King & Queen KQBR

_____, Beverley s/o Evalina POC owned by D.P.Wright b.d. Mar 1853; KQBR

_____, Catherine d/o Jane POC owned by John H. Watkins b.d. 1 Jan 1853; KQBR

_____, Ceasar POC owned by Dr. Durbridge b.d. 1713 SPPR

_____, Charlotte d/o Mary POC owned by John Wright b.d. May 1853; KQBR

_____, Charlotte POC owned by John Walker b.d. December 1853; KQBR

_____, Daniel s/o Sarah POC owned by Temple Walker b.d. Mar 1853; KQBR

_____, Dick POC owned by Mr. Whitlock b.d. 28 Oct 1708; SPPR

_____, Dolly d/o Emaline POC owned by Dr. William Dew b.d. May 1853; KQBR

_____, Duerson s/o Betsy POC owned by David A. Farinholt (who is recording the information

and listed as father) b.d. Feb 1853 POB King
& Queen; KQBR
_____, Emma d/o Henrietta POC owned by Mary A.
Hawes b.d. Dec 1853 POB King & Queen; KQBR
_____, Georgiana d/o Julia POC owned by J.H.Young
b.d. Jan 1853; KQBR
_____, Hagar POC owned by Madam Sarah Brays b.d.
1 Jan 1709 SPPR
_____, Hannah d/o Marissa owned by William
Boulware b.d. Aug 1853 POB King & Queen KQBR
_____, Hannah POC owned by Mrs. Alice Butts b.d.
22 Apr 1709 SPPR
_____, Henry s/o Eliza POC owned by Phebe Goldman
b.d. 25 Dec 1853 POB King & Queen; KQBR
_____, Hezekiah d/o Lavinia POC owned by Dr.
William Dew b.d. May 1853; KQBR
_____, Jacob s/o Hannah POC owned by John N.
Gresham b.d. Jul 1853 POB King & Queen; KQBR
_____, Kelam s/o Polly POC owned by Mariah A.W.
Hart (life estate) b.d. Jul 1853 POB King &
Queen; KQBR
_____, Lucinda d/o Creekley POC owned by
D.P.Wright b.d. Dec 1853; KQBR
_____, Lucy d/o Kesiah POC owned by Sarrah E.
Evans b.d. Sep 1853; KQBR
_____, Maria d/o Suckey POC owned by Samuel S.
Gresham b.d. Mar 1853; KQBR
_____, Martha d/o Louisa POC owned by James R.
Garnett b.d. 9 Mar 1853; KQBR
_____, Martin s/o Polly POC owned by Dr. William
Dew b.d. Jun 1853; KQBR
_____, Mary d/o Winney POC owned by Robert T.
Gwathmey b.d. Jan 1853; KQBR
_____, Munroe s/o Catherine POC owned by Lucy Dew
b.d. Nov 1853: KQBR
_____, Nanny POC owned by Richard Allin b.d. Sep
1711 SPPR
_____, Ned POC owned by Richard Allin b.d.20 Jun
1713 SPPR
_____, Ned s/o Aristeamia (?) POC owned by
Samuel Grey b.d. Jul 1853 POB King & Queen;
KQBR
_____, Otoway s/o Mary POC owned by Dr. William
J.B.Henry b.d. Sep 1853 POB Matthews Co; KQBR
_____, Paul POC owned by Madam Sarah Bray b.d. 20
Apr 1713 SPPR
_____, Peter POC owned by Charles Fleming b.d. 24
Jun 1703 SPPR
_____, Peter POC owned by David Craford b.d.10
Oct 1688 SPPR
_____, Peter s/o Catherine POC owned by Samuel
Grey b.d. May 1853 POB King & Queen; KQBR
_____, Phil s/o Charlotte POC owned by Dr.
William Dew b.d. Mar 1853; KQBR

4

_____, Pierce s/o Maria POC owned by John H.
Watkins b.d. Jul 1853; KQBR
_____, Pink d/o Mary POC owned by Dr. William Dew
b.d. May 1853; KQBR
_____, Rhoda d/o Letty POC owned by John W.
Watkins b.d. 23 Dec 1853; KQBR
_____, Richard POC owned by John Aldridge b.d.
Sep 1713 SPPR
_____, Robert s/o Julia POC owned by Samuel S.
Gresham b.d. Sep 1853 POB King & Queen; KQBR
_____, Rosella d/o Nancy POC owned by John W.
Garnett b.d. 31 Dec 1853 POB King & Queen;
KQBR
_____, Sam s/o Patsey POC owned by Tilman R.
Gardner b.d. Jan 1853 POB King & Queen; KQBR
_____, Sambo POC owned by orphans of Robert
Dudley (dec) exempt from taxes 19 Nov 1756;
SMP
_____, Sambo POC owned by Rowland Horsly b.d. 15
Aug 1691 SPPR
_____, Sarah mulatto POC owned by Major Field
b.d. 12 Mar 1705 SPPR
_____, Sarah POC owned by Robert Jarratt b.d
1708; SPPR
_____, Thomas s/o Maria POC owned by Luther C.
Dew b.d.Feb 1853; KQBR
_____, Travis s/o Martha POC owned by J.H. Young
b.d. Feb 1853; KQBR
_____, Travis s/o Rachel POC owned by John
Pollard b.d. 30 Aug 1853; KQBR
_____, Valeria d/o Jane POC owned by Elizabeth B.
Yarrington b.d. Jun 1853; KQBR
_____, Walter s/o Sally POC owned by Ann W.
Carlton (reported by Edward C. Fox hired in
1853) b.d. May 1853 POB King & Queen; KQBR
_____, Winney d/o Tilla POC owned by James
Guthrie b.d Oct 1853 POB King & Queen
father's POR King & Queen; KQBR
_____, Andrew POC owned by Samuel Overton b.d.
29 Mar 1700; SPPR
_____, Bob d/o Maria owned by Lawrence E.
Anderson POC b.d.Oct 1853 POB King & Queen
KQBR
_____, Claiborne s/o Anna owned by Robert Bland
POC b.d. Feb 1853 POB King & Queen KQBR
_____, Elanora d/o Ma_____ owned by Peter Bray
b.d. 29 Feb 1853 POB King & Queen KQBR
_____, Eliza d/o Isabella owned by James A.
Roane POC b.d. Mar 1853 POB King & Queen KQBR
_____, Hezekial s/o Mary owned by Agnes Anderson
POC b.d. Feb 1853 POB King & Queen KQBR
_____, Hunter s/o Sally owned by Philemon Bird
POC b.d. Jun 1853 POB King & Queen KQBR

5

_____, James s/o Sarah owned by Robert Bowden
POC b.d. Feb 1853 POB King & Queen KQBR
_____, Judy d/o Maria owned by Nancy Brown POC
b.d.20 Aug 1853 POB King & Queen KQBR
_____, Lucy d/o Sally owned by Roberet Bland POC
b.d. Nov 1853 POB King & Queen KQBR
_____, Margarett d/o Rachel owned by Ann R.
Bland POC b.d. Sep 1853 POB King & Queen KQBR
_____, Maria d/o Leria owned by Agnes Anderson
POC b.d. Jan 1853 POB King & Queen KQBR
_____, Martha d/o Agnes owned by Robert Bland
POC b.d. Apr 1853 POB King & Queen KQBR
_____, Mary d/o Grace owned by Handsford
Anderson POC b.d.Jul 1853 POB King & Queen
KQBR
_____, Peter POC owned by Madam Sarah Bray b.d.
31 May 1711 SPPR
_____, Peter, Musca-doras, Mary Phillis, Anne,
Elizabeth, Adult all POC owned by Mrs. Alice
Field bap 2 Jan 17__ SPPR
_____, Simon POC owned by Mrs. Alice Butts b.d.
16 Sep 1711 SPPR
_____, William s/o Phillis owned by William
Boulware b.d. Jan 1853 POB King & Queen KQBR
_____, Charles s/o Delphia owned by Polly
Garrett POC b.d. 1 Nov 1853 POB King & Queen
KQBR
AARON, G. bap 25 Nov 1788; VBHS
ABRAHAMS, Mary Frances d/o Mordecai Abrahams d.d.
7 Oct 1832 age 15 POD King William; KWC
ABRAHAMS, Mary Frances d/o Mordecai Abrahams POD
King William age 13 d.d. 7 Oct 1832; RE
ABRAMS, C.G. s/o James H. Abrams age 29 S overseer
POB King William POR King & Queen & **GARDNER**,
Ellen d/o Thomas Hundley age 33 W POB Essex
Co POR King & Queen; DOM 11 Jan 1860 POM King
& Queen KQMR
ABRAMS, Mordecai POR King William d.d. 16 Feb 1792
VGMA
ACRE, Ceyton d.d.1788 VBHS
ACRE, Rachel d.d. 22 Mar 1789 VBHS
ACREE, Lee s/o Ruffin & Mary(?) Ann Acree free POC
b.d. Mar 1853 POB King & Queen KQBR
ACREE, Nathaniel POR King William & **HEATH**, Maria
POR Hanover Co ML Hanover Co DOM 25 Feb 1830;
CTR
ADAMS, Anne d/o Ebenezar Adams & Tabitha Cocke
b.d. abt 1731 POB New Kent d.d. 1775 POD
Essex; KK1
ADAMS, Anne d/o Richard Adams & Elizabeth Griffin
of New Kent b.d. 27 Oct 1762 d.d. 22 Oct
1820; KK1

6

ADAMS, Bowler s/o Ebenezar Adams & Tabitha Cocke
b.d. 19 Apr 1722 POB New Kent d.d. 26 Nov
1726 POD New Kent; SPPR
ADAMS, Ebenezar s/o Richard Adams POB Abridge,
Essex, England POR New Kent d.d. 13 Jun 1735
POD "Winslow's", New Kent; SPPR
ADAMS, Elizabeth Pressin d/o Richard Adams &
Elizabeth Griffin b.d. 17 Dec 1757 POB New
Kent d.d. 1832; KK1
ADAMS, George d.d. 26 Aug 1709; SPPR
ADAMS, George s/o Valentine Adams b.d. 14 Apr 1726
POB New Kent; KK1
ADAMS, John & **MARTIN**, Mary POR New Kent ML New
Kent DOM 12 Nov 1831; CTR
ADAMS, John & **ROSE**, Ann P. POR King & Queen; DOM 8
Nov 1788; CCPR
ADAMS, John s/o Henry & Lucy Adams b.d. 26 Apr bap
15 Jun 1760 POB New Kent; SPPR
ADAMS, John s/o John & Frances Adams age 47 W POB
Hanover POR New Kent & **WADE**, Ann d/o Martin &
Eliza Wade age 43 S POB POR New Kent; DOM 2
Feb 1857 POM New Kent by James Fendall
Parkinson; NKMR
ADAMS, John s/o Richard Adams & Elizabeth Griffin
of New Kent b.d. 14 Jul 1773 d.d. 23 Jun 1825
POD Richmond; KK1
ADAMS, Patty d/o George & Lucy Adams b.d. 23 Nov
1758 POB New Kent; SPPR
ADAMS, Richard s/o Ebenezar Adams & Tabitha Cocke
b.d. 17 May 1726 POB New Kent d.d. 2 Aug 1800
POD Richmond; KK1
ADAMS, Richard s/o Ebenezar Adams & Tabitha Cocke
d.d. 12 Sep 1721 POD New Kent; SPPR
ADAMS, Richard s/o Ebenezar Adams & Tabitha Cocke
POB POR New Kent & **GRIFFIN**, Elizabeth; DOM 10
Apr 1755; KK1
ADAMS, Richard s/o Ebenezer Adams d.d. 12 Sep
1721; SPPR
ADAMS, Richard s/o Richard Adams & Elizabeth
Griffin of New Kent b.d. 26 Nov 1760 d.d. 9
Jan 1817; KK1
ADAMS, Sally d/o George & Lucy Adams b.d. 22 Feb
bap 14 May 1758 POB New Kent; SPPR
ADAMS, Samuel Griffin s/o Richard Adams &
Elizabeth Griffin of New Kent b.d. 5 May 1776
d.d. 15 Jul 1821; KK1
ADAMS, Sarah d/o Richard Adams & Elizabeth Griffin
of New Kent b.d. 14 Jan 1766 d.d. 30 Sep
1806; KK1
ADAMS, Tabitha d/o Ebenezar Adams & Tabitha Cocke
b.d. 7 Jul 1728 POB New Kent; SPPR
ADAMS, Tabitha d/o Richard Adams & Elizabeth
Griffin b.d. 18 Sep 1759 POB New Kent d.d. 17
Feb 1828; KK1

ADAMS, Thomas Bowler s/o Richard Adams & Elizabeth
Griffin of New Kent b.d. 18 Sep 1759 d.d. 28
Nov 1794 POD Richmond; KK1
ADAMS, Thomas POR King William & BARKER, Mildred
POR Hanover Co ML Hanover Co DOM 24 Apr 1832;
CTR
ADAMS, Thomas s/o Ebenezar Adams & Tabitha Cocke
b.d. abt 1730 POB New Kent; KK1
ADAMS, William s/o Ebenezar Adams & Tabitha Cocke
b.d. 4 Jul 1724 POB New Kent; SPPR
ADAMS, William s/o Richard Adams & Elizabeth
Griffin of New Kent b.d. 8 Jun 1764 d.d. 15
Jun 1787; KK1
ADDISON, Elizabeth d/o Thomas & Ann Addison d.d.
1730/3 POD New Kent; SPPR
ADDISON, James s/o Thomas & Ann Addison b.d. 28
Apr bap 29 May 1737 POB New Kent; SPPR
ADDISON, Peachy d/o John & Frances Addison b.d. 27
Apr 1756 POB New Kent; SPPR
ADDSION, Ruth d/o Thomas & Ann Addison b.d. 6 Jun
bap 221 Jul 1734 POB New Kent; SPPR
ALDRIDGE, John d.d. 16 Apr 1720; SPPR
ALEXANDER, James T. s/o Arthur Alexander age 26 S
miller POB POR King & Queen & MITCHELL, Mary
S. d/o Alex. Mitchell age 22 S POB POR King &
Queen; DOM 19 Jan 1860 POM King & Queen KQMR
ALEXANDER, John M. s/o John C. & Georgianna
Alexander b.d. 31 Dec 1855 POB King William;
NKMR
ALEXANDER, Sarah p.m. POR King William d.d. issue
dated 23 Jun 1837 RW
ALEXANDER, Sarah w/o Dudley Alexander POD The
Globe, King William d.d. 14 Jun 1853 age 24;
RW
ALFORD, Elizabeth d/o John & Grace Alford b.d. 1
Jul 1719 POB New Kent; SPPR
ALFORD, Isaac s/o John Alford d.d. 21 Aug 1723;
SPPR
ALFORD, James s/o James Alford b.d. 7 Apr 1713 bap
April 12th 1713 SPPR
ALFORD, James s/o James Alford b.d. 7 Feb 1713 POB
New Kent bap 12 Apr 1713; SPPR
ALFORD, John Sr. d.d. 14 Mar 1709/10; SPPR
ALFORD, Julius s/o James Alford b.d. Sep 1717 POB
New Kent d.d. 1771 POB Bute Co, NC; KK1
ALFORD, Lucy d/o Goodrich & Sarah Alford b.d. 25
Feb bap 27 Mar 1736 POB New Kent; SPPR
ALFORD, Susanna d/o Goodrich & Sarah Alford b.d. 5
Oct bap 18 Nov 1739 POB New Kent; SPPR
ALFORD, Warren s/o James Alford bap 28 Aug 1715
POB New Kent; SPPR
ALFORD, Warren s/o James Alford bap 28 Aug 1715
SPPR
ALFORD, William d.d. 11 Feb 1709/10; SPPR

ALLEN, Benjamin s/o Robert Allen b.d. 12 Apr 1711
SPPR

ALLEN, Betty d/o Richard Allen & Elizabeth Terrell
b.d. 26 Nov 1734 POB New Kent; BP

ALLEN, Drury s/o Robert Allen b.d. 6 Apr 1714 bap
2 May 1714 SPPR

ALLEN, Elizabeth T. POD King William d.d. 1 Aug
1840 age 26; RW

ALLEN, Hannah w/o William Allen d.d. 22 Mar 1719;
SPPR

ALLEN, James s/o Daniel Allen & Rebecca Richardson
b.d 1699 POR New Kent d.d. 1773; KK1

ALLEN, Joseph POR New Kent d.d. by Apr 1738 VG

ALLEN, Joseph s/o Robert Allen b.d. 12 Apr 1711
SPPR

ALLEN, Richard d.d. 6 Sep 1725; SPPR

ALLEN, Richard d.d. between 19 Oct 1772 and 29 Nov
1773; BP

ALLEN, Richard s/o Richard Allen & Elizabeth
Terrell b.d. 10 Dec 1741 POB New Kent; FB

ALLEN, William youngest s/o Col. Richard Allen
((dec)) POR New Kent d.d. 20 Jan 1809 POD
Bowling Green VGGA

ALLEN, Wilson s/o Richmond Allen & Elizabeth
Wilson b.d. 15 Feb 1774 POB New Kent d.d. 21
Jul 1844; FB

ALLEN, Wilson s/o Richmond Allen & Elizabeth
Wilson POB New Kent & **HOOMES**, Sophia d/o John
Hoomes & Judith Churchill Allen; DOM 22 Jan
1807; FB

ALLIN, Samuel s/o William Allin bap 20 Sep 1713
SPPR

AMESON, Thomas J. bap 25 Nov 1788; VBHS

AMETE, Henry s/o Levi Amete & Eliz. Abbott age 44
W shoemaker POB Dorchester, MD POR King &
Queen & **BIDJEST**, Maria d/o Leroy Bidjest &
C.Walden age 23 S POB POR King & Queen; DOM
19 Mar 1854 POM King & Queen by Thomas B.
Owens KQMR

AMMON, Lucy d/o Christopher Ammon POR New Kent
b.d. 27 Nov 1758 d.d.1826 SPPR

AMMONS, Christopher POB Middlesex POR New Kent &
BRISTOW, Mary d/o John Bristow & Mary Carter
b.d. 15 Aug 1715 POB Middlesex; DOM 29 Jan
1735 POM Middlesex by Bartholomew Yates; CCM

AMOS, Eliz. w/o Fra. Amos d.d. 28 Sep 1723; SPPR

AMOSS, Judith d/o Francis Amoss bap 24 Jan 1713
SPPR

ANDERSON, Andrew physician d.d. by 23 Feb 1784; BP

ANDERSON, Benjamin d.d. Oct 1839 POR King William
SMPR

ANDERSON, Charles E. POB POR Henrico S Dr. &
EPPES, Sallie Ann d/o John C. & Ann Eppes age

23 s POB POR New Kent; DOM 19 Nov 1856 POM
New Kent by Thomas Binford; NKMR

ANDERSON, Edward F. s/o Ro.S. & F.A. Anderson age
22 S farmer POB King & Queen & **GREY**, E.A.E.
d/o Samuel & Elizabeth Grey age 18 S POB King
& Queen; by William B. Todd KQMR

ANDERSON, Francis & **SPENCER**, Frances POR King &
Queen; DOM 10 Jan 1793 CCPR

ANDERSON, Hansford d.d. 25 Nov 1835 age 33 POD POR
King & Queen; RE

ANDERSON, James d.d. 1 May 1813 age 29 POD the
White House, New Kent VA

ANDERSON, James d.d. 15 Mar 1807 POD the White
House, New Kent age 63 VA

ANDERSON, James POR New Kent d.d. issue dated 7
May 1813 RE

ANDERSON, John POR King William d.d 26 Feb 1806 VA

ANDERSON, Lawrence E. s/o Edward F. & Eliza J.
Anderson age 27 W POB POR King & Queen &
BROWN (?), Sarah d/o John & Sarah Spencer age
31 W POR King & Queen; DOM 27 Dec 1857 POM
King & Queen by A.F.Scott KQMR

ANDERSON, Margaret w/o Thomas Anderson d.d. Jan
1710; SPPR

ANDERSON, Richard d.d.between 26 Sep 1755 and 19
Nov 1756; SMP

ANDERSON, Samuel B. s/o Samuel C. & Elizabeth
Anderson b.d. Feb 1855 POR New Kent; KK1

ANDERSON, William & **DABNEY**, Dorothy his wife POR
King & Queen by 25 Apr 1701 C&P3

ANDREWSON, Giles d.d. 23 Feb 1687/8; SPPR

APERSON, John d.d. 28 May 1722; SPPR

APPERSON, Anne d/o John Apperson b.d. 19 Mar
1710/11

APPERSON, Elizabeth d/o John Apperson b.d. 27 Apr
1708 SPPR

APPERSON, Elizabeth d/o William Apperson b.d. 17
Sep 1715 SPPR

APPERSON, Elizabeth w/o Thomas Apperson d.d. 22
Aug 1712; SPPR

APPERSON, Frances d/o Thomas Apperson b.d. 1 Apr
1716 SPPR

APPERSON, Francis [sic] d/o John Apperson b.d. 3
Dec 1706 SPPR

APPERSON, Henry s/o William Apperson b.d. 29 Mar
1713 SPPR

APPERSON, John s/o John Apperson Jr. b.d. 4 Feb
1713 bap 21 Mar 1713 SPPR

APPERSON, Mary d/o John Apperson b.d. 26 Feb 1715
SPPR

ARMISTEAD, Gill col. d.d. between 19 Oct 1761 and
12 Nov 1762; BP

ARMISTEAD, Gill s/o Cap. John Armistead &
Elizabeth Gill POR New Kent & **ALLEN**, Betty

d/o Richard Allen & Elizabeth Terrell b.d. 26
Nov 1734 POB New Kent; DOM 23 May 1751 POM
New Kent; KK1

ARMISTEAD, Robert Burbidge s/o Col. John Armistead
POR New Kent d.d. 1811; KK1

ARMISTEAD, Susannah d/o Gill Armistead & Betty
Allen of New Kent b.d. 1753; KK1

ARMISTEAD, William Capt. of New Kent & **ARMISTEAD**,
Polly Stith POR Elizabeth City; DOM 25 Aug
1783 VGAA

ARMISTEAD, William POR King & Queen d.d. issue
dated 6 Feb 1827 RW

ARMISTEAD, William s/o Col. John & Agnes Armistead
b.d. 5 Jan 1754 POB New Kent d.d. Jun 1793;
KK1

ARMISTEAD, William s/o Robert B. Armistead & Mary
Semple POB New Kent POR King & Queen & **BOYD**,
Lucy d/o Col. William Boyd & Mary Robinson
POB King & Queen; DOM 6 May 1824 POM
"Clifton", King & Queen; KK1

ARMISTEAD, William s/o Robert Burbidge Armistead &
Mary Semple b.d. 1797 POB New Kent; KK1

ARMSTRONG, William B. POR King William & **FOX**,
Polly POR King William ; 29 Jul 1823 ML King
William CT

ARNOLD, Anthony POD West Point, VA before 1677 had
4 children one of whom was Benjamin Arnold;
Petition to Commissioners, Williamsburg

ARNOTT, Thomas Dr. POR New Kent d.d. 29 Jan 1745
age 58 or 38 ; KK1 SPPR

ASHCRAFT, Johannah w/o Thomas Ashcraft d.d. 25 Sep
1716; SPPR

ASHCROFT, Mrs. w/o Richard Ashcroft d.d. Oct 1721;
SPPR

ASHLING, Mary d/o Joseph & Anne Ashling b.d. 12
Jan 1715 SPPR

ASKEW, John d.d. 25 Feb 1719; SPPR

ASKEW, Sarah d.d. 16 Jan 1709/10; SPPR

ATKINS, James s/o Alexander & Susan Atkins free
POC b.d. Nov 1853 POB King & Queen KQBR

ATKINS, John b.d. 12 Jan 1817 FB VSA #34117

ATKINS, Malindy b.d. 30 Mar 1827 FB VSA #34117

ATKINSON, Henry d.d. 10 Feb 1718; SPPR

ATKINSON, Susannah w/o William Atkinson d.d. 25
Jan 1719; SPPR

ATKINSON, William A. b.d. 5 Jun 1796 POR New Kent
d.d. 20 Jun 1860; KK1

ATKINSON, William POR New Kent & **MOORE**, Elizabeth;
DOM 14 Mar 1821 by William Ratcliffe; KK1

AUSTIN, Gervis d.d. 30 Dec 1722; SPPR

AUSTIN, Israell d.d. 29 Feb 1687/8; SPPR

AUSTIN, James A. s/o Lancelot & Patsy Austin POB
New Kent & **PEAY**, Lucy; DOM issue dated 21 Dec
1843 POM New Kent by Thomas S. Morris; RH

AUSTIN, Lewis Delaware POR New Kent d.d. 21 Jun
1888 & CAUL, Mary N.; DOM issue dated 9 Nov
1854 POM New Kent by Thomas Morris; KK1
AUSTIN, William S. POR New Kent & GILLIAM,
Elizabeth E.; DOM consent dated 18 Aug 1853
POM New Kent; KK1
AXFORD, Higins s/o John Axford bap 19 Sep 1714
SPPR
AYLETT, Elizabeth H. 2nd d/o Philip Aylett d.d. 13
Nov 1818 age 21 POD Montville, King William
RE
AYLETT, Louisa d.d. 18 Aug 1822 age 18 POR King
William POD Montville, King William; RE
AYLETT, Philip & DANDRIDGE, Martha d/o Col.William
Dandridge POR Elsing Green & Unity West; DOM
1739 KWH
AYLETT, Philip Jr. (Col.) POR King William &
WALLER, J.P. only d/o Benjamin Waller ((dec))
POR King William DOM 20 Apr 1822 by Rev.
Robert B. Semple; VG
AYLETT, Philip s/o Philip & Elizabeth Aylett &
WALLER, Judith Page; DOM 1823 KWH
AYLETT, Philip s/o William & Mary Aylett & HENRY,
Elizabeth d/o Patrick Henry; DOM 1786 KWH
AYLETT, William POR King William & POSLY, Martha S
POR New Kent; DOM 29 Apr 1802 VA
AYLETT, William s/o Philip & Judith Aylett &
BROCKENBROUGH, Alice; DOM 1860 KWH
AYLETT, William s/o Philip & Martha Aylett &
MACON, Mary; DOM 1766 KWH
AYLETT, William will dated 12 Apr 1780 will
probated 15 Jun 1780 at King William
(children stated as Philip, Elizabeth,
William, Ann, Rebecca, wife Mary); VSA Land
Office Military Box 3
BACON, Albert Gallatin s/o John Bacon & Elizabeth
Ware of New Kent b.d. 8 Dec 1816 d.d. 28 Dec
1861; KK2
BACON, Edmund capt. POR Black Creek, New Kent &
LYDDALL, Ann; DOM 12 May 1682 New Kent; KK2
BACON, Edmund s/o Lydall Bacon & Ann Apperson b.d.
26 Aug 1780 POB New Kent; FB
BACON, Elizabeth B. d/o John Bacon & Elizabeth
Ware of New Kent b.d. 7 May 1814 d.d. 15 Oct
1850; KK2
BACON, James W. s/o John Bacon & Elizabeth Ware of
New Kent b.d. 22 Mar 1807 d.d. Oct 1863; KK2
BACON, James W. s/o John Bacon & Elizabeth Ware of
New Kent & RIGGS, Alica; DOM 24 Mar 1836; KK2
BACON, John & PARKE, Susanna; DOM 4 Jul 1710; SPPR
BACON, John Mosby s/o John Bacon & Elizabeth Ware
of New Kent b.d. 31 Oct 1811 & HAGGIN, Sarah
Jane; DOM 29 Mar 1835; KK2

BACON, John s/o John & Susanna Bacon b.d. 14 May
1711 SPPR
BACON, John s/o Lydall Bacon & Ann Apperson POB
New Kent & PATTESON, Ann; DOM 13 Nov 1794;
KK2
BACON, John s/o Lydall Bacon & Ann Apperson POR
New Kent & WARE, Elizabeth d/o William Ware &
Sarah Samuel d.d. 30 Jul 1849; DOM 31 May
1799; KK2
BACON, John s/o Lyddall & Ann Bacon b.d. 10 Mar
1767 POR New Kent d.d. 9 May 1817; FB
BACON, Langston s/o Lydall Bacon & Ann Apperson
b.d. 20 Feb 1777 POB New Kent; KK2
BACON, Langston s/o Lyddall Bacon & Ann Apperson
b.d. 20 Feb 1777 POB New Kent d.d. 1845; FB
BACON, Lydall s/o Lydall Bacon & Ann Apperson of
New Kent b.d. 29 Aug 1775 POB New Kent; KK2
BACON, Lyddall s/o John Bacon & Susannah Parke
b.d. 1717 POB New Kent d.d. will probated 12
Oct 1775 POD Lunenburg; KK2
BACON, Richard Apperson s/o John Bacon & Elizabeth
Ware b.d. 2 Jul 1809 d.d. Oct 1865; Kk2
BACON, Richard Apperson s/o John Bacon & Elizabeth
Ware of New Kent & TERRELL, Elizabeth E.; DOM
15 Apr 1830; KK2
BACON, Sally d/o John Bacon & Elizabeth Ware of
New Kent b.d. 24 Mar 1802; KK2
BACON, Sarah d/o John & Susanna Bacon b.d. 28 Dec
1712 SPPR
BACON, William S. s/o Edmund Bacon & Elizabath
Allen POR Barhamsville, New Kent & MARSTON,
Maria A. POR James City Co.; DOM 30 Dec 1830
by William Peyton; KK2
BACON, Williamson s/o John Bacon & Elizabeth Ware
of New Kent b.d. 7 Mar 1804 & NOEL, Anna
Maria; DOM 3 Nov 1824; KK2
BAGBY, Alfred minister POB Stevensville, King &
Queen b.d. 15 Jun 1828; HMBC
BAGBY, Elizabeth p.m. POR King & Queen d.d. issue
dated 11 Oct 1836 RW
BAGBY, George F. s/o John & Elizabeth Bagby age
21y 10m S teacher POB POR King & Queen &
COURTNEY, Mary C. d/o William P. & Martha E.
Courtney age 24 S POR King & Queen; DOM 15
Dec 1857 POM King & Queen by Alfred Bagby
KQMR
BAGBY, John Robert s/o John & Eliz Bagby age 26 S
merchant POB POR King & Queen & FLEET, Betty
P. d/o Col A. & Betty Fleet age 20 S POB POR
King & Queen; DOM Apr 1854 POM King & Queen
by Robert B. Semple KQMR
BAGBY, Richard & FLEET, Dorethea Ann d/o Capt.
William Fleet POR King & Queen; DOM 15 Feb
1821 POM Fleetwood by R.B.Semple; VCA

13

BAGBY, Richard POR King & Queen & **FLEET**, Dorothea
Ann 3rd d/o Capt. William Fleet POR King &
Queen; DOM 15 Feb 1821 POM Fleetwood RCC
BAGWELL, Drury & **WARE**, Catherine POR King & Queen;
DOM 28 Feb 1786 CCPR
BAILEY, Anselm J. s/o Anselm & Susannah Bailey POB
POR New Kent & **WRIGHT**, Lucy Ann POR Henrico
consent signed by William Wright; Dom consent
dated 15 Nov 1852 POM New Kent; KK2
BAILEY, Anselm s/o John Bailey Jr. bap 8 Apr 1711;
SPPR
BAILEY, Delaware A. s/o Anselm J. Bailey & Lucy
Ann Wright b.d. 11 Nov 1856 POB New Kent d.d.
5 Oct 1905; KK2
BAILEY, Delaware Allen b.d. 14 Nov 1856 POB
Quinton POR Mountcastle, New Kent d.d. 5 Oct
1908; FB
BAILEY, John & **JACKSON**, Mary; DOM 29 Dec 1709;
SPPR
BAILEY, Lucy d/o Thomas Bailey b.d. 28 Aug 1715;
SPPR
BAILEY, Tabitha d/o John & Mary Bailey bap 4 Aug
1713; SPPR
BAILEY, Thomas s/o John & Susan Bailey age 29 S
POB POR New Kent carpenter & **ARNOLD**, Eliza
d/o Robert & Virginia Arnold age 26 S POB
King William POR New Kent; DOM 19 Jan 1859
POM Olivet Ch, New Kent by Isaac O. Sloan;
NKMR
BAIZEY, Jane d/o George Baizey bap 24 Aug 1709;
SPPR
BALL, George attorney POR Gloucester & **HOOMES**,
Maria M. d/o Capt. Benjamin Hoomes POR King &
Queen; DOM 24 Dec 1807 POM Point of View,
King & Queen by Robert Semple; VA
BALL, Lewis C. s/o Carter & Martha Ball age 22 S
farmer & **BARNETT**, Louisa C. d/o Gatewood &
Margaret Barnett age 21 S POB King & Queen;
DOM 21 Aug 1856 POM King & Queen by Robert Y.
Henley; KQMR
BANKS, Tunstall & **CURTIS**, Polly Murray; DOM 22 May
1793 POM King & Queen; VM
BARDRICK, Constantine s/o Henry Bardrick bap 15
Mar 1712; SPPR
BARDRICK, Elizabeth d/o Henry Bardrick bap 29 Oct
1710; SPPR
BAREFOOT, Edward s/o William & Susan Barefoot age
45 W farmer POB POR King & Queen & **NOEL**,
Frances d/o Philip & Frances Noel age 20 S
POB POR King & Queen; DOM 14 May 1856 POM
King & Queen by H. Montague; KQMR
BARKER, Elizabeth buried by 15 Oct 1755; BP
BARKER, Frances bastard d/o Susanna Barker (dec)
bound to David Edwards 10 Oct 1733; SMP

14

BARKER, James Roberson & Frances Barker
illegitimate children of Susannah Barker
bound to Job Jackson 10 Oct 1734 SMP
BARKER, William s/o Randolph & Lotsy Barker age 28
S POB Hanover POR New Kent farmer & MARTIN,
Elizabeth E. d/o James & Charity Chadick age
48 W POB James City Co. POR New Kent; DOM 20
Sep 1856 POM New Kent by J.W.Fussell; NKMR
BARNS, Rebecca d/o Thomas Barns bap 1 Mar 1712;
SPPR
BARRAM, Thomas illegitimate s/o Thomas Barram
bound to Abram Basket 16 Nov 1757; SMP
BARRETT, Lucy single d.d. Sep 1832 age 18 POR King
William; SMPR
BARRICK, William E. s/o John & Emiline Barrick age
20 S house joiner POB Middlesex & WALDEN,
J.A.E. d/o Th.B. & S.A.Walden age 18 S POB
King & Queen; DOM 23 Sep POM King & Queen by
A.F.Scott; KQMR
BASSETT, Alfred s/o John Bassett & Elizabeth
Carter Browne of New Kent b.d. 18 Jul 1805
d.d. 25 Sep 1805; KK2
BASSETT, Anna Maria d/o Burwell Bassett & Anna
Maria Dandridge b.d. 16 May 1760 d.d. 23 Jul
1760; FB
BASSETT, Anna Maria d/o Burwell Bassett & Anna
Maria Dandridge of New Kent b.d. 26 Feb 1763;
FB
BASSETT, Anne d/o Thomas & Ellenor Bassett bap 20
Jun 1703 POR New Kent; SPPR
BASSETT, Anne d/o Thomas Bassett bap 20 Jun 1703
SPPR
BASSETT, Betty Carter d/o John Bassett & Elizabeth
Carter Browne of New Kent b.d. 5 Jan 1807;
KK2
BASSETT, Burwell POR New Kent & DANDRIDGE, Anna
Maria; DOM 7 Jan (or Jun) 1757; FB
BASSETT, Burwell s/o Burwell Bassett & Ann K.
Chamberlayne b.d. 3 Mar 1734 POB "Eltham" New
Kent; FB
BASSETT, Burwell s/o Burwell Bassett & Anna Maria
Dandridge of New Kent b.d. 18 Mar 1764; FB
BASSETT, Burwell s/o John Bassett & Elizabeth
Carter Browne b.d. 22 Jan 1802 d.d. 1 Oct
1802 POD "Elsing Green" King William; KK2
BASSETT, Burwell s/o William Bassett & Elizabeth
Churchill b.d. 8 Mar 1712 New Kent d.d. 4 Jan
1793 POD "Eltham", New Kent; FB
BASSETT, Burwell s/o William Bassett & Elizabeth
Churchill POB POR New Kent & CHAMBERLAYNE,
Ann Kidley d/o William Chamberlayne &
Elizabeth Littlepage POB New Kent; DOM 26 Jun
1755; FB

BASSETT, David s/o Thomas & Mary Bassett (d.d. of
Mary 18 Nov 1719) b.d. 7 Nov 1719 POB New
Kent; SPPR
BASSETT, Elizabeth d/o Burwell Bassett & Ann K.
Chamberlayne b.d. 17 Oct 1756 POB New Kent;
FB
BASSETT, Elizabeth d/o Burwell Bassett & Anna
Maria Dandridge b.d. 26 Jan 1759; FB
BASSETT, Elizabeth d/o William & Joanna (Burwell)
Bassett POR New Kent b.d. 4 Jul 1697 bap 13
Jul 1697 d.d. 14 Oct 1738 POD "Claremont",
Surry ; FB
BASSETT, Elizabeth d/o William Bassett & Joanna
Burwell of New Kent b.d. 4 Jul 1697 bap 13
Jul 1697; KK2
BASSETT, Frances Carter d/o John Bassett &
Elizabeth Carter Browne b.d. 9 Dec 1792 POB
"Wakefield" d.d. 4 Jan 1795; KK2
BASSETT, Francis s/o Burwell Bassett & Anna Maria
Dandridge of New Kent b.d. 19 Dec 1767; FB
BASSETT, George s/o Burwell Bassett & Anna Maria
Dandridge of New Kent b.d. 7 Aug 1766 d.d 7
Aug 1766; FB
BASSETT, George Washington s/o John Bassett &
Elizabeth Carter Browne of New Kent b.d. 23
Aug 1800 POB "Farmington" Hanover; KK2
BASSETT, Hannah d/o William Bassett & Joanna
Burwell POR New Kent b.d. 9 Mar 1713/14 bap
19 Mar 1713/14; KK2
BASSETT, Henry Alfred s/o John Bassett & Elizabeth
Carter Browne of New Kent b.d. 17 Nov 1803
POB "Farmington" Hanover d.d. at 15 months;
KK2
BASSETT, Jane d/o Thomas & Ellenor Bassett (d.d.
of Ellenor 20 Sep 1713) POR New Kent bap 29
Apr 1711: SPPR
BASSETT, Jane d/o Thomas Bassett bap 29 Apr 1711
SPPR
BASSETT, Joanna d/o William Bassett & Joanna
Burwell POR New Kent b.d. 12 Oct 1701 bap 25
Oct 1701 d.d. 25 Oct 1702; KK2
BASSETT, Joanna d/o William Bassett & Joanna
Burwell POR New Kent b.d. 2 Oct 1703 bap 19
Oct 1703 d.d. 4 Oct 1708; KK2
BASSETT, John Burwell s/o John Bassett & Elizabeth
Carter Browne b.d. 27 Dec 1794 POB
"Farmington" Hanover d.d. 12 Apr 1796 POD
"Farmington" Hanover; KK2
BASSETT, John Churchill s/o John Bassett &
Elizabeth Carter Browne of New Kent POB
"Farmington" Hanover b.d. 1 May 1797 d.d. 12
Sep 1798 POD "Farmington" Hanover; KK2
BASSETT, John s/o Burwell Bassett & Anna Maria
Dandridge b.d. 30 Aug 1765 POB "Eltham" New

Kent & **BROWNE**, Elizabeth Carter d/o William
Burnet Browne & Judith Carter b.d. 22 Dec
1768; DOM 12 Sep 1786; KK2
BASSETT, John s/o Burwell Bassett & Anna Maria
Dandridge of New Kent b.d. 30 Aug 1765; FB
BASSETT, John s/o Thomas & Ellenor Bassett b.d. 8
Feb POB New Kent d.d. 17 Mar 1716 POD New
Kent; SPPR
BASSETT, Judith Carter d/o John Bassett &
Elizabeth Carter Browne of New Kent b.d 5 Jan
1799 POB "Farmington" Hanover d.d. 21 Aug
1800; KK2
BASSETT, Lewis s/o William Bassett & Joanna
Burwell b.d. 8 Mar 1707 POR New Kent bap 19
Aug 1707 d.d. 8 Sep 1708; KK2
BASSETT, Lucy d/o William Bassett & Joanna Burwell
POR New Kent b.d. 20 May 1699 bap 13 Jul
1699; KK2
BASSETT, Mary d/o Thomas & Elizabeth Bassett (d.d.
of Elizabeth 7 Apr 1717) POR New Kent b.d. 4
Apr 1717; SPPR
BASSETT, Nathaniel s/o William Bassett & Joanna
Burwell POR New Kent b.d. 16 Jan 1718/19; KK2
BASSETT, Thomas s/o William & Anne Bassett &
HOWLE, Lidia; DOM 25 Feb 1719/20 POM St.
Peter's Parish, New Kent; SPPR
BASSETT, Thomas s/o William & Anne Bassett POR New
Kent d.d. 20 Apr 1720 POD New Kent; KK2
BASSETT, Ursula d/o Thomas & Elizabeth Bassett POR
New Kent b.d. 15 Sep 1715; SPPR
BASSETT, Ursula d/o Thomas Bassett b.d. 15 Sep
1715; SPPR
BASSETT, William d.d. between 10 Oct 1722 and Dec
1724; BP
BASSETT, William d.d. between 18 Oct 1743 and 15
Oct 1744; BP
BASSETT, William POR "Eltham", New Kent b.d.1670
in VA; CVR
BASSETT, William s/o Burwell Bassett & Anna Maria
Dandridge of New Kent b.d. 19 Sep 1761; FB
BASSETT, William s/o John Bassett & Elzabeth
Carter Browne b.d. 10 Oct 1790 POB "Elsing
Green", King William d.d. 21 Nov 1812 POD
"Middleway" Gloucester; KK2
BASSETT, William s/o Thomas & Ellenor Bassett POR
New Kent d.d. 8 Mar 1716; SPPR
BASSETT, William s/o William Bassett & Bridget
Cary b.d. 1670 POB Southampton Co.,England
POR "Eltham", New Kent d.d. 11 Oct 1723 POD
"Eltham" New Kent; KK2
BASSETT, William s/o William Bassett & Bridget
Cary POR New Kent & **BURWELL**, Joanna d/o Lewis
Burwell & Abigail Smith; DOM 28 Nov 1693; KK2

17

BASSETT, William s/o William Bassett & Joanna
    Burwell b.d. 8 Mar 1709 POR New Kent &
    CHURCHILL, Elizabeth; DOM 29 Jan 1729 POM
    Middlesex; KK2
BASSETT, William s/o William Bassett & Joanna
    Burwell POR New Kent b.d. 17 Mar 1705 bap 11
    Apr 1705 d.d. 8 Sep 1708; KK2
BASSETT, William s/o William Bassett POB
    Southampton Co.,England d.d. will dated 28
    Aug 1671 will probated 4 Jan 1671/2; KK2
BATES, John buried by 9 Oct 1759; BP
BATES, Thomas buried by 12 Oct 1738; BP
BATES, William POR King & Queen & BOULWARE, Susan
    d/o Mark Boulware; DOM 10 Feb 1830 POM
    Caroline by John Micou; VCA
BATHURST, Lancelot s/o Sir Edward Bathurst & Susan
    Rich b.d. 1646 POB Gloucestershire, England
    POR New Kent; KK2
BAUGHAN, Joseph b.d. 17 Feb 1702 SPPR
BAYLOR, John POR King & Queen & PRITCHET, Sally S
    POR Middlesex; DOM "married lately" issue
    date 13 Apr 1782 VGAA
BAYLOR, John POR King & Queen d.d. 1709; EHR
BAYLOR, John s/o John Baylor & Lucy Todd POB
    Walkerton, King & Queen b.d. 12 May 1705;
    ONKH
BAYLOR, Robert s/o Robert Baylor POR Ricahock,
    King & Queen d.d. 1762; ONKH
BAYLOR, Thomas L. POR King & Queen d.d. issue
    dated 3 Sep 1822 RE
BAYLY, Edward s/o John Bayly bap 30 May 16__ SPPR
BELL, David s/o David & Bethea Bell bap 10 Jul
    1698 SPPR
BELL, Edward s/o Edward & Mary Bell bap 16__ SPPR
BEN (?), Richard C. s/o James & Mary Ben(?) age 19
    S farmer POB POR King & Queen & HOG (?),
    Elizabeth d/o Thomas & Susan Hog (?) age 26 S
    POR King & Queen; DOM 26 Dec 1857 POM King &
    Queen by Thomas B. Evans KQMR
BERKELEY, Thomas Nelson s/o Nelson Berkeley of
    King William d.d. 18 Sep 1823 POR POD
    Airwell, Hanover; KWC
BERRELL, Benjamin & ALKINSON, Elizabeth; DOM 21
    Mar 1711; SPPR
BETTES, Edward & JACKSON, Rachel; DOM 4 Mar
    1708/9; SPPR
BETTES, Gedion s/o Edward Bettes bap 3 Aug 1711
    SPPR
BETTES, Hester d/o Edward & Rachel Bettes bap 14
    Aug 1709 SPPR
BETTES, Uriah s/o Edward & rachelk Bettes bap 14
    Aug 1709 SPPR
BEVERLEY, Robert s/o William Beverley & Elizabeth
    Beverley b.d. 21 Auf 1740; FB

18

BIBEY, John bap 5 Jan 1706/7 SPPR
BIGGER, William s/o Will Bigger b.d. 28 Jan 16__
SPPR
BINGHAM, Will & Jane his wife 16__ Spp
BINNS, Allen P. s/o William Binns & Mary Salter
b.d. 26 Nov 1804 d.d. 25 Dec 1843 POD Sumpter
Co., AL; KK2
BINNS, Ann Kidley d/o Daniel Binns & Ann Kidley
Cooke b.d. abt 1806 POB New Kent POD Potter's
Farm, Charles City Co; KK2
BINNS, Charles Henry s/o William Binns & Mary
Salter & COLGIN, Adelaide Broadnax; DOM 29
Mar 1838 POM Sumpter Co.,AL; KK2
BINNS, Charles Henry s/o William Binns & Mary
Salter b.d. 4 Jan 1812 & BINNS, Martha
Eleanor d/o Daniel Binns & Martha Harman b.d.
24 Sep 1814; DOM 15 Jan 1835 POM New Kent;
KK2
BINNS, Charles s/o Thomas Binns & Frances Pearson
b.d. 5 Feb 1778 POR New Kent d.d. 7 Mar 1854;
KK2
BINNS, Daniel s/o Thomas Binns & Frances Pearson
b.d. 19 Jun 1767 bap 18 Jun 1769 New Kent;
KK2
BINNS, Elizabeth d/o Thomas Binns & Frances
Pearson b.d. 22 Dec 1770 d.d. 22 Dec 1770;
KK2
BINNS, George Fleming s/o William Binns & Mary
Salter b.d. 30 Mar 1815 d.d. Aug 1838 POD
Sumpter Co.,AL; KK2
BINNS, George s/o Thomas Binns & Frances Pearson
b.d. 14 Sep 1764; KK2
BINNS, Gideon Christian s/o William Binns & Mary
Salter b.d. 26 Oct 1819 d.d. 3 Apr 1869 POD
Sumpter Co.,AL; KK2
BINNS, John s/o Thomas Binns & Frances Pearson
b.d. 13 May 1775 d.d. 1828 POD New Kent; KK2
BINNS, Otway s/o Daniel Binns & Martha Harman of
New Kent b.d.1812 POB Charles City Co &
LIPSCOMB, Aurelia Ann; DOM 1844; KK2
BINNS, Polly d/o Thomas Binns & Frances Pearson
b.d. 19 Jan 1785; KK2
BINNS, Richard Graves s/o William Binns & Mary
Salter b.d. 4 May 1814 d.d. 10 Oct 1824; KK2
BINNS, Richard s/o Thomas Binns & Frances Pearson
b.d. 7 Jun 1781 POD Charles City Co.; KK2
BINNS, Thomas s/o William & Sarah Binns & PEARSON,
Frances d/o Charles & Rebecca Pearson; DOM 5
Feb 1762 POM New Kent; FB
BINNS, Thomas s/o William & Sarah Binns b.d. 13
Nov 1734 POB New Kent bap 11 Jan 1835 at
St.Peter's Parish; KK2

BINNS, Thomas Salter (twin) s/o William Binns &
    Mary Salter b.d. 26 Feb 1809 d.d. 26 Sep 1833
    POD Surry; KK2
BINNS, William E. s/o Dennis Binns & Martha
    "Patsy" Truman age 21 s farmer POB POR New
    Kent & FUSSELL, Frances d/o John K. & Mary
    Fussell age 24 s POB Charles City Co POR New
    Kent; DOM 30 Dec 1858 POM New Kent by James
    F. Parkinson; NKMR
BINNS, William s/o Thomas Binns & Frances Pearson
    & SALTER, Mary d/o William & Mary Salter; DOM
    24 Dec 1797; KK2
BINNS, William s/o Thomas Binns & Frances Pearson
    b.d.8 May 1769 POB New Kent bap 18 Jun 1769
    St. Peter's Parish d.d. 5 Oct 1824 POD Surry;
    KK2
BINNS, William Salter (twin) s/o William Binns &
    Mary Salter b.d. 26 Feb 1809 d.d. 16 Oct 1830
    POD Surry; KK2
BIRD, Braxton, & PRICE, Mary; DOM 18 Apr 1760 POM
    King & Queen VM
BIRD, Sarah d.d. 8 Nov 1771; SMP
BIRD, Uriah s/o James Bird & Anna Hudgins age 29 s
    POB King & Queen POR Middlesex ditcher free
    POC & DAVENPORT, Mary A. d/o Thomas Davenport
    & Fanny Brocow age 23 s POB Gloucester Co POR
    King & Queen free POC; DOM 23 Jan 1853 POM
    King & Queen by Thomas B. Evans KQMR
BLACKBURNE, Rowland & GLEN, Anne; DOM 6 Feb 1713;
    SPPR
BLACKWELL, James & Lydia, his wife 16__ SPPR
BLACKWELL, James Jr. & GLENN, Mary; DOM 18 Apr
    1699; SPPR
BLACKWELL, Thomas POR King William d.d. 14 May
    1819 POD Richmond leaving wife and 2 children
    RE
BLAND, George F. s/o Zachary & Delila A.C.Bland
    b.d. 17 Mar 1853 POB King & Queen father's
    occupation farmer KQBR
BLAND, Robert F. s/o Archer Bland & Mary Chapman
    age 23 S farmer POB Gloucester POR Middlesex
    & BLAND, Mary F. d/o A. Bland & ___ Clayton
    age 19 S POB Gloucester POR King & Queen; DOM
    7 Dec 1854 POM King & Queen by William
    Parkwood KQMR
BLAND, Roderick Jr. s/o Roderick Bland & Juliza
    Clayton age 22 S farmer POB King & Queen &
    CARR, Ann B. d/o Thomas Carr & Mary A.
    Shackleford age 23 S POB King & Queen Co; DOM
    23 Oct 1853 by Archer Bland KQMR
BOHANNON, Thomas & FOX, Maria 2nd d/o Maj.
    Nathanial Fox S POR King William; DOM 1 Sep
    1808 by John D. Blair VA
BON, Jane d/o Henry Bon bap 4 Apr 1703 SPPR

20

BORER, Robert & **ROW**, Elizabeth; DOM 22 Nov 1698;
     SPPR
BOSHER, James Gideon POR Richmond & **DABNEY**, Mary
     Booth S POR King William; POM Dorrell, King
     William 12 May 1840 RW
BOSHER, James Gideon POR Richmond & **DABNEY**, Mary
     Booth s POR King William; DOM 12 May 1840 POM
     Dorrell, King William by Rev. J.B.Jeter; KWC
BOUGHTON, John P. POR King William & **SPILLER**, A.D.
     p.m. POR King William; DOM 5 Nov 1833 RE
BOULES, John Jr. bap 13 Feb 1703/4 SPPR
BOULWARE, William professor POR Columbian College,
     Washington D.C. & **GATEWOOD**, Mary M. p.m. POR
     Travelers Rest, King & Queen; DOM 25 Oct 1832
     RE
BOURN, Anne d/o William Bourn Jr. bap 1 Mar 1712
     SPPR
BOURN, Francis [sic] d/o William BOurn Jr. bap 8
     Aug 1714 SPPR
BOWERY, Ida B. d/o William W. & Georgianna Bailey
     b.d. 15 Dec 1857 POB New Kent d.d. 24 Jan
     1926; KK2
BOWLES, Hannah buried by 31 Oct 1749; BP
BOYD, Lucy Ann p.m. POR New Kent d.d. issue dated
     31 Oct 1834 RW
BOYD, Mary H. p.m. POR King & Queen d.d. issue
     dated 27 Feb 1821 RE
BOYD, Mary H. w/o Col. William Boyd only surviving
     d/o John Robinson d.d. issue dated 27 Feb
     1821 POD Clifton, King & Queen; VCA
BOYD, Mary H. w/o William Boyd d/o John Robinson
     d.d. 19 Feb 1821 POD Clifton, King & Queen
     RCC
BOYD, Robert B. POR King & Queen d.d. issue dated
     22 Jun 1838 RW
BOYD, Robert Bolling POR New Kent d.d. issue dated
     20 Jan 1837 RW
BOYD, Robert POB Scotland POR New Kent d.d. 17 Nov
     1812 age 62 POD New Kent VP
BOYD, Spencer d.d. between 7 Jul 1775 and 28 Sep
     1779; SMP
BOYD, William POR New Kent & _____. Lucy Ann POR
     Richmond; DOM 28 Jul 1831 RE
BOYDE, James Dr. POR King & Queen d.d. issue dated
     14 Feb 1737 VG
BRADGER, Margret molatto [sic] bastard of Ann
     Bradger bound to Stephen Haynes 27 Mar 1744
     SMP
BRAXTON, Carter & **CORBIN**, Betty d/o Richard Corbin
     & Betty Tayloe DOM 1761; VG
BRAXTON, Carter & **SAYRE**, Mary Grynmes; DOM 21 May
     1823 POM King & Queen VM
BRAXTON, Carter s/o Mary Braxton b.d. 16 Sep 1736;
     MBC

BRAXTON, Carter s/o Mary Carter & ____ Braxton
    b.d. 16 Sep 1736; VCA
BRAXTON, Carter s/o s/o George Braxton & Mary
    Carter b.d. 1736 POR King & Queen d.d. 1797,
    Burgess, Member of VA Convention 1775, signer
    of Declaration of Independance; SAR
BRAXTON, Corbin POD Florida d.d. issue dated 9 Jul
    1822; KWC
BRAXTON, Elizabeth d/o George Braxton Sr. 1678-
    1748 POR King & Queen SAR
BRAXTON, Elizabeth Pope p.m. POR King William d.d.
    issue dated 22 Dec 1831 RW
BRAXTON, George d.d. 1 Jul 1748 age 71 left a son
    and two daughters; MBC
BRAXTON, George d.d. 1 Jul 1748 age 71; VCA
BRAXTON, George POR King & Queen b.d. 1678 d.d.
    1748; SAR
BRAXTON, George s/o George Braxton POR King &
    Queen & King William d.d. 1761; SAR
BRAXTON, George s/o Mary Braxton b.d. 13 Jan 1734;
    MBC
BRAXTON, George s/o Mary Carter & _____ Braxton
    b.d. 13 Jan 1734; VCA
BRAXTON, infant s/o George Braxton & Mary Carter
    d.d. 20 Sep 1736; VG
BRAXTON, Mary (Mrs.) d/o Hon. Robert Carter d.d.
    17 Sep 1736 age 34; VCA
BRAXTON, Mary d/o late Col. Carter w/o George
    Braxton POR King & Queen d.d. 17 Sep 1736; VG
BRAXTON, Mary d/o Robert Carter d.d. 17 Sep 1736;
    MBC
BRAXTON, William Fitzhugh s/o Carter Braxton (dec)
    d.d. 11 Jan 1821 from the Philadelphia
    National Gazette; KWC
BRAXTON, William P. Dr. POR King William &
    COALTER, Virginia B. youngest d/o George T.
    Coalter (dec) POR Stafford; POM Stanley,
    Hanover DOM 12 Jun 1855 VH
BREEDEN, Sarah wife of Moody Breeden POR King
    William d.d. 15 Oct 1808 age 79 VA
BRISTOW, Robert B. POR King & Queen d.d. issue
    dated 23 Nov 1827 RE
BROACH, Albert POD King & Queen d.d."on Wednesday
    last" issue dated 31 Mar 1860; WA
BROACH, Allen s/o Anderson Broach & Susan Thornton
    age 31 S farmer POB POR King & Queen &
    DARNEL, Harriet d/o Ben Thurston & Nancy Bray
    age 32 W POB POR King & Queen; DOM 28 Aug
    1856 POM Middlesex by Archer Bland KQMR
BROACH, Martin s/o Benoni & Mary Broach age 49 W
    farmer POB King & Queen & **CROW**, Elliz age 33
    S POB King & Queen; DOM 30 Jan 1854 POM King
    & Queen by R.H.Bagby KQMR
BROACH, Patty bap 25 Nov 1788; VBHS

BROCK, Joshua s/o George Brock bap 3 Jul 1703 SPPR

BROGMAN, Thomas bap 25 Feb 1704/5 SPPR

BROKENBOROUGH, Eugenia d/o John & Frances Brokenborough bap. 22 Jul 1838 POR King William SMPR

BROOK, Mary E. d/o George W. & Mary C. Brook b.d. 5 Jul 1853 POB King & Queen father's occupation school teacher KQBR

BROOKE, Christopher & **SAUNDERS**, Elizabeth; DOM 23 Dec 1782 POM King & Queen VM

BROOKE, Christopher POR King & Queen & **SAUNDERS**, Elizabeth s; DOM 23 Dec 1782; Middlesex Marriage Register

BROOKE, Humphrey & **PAGE**, Sarah; DOM 7 Feb 1799 POM King William VM

BROOKE, Humphrey d.d issue dated 26 Oct 1738 POR POD King William; KWC

BROOKE, Humphrey died 1738 POR King William s/o Robert Brooke & Catherine Boothe; SAR

BROOKE, Humphrey POR King William was a Justice of the Peace d.d. 21 Oct 1738 VG

BROOKE, William s/o Temple Brooke age 23 S carpenter POB Gloucester POR King & Queen & **COOKE**, Clarilla d/o Dawson Cooke age 21 S POB POR King & Queen; DOM 30 Oct 1860 POM King & Queen KQMR

BROOKER, Antapass d/o Richard Brooker bap 13 Dec 1713 SPPR

BROOKER, Peter s/o Richard Brooker bap 8 Apr 1711 SPPR

BROOKING, Frances (Mrs.) POR King & Queen d.d.25 Oct 1804 age 85 VA

BROOKING, Robert POR King & Queen & **VIVION**, Frances d/o Thomas Vivion POR King George; DOM deed found 1741 POM deed found Essex; Essex Deed Book 22

BROOKS, Ruth d.d. before 3 Oct 1752; BP

BROTHERS, Francis s/o Nathaniel Brothers b.d. 16 Feb 1711 SPPR

BROWN, Archibald merchant POR King William & **SAUNDERS**, Ann S POR King & Queen; DOM 18 Dec 1816 by Robert B. Semple RE

BROWN, Archibald merchant POR King William & **SAUNDERS**, Ann s POR King & Queen; DOM 18 Dec 1816 by Rev. Ro. B. Semple; KWC

BROWN, Archibald POR King William & **SAUNDERS**, Ann POR King & Queen s DOM 18 Dec 1816; VG

BROWN, Basil POR King William & **DANDRIDGE**, Fanny R. d/o Capt. John Dandridge POR Henrico; DOM 22 Dec 1803 VGGA

BROWN, Carver C. s/o Carver W. & Sally S. Brown (Carver W. is a farmer) POB POR King William b.d. Aug 1853; ROBKW

BROWN, Eliza R. p.m. POR King William d.d. issue
  dated 18 Feb 1815 RE

BROWN, Eliza R. wife of William B.Brown d.d. 29
  Jan 1815 POD Elsing Green, King William RE

BROWN, Elizabeth d/o Ann Brown bound to Zach.
  Shackleford 10 Oct 1744 SMP

BROWN, Elizabeth d/o Robert Brown kept by Robert
  Garrett 10 Oct 1741 SMP

BROWN, Emily Lewis d/o Lewis Brown & Nancy Nunn
  b.d. 10 Apr 1816 POB King & Queen GN VSA
  #34327

BROWN, Henry (dec) by 30 Sep 1751; SMP

BROWN, Henry POR King & Queen d.d.between 8 Oct
  1750 and 30 Sep 1751 SMP

BROWN, James d.d. 1751; BP

BROWN, John & **WHORTON**, Mary; DOM 4 Jan 1708/9;
  SPPR

BROWN, Lewis b.d. 25 Jan 1773 POB King & Queen GN
  VSA #34327

BROWN, Lewis b.d. 25 Jan 1773; IR Flores

BROWN, Rebecca d/o Henry Brown bap 28 Mar 1702/3
  SPPR

BROWN, Sarah Ann d/o Lewis Brown & Nancy Nunn b.d.
  15 Nov 1821; IR Flores

BROWN, Sarah d/o Lewis Brown & Nancy Nunn b.d. 15
  Nov 1821 POB King & Queen GN VSA #34327

BROWN, Thomas s/o Lewis Brown & Nancy Nunn b.d. 4
  Nov 1810 POB King & Queen GN VSA #34327

BROWN, Thomas s/o Lewis Brown & Nancy Nunn b.d. 4
  Nov 1810; IR Flores

BROWN, William & **VAUGHAN**, Mary; DOM 28 Dec 1711;
  SPPR

BROWNE, Andrew C. POR King & Queen & **GARNETT**, Lucy
  S POR King & Queen; DOM 11 Nov 1818 by
  William Tude RE

BROWNE, Thomas s/o Thomas Browne bap 27 Nov 168_
  SPPR

BROWNE, William B. POR King William d.d. issue
  dated 18 Oct 1833 RW

BRYAN, B.H. & **BACON**, Elizabeth B. d/o John Bacon &
  Elizabeth Ware; DOM 31 Dec 1839; KK2

BUGG, John s/o Samm. Bugg b.d. 5 May 1715 SPPR

BUGG, Sherwood b.d. 8 Jul 1720; marker found in
  St. Peter's Churchyard, New Kent

BULLOCK, Alice d.d. 22 Aug 1759 age 79; Camm FB

BULLOCK, Richard d.d. 22 Aug 1759 & _____,
  Alice; DOM 1701; Camm FB

BULLOCK, Richard d/o Edward & Sarah Bullock bap 16
  Apr no year stated; SPPR

BURBIDGE, John s/o Robert & Mary Burbidge b.d. 26
  Aug 1714; SPPR

BURBIDGE, Robert & **KING**, Mary; DOM 11 Aug 1711;
  SPPR

BURCH, Jonathan s/o William Burch & Kitty Richason
age 35 W farmer POB King & Queen & **CORDON**,
Willy Ann d/o Richard Cordon & Mary Eubank
age 18 S POB King & Queen Co; DOM 23 Oct 1853
POM King & Queen by Isaac Diggs; KQMR
BURCHELL, John s/o N. & Mary Burchell age 29 W
farmer POB POR King George & **BURCH**, Ann E.
d/o Henry & F. Burch age 21 POB King & Queen
POR King George; DOM 25 Sep 1859 POM King
George taken from the marriage register at
King George
BURDETT, Howard buried by 16 Oct 1751; BP
BURGESS, Matthew buried by 22 Feb 1762; SMP
BURKE, Anne Roy d/o Robert Burke POR King William
b.d. 1840 d.d.1844; KWH
BURKE, Ariana d/o Robert Burke b.d. 1835 POR King
William; KWH
BURKE, Emma Roy d/o Robert Burke b.d. 1 Oct 1844
POR King William; KWH
BURKE, Felix Roscoe s/o Robert Burke POR King
William b.d. 1836; KWH
BURKE, George Haviland s/o Robert Burke b.d. 13
Apr 1857 POR "Spring Bank" King William; KWH
BURKE, Herbert s/o Robert Burke b.d. 1847 d.d.
1849; KWH
BURKE, Herbert s/o Waller Burke & Mary Edwards
b.d. 1814 d.d 1829 POR King William; KWH
BURKE, John Waller s/o Robert Burke POR King
William b.d. 14 Mar 1842; KWH
BURKE, Lucius C. s/o Robert Burke b.d. 27 Jul 1849
POR King William; KWH
BURKE, Mary Jane d/o Waller Burke & Mary Edwards
b.d 1826 POR King William d.d. 1838; KWH
BURKE, Mary Wiley d/o Robert Burke b.d. Jul 1838
POR King William; KWH
BURKE, Robert s/o Waller & Mary Burke POR "Spring
Bank" King William & **LIPSCOMB**, Margaret; DOM
Jun 1831; KWH
BURKE, Robert s/o Waller Burke & Mary Edwards POR
King William b.d. 3 May 1808; KWH
BURKE, Waller b/o William Burke b.d. 4 Feb 1778
d.d. 30 Mar 1829 POR "Spring Bank" King
William; KWH
BURKE, Waller POR "Spring Bank" King William &
EDWARDS, Mary d/o Samuel Edwards; DOM Dec
1806; KWH
BURNET, Elizabeth buried by 21 Nov 1758; SMP
BURRUS, _____ d/o Harris D. & Mary E. Burrus
(Harris is a farmer) POB POR King WIlliam
b.d. Sep 1853; ROBKW
BURRUS, Richard D. s/o George & Frances Burrus
b.d. 20 Mar 1815; VCA
BURTON, Hutchens & **ALLEN**, Susanna; DOM 31 Mar
1719; SPPR

BURWELL, Ann [nee Jones] wi/o James Burwell POR
York d.d. issue dated 30 Oct 1779; KWC

BURWELL, Joanna d/o Major Lewis Burwell & Abigail
Smith b.d 1675 POR Carter's Creek, Gloucester
d.d. 7 Oct 1727 [probable POD New Kent]; KK2

BURWELL, Margaret wi/o Col. Nathaniel Burwell POR
POD King William d.d. issue dated 3 Jul 1779;
KWC

BURWELL, Nathaniel (Captain of the artillary) &
DIGGS, Patty d/o Dudly Diggs POR
Williamsburg; issue date 11 Mar 1780; VG

BUTLER, David S. POR King William & **DUGAR**,
Frances I.or J. POR King William ; 27 Nov
1823 ML King William; CTR

BUTLER, James M. POR King & Queen d.d. issue dated
13 Apr 1838; RW

BUTLER, Mary N. p.m. POR King & Queen d.d. issue
dated 1 Sep 1829; RW

BUTLER, Mary S. d/o Benjamin & Mary W. Butler d.d.
24 Aug 1829 age 3 years; KWC

BUTLER, Mary S. POR King William d.d. issue dated
1 Sep 1829; RW

BUTLER, Mary W. w/o Benjamin Butler d.d. 21 Aug
1829 age 22; KWC

BUTLER, Reuben major former POR North Carolina
d.d. 20 Dec 1828 b.d. 13 Dec 1749 POD King
William; KWC

BUTMAN, Thomas C. s/o Thomas & Margaret Butman age
43 W farmer POB King & Queen & **MORRIS**, Vester
Ann R. d/o William & Mary Newcomb age 39 W
POB King & Queen; DOM 23 Aug 1856 POM King &
Queen by John P. Woodward; KQMR

BUTTLER, Mary d/o Thomas & Mary Buttler bap 7 ___
16__; SPPR

BUTTLER, Thomas & **CRUE**, Margery; DOM 1 Mar 1685/6;
SPPR

BUTTS, Peter s/o Thomas & Catharine Butts b.d. 1
Sep 1714; SPPR

BUTTS, Thomas & **MACLAGHE**, Catherine; DOM 2 Apr
1713; SPPR

CADE, Margarett d/o Robert Cade bap 27 Nov 169_;
SPPR

CADE, Robert & **CRUMP**, Susanna; DOM 17 Sep 1713;
SPPR

CAMBO, Elizabeth d/o Richard Cambo bap 15 Feb
168_; SPPR

CAMM, Ann d/o John Camm & Mary Bullock b.d. 5 Jan
1723; Camm FB

CAMM, Elizabeth d/o John Camm & Mary Bullock b.d.
12 Feb 1729; Camm FB

CAMM, John & **BULLOCK**, Mary; DOM 22 May 1722 by
Lewis LaHany; Camm FB

CAMM, John POR North Bank, King & Queen will dated
    17 Mar 1766 daughters Ann Booker, Mary
    Garlick, Elizabeth White; BKQCHS
CAMM, John s/o John Camm & Mary Bullock b.d. 17
    Jan 1745 d.d. 30 Jul 1748; Camm FB
CAMM, John s/o John Camm & Mary Bullock b.d. 30
    May 1732 d.d. 5 Dec 1735; Camm FB
CAMM, John s/o John Camm & Mary Bullock b.d. 4 May
    1731 d.d. 30 May 1731; Camm FB
CAMM, Mary d/o John Camm & Mary Bullock b.d. 15
    Oct 1724 d.d. 22 Aug 1726; Camm FB
CAMM, Mary d/o John Camm & Mary Bullock b.d. 15
    Oct 1727; Camm FB
CAMM, Mary w/o John Camm d.d. 1 Jan 1753 age 49y 1
    mo 17 days; Camm FB
CAMM, Sarah d/o John Camm & Mary Bullock b.d. 28
    Feb 1738 d.d. 13 Oct 1756 w/o John Walker;
    Camm FB
CAMM. Richard s/o John Camm & Mary Bullock b.d. 1
    Jul 1736 d.d. 12years 1 mo 21 days; Camm FB
CAMPBELL, James mollatto basterd [sic] s/o
    Margaret Campbell bound to Richard Guthrie 17
    Nov 1752; SMP
CAMPBELL, James mulatto illegitimate s/o Margarett
    Campbell bound 17 Nov 1752; SMP
CAMPBELL, Peter POR King & Queen & HENLEY, Mary S
    POR Essex; DOM 10 Dec 1816 by Philip
    Montague; RE
CAMPBELL, Thomas R. POR King & Queen d.d. issue
    dated 8 Mar 1833; RW
CAMPBELL, William POR King & Queen & COURTNEY,
    Priscilla 2nd d/o Capt Robert Courtney POR
    King & Queen; DOM 22 Sep 1818 by Rev.
    Montague; RE
CARLTON, Alice b.d. 31 Jan 1856 d.d. 27 Sep 1881;
    MBC
CARLTON, Christopher s/o Christopher Carlton &
    Jane Hart age 47 W carpenter POB POR King &
    Queen & EUBANK, Susan d/o Thomas Jeffries &
    Susan Carlton age 44 W POB POR King & Queen;
    DOM 22 Dec 1853 POM King & Queen by William
    B. Todd; KQMR
CARLTON, Cornelius H. b.d. 28 Mar 1826 d.d. 2 Jun
    1887; MBC
CARLTON, Humphrey ; DOM 1 Feb 1778 POM King &
    Queen; VM
CARLTON, Isaac s/o Richard & Mary Carlton age 26 S
    farmer POB POR King & Queen & GARRETT, Mary
    C. d/o Lorenzo W. & Mary E. Garrett age 16 S
    POB POR King & Queen; DOM 10 Apr 1856 POM
    King & Queen by John B. Laurens; KQMR
CARLTON, William H. s/o Richard Carlton age 25 S
    farmer POB POR King & Queen & HILYARD,
    Elizabeth d/o William Hilyard age 18 S POB

27

POR King & Queen; DOM 28 Dec 1859 POM King &
Queen by Isaac Digges; KQMR
CARPENTER, Peter d.d. between 24 Apr 1725 and 24
Jun 1726; BP
CARR, Thomas s/o Thomas Carr & Mary Bland age 46 W
farmer POB King & Queen & **BLAND**, Mary C. d/o
Charles Kercheval & Lucy A. Orrel age 26 W
POB King & Queen; DOM 16 Dec 1856 POM King &
Queen by Archer Bland; KQMR
CARRINGTON, Mayo & **ADAMS**, Ann d/o Richard Adams &
Elizabeth Griffin POR New Kent; DOM 30 Sep
1787; KK1
CARTER, John POR King George Co & **CLAIBORNE**,
Philadelphia d/o Philip Whithead Claiborne s
POR King William; DOM 3 Oct 1771; VG
CARTER, Robert E. POR King & Queen d.d. issue
dated 5 Mar 1814; RE
CARTER, Thomas N. POR Pampatike & **GAINES**, Juliet
M. d/o Henry Gaines POR Gloucester Co POM
King William issue date 25 Feb 1826; VG
CASE, Barbara d/o Thomas & Mary Case b.d.9 Dec
169_ bap 10 Jan 1698; SPPR
CASE, Mary d/o Thomas Case [probably sister of
Barbara and Thomas] bap. 18 ___, ___; SPPR
CASE, Thomas s/o Thomas Case 16 Nov 169_; SPPR
CASE, William s/o Hugh Case bap 24 ___, ___; SPPR
CATLETT, Caroline eldest d/o Ann Catlett POR King
William d.d.6 Oct 1823; KWC
CATLETT, Caroline POR King William d.d. issue
dated 17 Oct 1823; RE
CATLETT, John POR King William & **BAITUP**, Martha
POR Gloucester s DOM 19 Feb 1818; VG
CATLETT, John POR King William & **BAITLE**, Martha S
POR Gloucester; DOM 18 Feb 1818 RE
CATLETT, Mary (Mrs.) d.d. Apr 1820 POD King
William age 89; RE
CHADICK, Thomas D. POR New Kent & **MARTIN**, Sarah
POR New Kent ML New Kent DOM 4 Oct 1828; CTR
CHAFORD, Angelina d/o John Chaford bap 21 Nov
1689; SPPR
CHAMBERLAYNE, Ann d/o Will and Eliz Chamberlayne
d.d. 8 Oct 1725 age 1 year 6 months 25 days;
SPPR
CHAMBERLAYNE, Ann Kidley d/o William Chamberlayne
& Elizabeth Littlepage b.d. 10 Apr 1736 POB
New Kent d.d. 1756 POD "Eltham", New Kent;
KK2
CHAMBERLAYNE, Edward P. POR King William d.d. 4
Jun 1806 age 48 leaving a widow and 8
children; RE
CHAMBERLAYNE, Elizabeth (Mrs.) POR King William
d.d. (issue date) 24 Jun 1807 age 49 leaving
5 children; VA

CHAMBERLAYNE, Frances d/o Will and Eliz
     Chamberlayne d.d. 17 Nov 1722 age 30 days;
     SPPR
CHAMBERLAYNE, Lewis W. Dr. POR Richmond & DABNEY,
     Martha B.; DOM 11 Apr 1820 POM Mt. Prospect,
     New Kent by Rev. R.C.Moore; RC
CHAMBERLAYNE, Sarah d/o Thomas Delaware
     Chamberlayne d.d. 28 Aug 1828 age 13y 5 mo
     POD King William; KWC
CHAMBERLAYNE, Sarah p.m. POR King William d.d.
     issue dated 9 Sep 1828; RE
CHAMBERLAYNE, William d.d. 2 Aug 1736 age 36; SPPR
CHAMBERLAYNE, William general POR New Kent d.d.
     issue dated 6 Sep 1836; RW
CHAMBERLAYNE, William POR New Kent & WILKINSON,
     Peggy S POR Hnerico; issue date 7 Aug 1784;
     VGAA
CHAMBERS, James s/o Edward & Eliz. Chambers bap 7
     Aug 169_; SPPR
CHANDLER, David d.d. by 23 Feb 1784; BP
CHANDLER, James POR New Kent & RICHARDSON, Mary
     A.C. S POR New Kent DOM 10 Aug 1836 by
     Rev.Stephen W.Jones; VCS
CHANDLER, James POR New Kent d.d. issue dated 10
     Sep 1813; RE
CHANDLER, John s/o Robert Chandler bap 11 Jan 16__
     ;SPPR
CHANDLER, Joseph s/o Robert Chandler bap 11 Aug
     ____; SPPR
CHANDLER, Robert s/o Robert Chandler bap 30 May
     168_ ;SPPR
CHANDLER, Timothy s/o Robert & Elizabeth Chandler
     bap 17 Oct 168_ ;SPPR
CHANDLER, William s/o Robert Chandler bap 26 Jun
     169_; SPPR
CHAPELL, Samuel s/o Burnell Chapell bap 4 ___,
     16__; SPPR
CHAPPELL, Stephen (a parish child) b.d. May 1705
     bap Jun 1712; SPPR
CHAPPELL, Carrell F. POR New Kent d.d. issue dated
     26 Oct 1830; RW
CHAPPILL, William POR New Kent & BOZE, Jane POR
     New Kent ML New Kent DOM 27 Jun 1831; CTR
CHARLES, Gatewood bap 25 Nov 1788; VBHS
CHARLTON, William buried by 21 Nov 1763; BP
CHASLIN, Sara d/o Richard Chaslin bap 13 May 168_;
     SPPR
CHENEY, Francis s/o Thomas Cheney bap 15 Dec ___
     ;SPPR
CHILDES, James s/o Henry Childes Gent.[probably
     br/o Walter and Henry] bap 4 ___, ____; SPPR
CHILDES, Walter s/o Henry Childes [probably br/o
     James and Henry] bap 5 Jan ___; SPPR

CHILDS, Henry s/o Henry Childs [probably br/o Walter and James Childes] bap 13 Nov 169_; SPPR

CHILTON, Charles & **FOX**, Levina POR King & Queen; DOM 30 Sep 1819 by R.B.Semple; VCA

CHILTON, Charles S. POR King & Queen & **FOX**, Levinia S POR King & Queen; DOM 30 Sep 1819 by Rev.Robert B.Semple; RE

CHRISTIAN, D. Collier POR New Kent d.d.12 Jul 1814 age 49; VP

CHRISTIAN, James R. POR New Kent d.d. issue dated 13 May 1834; RW

CHRISTIAN, John Fleming physicain POR New Kent & **PLEASANTS**, Sarah Ann d/o Samuel Pleasants (dec) POR Richmond; DOM 21 Oct 1819 by John D. Blair; RC

CHRISTIAN, John H. major POR New Kent & **BATES**, Mary H. p.m.; DOM 28 Feb 1811 POM Goochland by Rev.Reuben Ford; RE

CHRISTIAN, Judith d/o James Christian bap 21 May 1711; SPPR

CHRISTIAN, Mary wife of Robert Christian POR New Kent d.d. 19 May 1816; VP

CHRISTIAN, Robert POR New Kent d.d issue dated 6 Aug 1822; RW

CHRISTIAN, Susan POR New Kent d.d. issue dated 12 Sep 1817; RE

CLAIBORNE, Euphania p.m. POR King & Queen d.d. issue dated 1 May 1832; RW

CLAIBORNE, Frances p.m. POR King William d.d. issue dated 18 Jun 1819; RE

CLAIBORNE, Frances wife of William Claiborne POR King William d.d.11 Jun 1819 age 29 leaving husband and 3 infant daughters, one a few hours old.; RE

CLAIBORNE, Herbert POR Sussex Co & **RUFFIN**, Molly S POR King William DOM issue date 25 Nov 1773; VG

CLAIBORNE, Mary wife of William Claiborne POR New Kent d.d. (issue date) 20 Apr 1782; VGA

CLAIBORNE, Philip Whitehead POR King William d.d. 5 Dec 1771; EHR

CLAIBORNE, Philip Whitehead representative POR King William d.d. issue dated 5 Dec 1771; KWC

CLAIBORNE, Sterling & **ROW**, Jane Maria; DOM 5 May 1808; VG

CLAIBORNE, Sterling s/o Buller & Patsy Claiborne & **ROW**, Jane Maria d/o Charles & Sarah Row; 5 May 1808; BF

CLAIBORNE, Sterling s/o Buller & Patsy Cliaborne b.d.15 Oct 1785; BF

CLAIBORNE, Willaim Dandridge d.d. 11 Jun 1811 POR King WIlliam POD Liberty Hall, King William age 55; RE

CLAIBORNE, William POB England b.d.abt 1587 POR
New Kent d.d. abt 1677 POD Virginia; CVR
CLAIBORNE, William Presley Dr. POR King William
d.d. 27 Apr 1817 POD Santa Cruz, Island of
Teneriffe; RE
CLAIBORNE, William Presley Dr. POR King William
d.d. 27 Apr 1817 POD Santo Domingo, Island of
Teneriffe; KWC
CLARK, Benjamin s/o Benjamin Clark bap 20 Sep
___; SPPR
CLARK, Hannah d/o Benjamin & Eliz. Clark bap 12
Mar 169_; SPPR
CLARK, Samuel Sanford POR Boston, Mass. & **GRAVES**,
Mary Ann POR New Kent POM Richmond DOM 18 Nov
1836 by Rev.J.B.Taylor; VCS
CLARK, Sarah d/o Henry Clark b.d. 13 Feb 1715;
SPPR
CLARK, Sarah d/o Henry Clark b.d. 13 Feb 1715;
SPPR
CLARK, William s/o Benjamin Clark and Mary bap 25
Jun 169_; SPPR
CLARKE, Howard & **ROWE**, Evelyn S.; DOM 1857 POM
King & Queen; KQMR
CLARKSON, David & **JACKSON**, Elizabeth; DOM 18 Nov
1713; SPPR
CLARKSON, John s/o David Clarkson bap Feb 1710;
SPPR
CLAYBROOKE, Richard & **SHEPHERD**, Julia D.; DOM 1
Oct 1811 POM King & Queen; VM
CLAYTON, Philip s/o Samuel and Susanna **CLAYTON**
born 1746 ; died 13 Sep 1807; SAR
CLAYTON, Samuel s/o Samuel & Susanna Clayton 1689-
1735 POR King & Queen and Essex married
Elizabeth **PENDLETON** 1690-1761 d/o Philip
Pendleton (1650-1721); SAR
CLAYTON, Samuel s/o Samuel Clayton & Elizabeth
Pendleton 1715-1782 POR King & Queen, Essex,
Culpeper & Frederick Counties; SAR
CLEGG, Hillary POR King & Queen & **WARDE**, Sarah POR
Hanover Co ML Hanover Co DOM 14 Feb 1826; CTR
CLEMENT, Benjamin s/o William Clement POR King
William (will dated 1780 in Pittsylvania
Co,VA) & **HILL**, Susannah d/o Col.Isaac Hill
POR King & Queen; DOM pre 1760 from
unpublished Clements notes in DAR
CLEMENT, William s/o Benjamin Clement POR King
William d.d. 1760 from unpublished Clement
notes in DAR
CLERK, Benjamin & Mary his wife imported to King &
Queen by John Thomson before 25 Apr 1701;
C&P3
CLOPTON, Bathyah (Birtha) d/o Robert Clopton b.d.
19 Aug bap 28 Sep 1712; SPPR

CLOPTON, Henley D. POR New Kent & **PARSONS**, Mary
POR Hanover Co s ML Hanover Co DOM 1838; CTR

CLOPTON, John d.d. 12 Sep 1816 POD New Kent member
of Congress, State Legislature, Executive
Council, and in Revolution; VA

CLOPTON, John s/o William Clopton & Elizabeth D.
Jones POR "Roslyn" New Kent & **BACON**, Sarah
d/o Edmund Bacon & Elizabeth Edloe; DOM 15
May 1784; KK2

CLOPTON, John s/o William Clopton & Elizabeth
Darrell (Ford) Jones b.d. 7 Feb 1756 POR New
Kent d.d. 11 Sep 1816 POD "Roslyn"; KK2

CLOPTON, Robert & **SCOTT**, Sarah; DOM 18 Dec 1711;
SPPR

CLOPTON, Walter & **JARRETT**, Mary; DOM 4 Sep 1711;
SPPR

CLOPTON, William Jr. & **WILKINSON**, Joice; DOM 27
Jan 1718; SPPR

CLOPTON, William POR New Kent & **ACREE**, H.R. POR
Henrico s ML Henrico Co DOM 8 Mar 1832; CTR

CLOUGH, George d.d. between 8 Oct 1739 and 29 Sep
1740; BP

CLOUGH, Richard & **POINDEXTER**, Anne; DOM Jun 1718;
SPPR

CLUVERINES, Richard S. s/o Alward & Fanny
Cluverines age 36 S tailor POB Gloucester &
BAGLEY, Martha d/o Isham & Martha Bagby age
20 S POB King & Queen Co; DOM 27 Dec 1853 POM
King & Queen by Ro. Y. Henly; KQMR

COALTER, St. George T. POR Stafford & **TOMLIN**, Judy
H. youngest d/o John H. Tomlin (dec); DOM 16
Dec 1829 POM Chericoke, King William; RW

COLEMAN, Archer POR Amelia & **QUARLES**, Margaret S
d/o Isaac Quarles POR King William; DOM 18
May 1809 by Simon Morgan; VCA

COLEMAN, Armistead Capt. POR Amelia & **QUARLES**,
Betsy S. S ; DOM 4 Feb 1818 POM Woodberry
(late residence of Isaac Quarles (dec)) King
William; RE

COLEMAN, Armistead captain POR Amelia & **QUARLES**,
Betsy L.; DOM 14 Feb 1818 POM Woodberry POR
Isaac Quarles, (dec); KWC

COLEMAN, Armistead POR Amelia Co & **QUARLES**, Betsey
L. S POM Woodberry, King William DOM 14 Feb
1818; VG

COLEMAN, John R. b.d. 15 Mar 1847 d.d. 26 Feb
1926; GN VSA #34327

COLLIER, Charles POR King & Queen d.d. between 21
Jan 1746 & 9 Oct 1747; SMP

COLLIER, William d.d. between 24 Nov 1760 and 22
Feb 1762; SMP

COLLINS, Thomas POR King & Queen d.d 1831; King &
Queen Loose Papers, clerk's office

COLLY, William A. s/o Charles Colly & Ann Colly
age 36 W farmer POB POR King & Queen &
JOHNSON, Mary F. d/o Richard & Frances
Johnson age 20 S POR King & Queen; DOM 10 Jan
1856 POM King & Queen by Isaac Diggs; KQMR

COOK, Hannah d/o Abraham Cook bap 21 Dec ____;
SPPR

COOK, Mathew s/o Abraham Cook b.d. 27 Jun; SPPR

COOK, Richard P. (Capt.) POR New Kent & **CHANDLER**,
Sarah A.E. S POR New Kent DOM 22 Nov 1836 by
Rev.S.W.Jones; VCS

COOK, William B. POR Richmond & **TIBBS**, Emily F.
d/o Cap. Foushee G. Tibbs; DOM 3 Mar 1824 POM
Paradise, Essex; KWC

COOKE, Fountain W. s/o Henry & Polly Cooke age 25
S farmer POB King & Queen & **JONES**, Ann Judson
d/o Mary & Markmen(?) Jones age 18 S POB King
& Queen; DOM 14 Aug 1856 POM King & Queen;
KQMR

COOKE, George Washington b.d. 24 Mar 1827; MBC

COOKER, Bryan s/o William Cooker bap 10 Oct ____;
SPPR

CORBAT, Joane buried by 13 Nov 1728; BP

CORBIN, Betty ne Betty **TAYLOE** d.d. 13 May 1784 age
65; VG

CORBIN, Gawin POR King & Queen & **BASSETT**, Martha
d/o William Bassett & Joanna Burwell b.d. 2
Dec 1694 bap 16 Jan 1694; KK2

CORBIN, Gawin s/o Henry Corbin (1629-1675) POR
Middlesex Co d.d.1744; VG

CORBIN, John s/o Maj. Richard Corbin POR
Lanesville, King & Queen d.d. 8 Dec 1815 from
a duel wound at Carlisle College; RE

CORBIN, John Taylor & **MUSE**, Juliet; DOM 26 Jan
1799 POM King & Queen; VM

CORBIN, Rebecca Park POR King & Queen d.d. issue
dated 26 Apr 1822; RE

CORBIN, Richard eldest s/o Gawin Corbin & **TAYLOE**,
Betty d/o John Taloe S POR Mt. Airy DOM 29
Jul 1737 POM Williamsburg; VG

CORBIN, Richard maj. d.d.10 Jun 1819 age 48 POD
Lanesville, King & Queen leaving a wife and 4
children; RE

CORBIN, Richard POR Lanesville, King & Queen
d.d.18 May 1790 age 77; VICGA

CORBIN, Richard R. & **FAUNTLEROY**, Catherine; DOM 28
May 1821 POM King & Queen; VM

CORBIN, Richard s/o Gawin Corbin & Jane **LANE** POB
King & Queen b.d.1714; VG

CORBIN, Richard s/o Gawin Corbin d.d. 20 May 1790;
VG

CORBIN, Richard, Major POR Laneville, King &
Queen d.d. 10 Jun 1819; VCA

CORR, James E.P. s/o John Corr age 30 S farmer POB POR King & Queen & **PEARCE,** Mary E. d/o John Pierce age 18 S POB POR King & Queen; DOM 20 Sep 1860 POM King & Queen; KQMR

CORSON, Cornelius s/o John Corson age 21 S capt. vessell (sic) POB New York State & **DUDLEY,** Sarah d/o Robert Dudley age 21 S POB POR King & Queen Co; DOM 1 Feb 1855 POM King & Queen by William Eastwood; KQMR

CORTLON, James s/o Richard & Mary Cortlan age 25 S farmer POB POR King & Queen & **DAVIS,** Mary P. d/o Peter & Sarah Davis age 19 S POB POR King & Queen; DOM 25 May 1856 POM King & Queen by Isaac Digges; KQMR

CORTLON, William B. s/o John W. & Elizabeth W. Cortlon age 29 S farmer POB King & Queen & **CARLTON,** Mary P. d/o Richard & Mary Carlton age 29 W POB King & Queen; DOM 23 Sep 1856 POM King & Queen by John Bayley; KQMR

COSBY, Leland b.d.1813-b.d. 1900; GN VSA #34327

COSBY, Martha E. w/o Leland Cosby b.d.1812- d.d.1886; GN VSA #34327

COSEY, J.E. b.d. 17 Oct 1856; FB VSA #34117

COSTULA, Lucey d/o Bridget Costula kept by Thomas Collins 10 Oct 1743; SMP

COTTERELL, Charles s/o Richard Cotterell Jr. bap 27 Dec 1713; SPPR

COTTERELL, Gilbert s/o Thomas Cotterell bap 1 Mar 1712; SPPR

COTTERELL, Richard s/o Richard Cotterell bap 17 Dec 1710; SPPR

COTTERELL, Susana d/o Thomas Cotterell bap 1 Apr 1710; SPPR

COTTERELL, Thomas & **HACHER,** Martha; DOM 25 May 1709; SPPR

COTTERELL, Thomas s/o Thomas Cotterell bap 22 Apr 1711; SPPR

COTTORILL, Thomas s/o Richard & Mary Cottorill bap 11 Apr 169_; SPPR

COTTRELL, William & **REYNOLDS,** Nancy; DOM 29 May 1780 POM King William; VM

COUNCIL, James C. s/o John & Sarah Council age 28 S teacher POB Southampton & **SMITH,** Mary E. d/o James & Priscilla Smith age 20 S POB King & Queen; DOM 11 May 1854 POM King & Queen by William B. Todd; KQMR

COURTNEY, Dandridge P. & **LUMPKIN,** Sally Coleman S; POM King & Queen issue date 8 Mar 1808; RE

COURTNEY, Philip POR King & Queen d.d. 4 Feb 1809 age 56 POD drowned in Mattapony River; RE

COURTNEY, Polly wife of Thomas Courtney d.d.29 Aug 1806 POD New Kent age 22 after 13 months of marriage; VA

34

COURTNEY, Robert POR Richmond & **CAMPBELL**, Sarah S POR King & Queen; DOM 9 Apr 1812 by Robert Semple; VA

COURTNEY, Thomas Baptist minister of Church of Christ, Black Creek, New Kent d.d. 25 Apr 1797; VA

COURTNEY, Thomas W. POR King & Queen & **BOULWARE**, Elizabeth H. POR Richmond; DOM 15 May 1823 POM Charles City Co. by William Willis; RCC

COURTNEY, William H. POR New Kent & **ANDERSON**, Martha M. POR New Kent ML New Kent DOM 11 Mar 1830; CTR

COX, Abraham s/o Abraham Cox bap 13 Dec 169_; SPPR

COX, John s/o Nicholas & Mary Cox bap 31 Oct 168_; SPPR

COX, Rachel d/o George Cox bap 1 Jun 1690; SPPR

COX, William POR King & Queen merchant & **BROADDUS**, Fanny T. 3rd d/o Rev. Andrew Broaddus S; DOM 18 Apr 1821 POM Richmond by Mr. Bryce; RCC

COYLE, Edward & **BROWN**, Mary; DOM 21 Sep 1710; SPPR

CRAFTON, William B. POR New Kent d.d. Issue dated 15 Jun 1838; RW

CRANE, A. Judian s/o William C. Crane & Lydia Terrell age 38 W lawyer POB Richmond & **SMITH**, Sarah E. d/o Thomas Smith & Martha G. Fleet age 20 S POB King & Queen Co; DOM 12 Dec 1853 POM King & Queen by H.W.L.Temple; KQMR

CRANSHAW, Thomas s/o Thomas Cranshaw bap 25 Dec 169_; SPPR

CRITTENDEN, George D. s/o James Crittenden & Lucy Collins age 19 S farmer POB Middlesex POR King & Queen & **YORRINGTON**, Milisa S. d/o James S. Yorrington & Mary R. Burton age 21 S POB POR KIng & Queen; DOM 21 May 1856 POM King & Queen by Thomas B. Evans; KQMR

CRITTENDEN, James C. s/o William & Ann Crittendon age 34 W farmer POB Gloucester & **DIGGS**, Lucy J. d/o Dudley & Catherine Diggs age 25 S POB King & Queen; DOM 2_ May 1854 PPOM King & Queen by Isaac Diggs; KQMR

CRITTENDON, George H. & **CRITTENDON**, Emeline; DOM 5 Feb 1857 POM King & Queen; KQMR

CRITTENDON, James & **COLLINS**, Lucy d/o Thomas Collins POR King & Queen; DOM pre 1831; King & Queen Loose papers, clerk's office

CRITTENDON, John & **FRITER**, Frances; DOM 1857 POM King & Queen; KQMR

CROMPTON, Anne d/o Henry Crompton bap 25 Dec ___; SPPR

CROUCH, Baylor & **NUNN**, Lucy White d/o Thomas Nunn & Sarah Smith d.d. 12 Oct 1856; DOM 1827-28; IR Flores

CROW, Charles R. illegitimate s/o Elisabeth Crow b.d. Mar 1853 POB King & Queen; KQBR

CROW, Fielding S. & **LUMPKIN**, Polly DOM 1808; FB
CROW, Fielding S. b.d.1785; FB
CROW, Martha POR King & Queen d.d. issue dated 9
    Aug 1836; RW
CROXTON, Martha Edwards d/o Ambrose Edwards w/o
    Philip Croxton POR "Belmont" King William
    d.d. 27 Sep 1844; KWH
CROXTON, William Virginius s/o William E. Croxton
    b.d. 10 Feb 1840 POB King William; KWH
CRUE, Sarah d/o Arthur Crue b.d. 21 Apr 1712; SPPR
CRUMP, Agnes d/o James Crump bap 10 May 1713; SPPR
CRUMP, Agnes d/o Stephen Crump bap 25 Nov 1711;
    SPPR
CRUMP, Anne d/o William Crump b.d. 8 Sep bap 4 Oct
    1713; SPPR
CRUMP, Bart s/o William Crump bap 12 May ___; SPPR
CRUMP, Benedict POR New Kent d.d. issue dated 1
    Aug 1837; RW
CRUMP, Benjamin & **PARKE**, Susannah; DOM 21 May
    1771; SPPR
CRUMP, Beverly POR New Kent d.d. issue dated 7 Mar
    1837 & 28 Feb 1837; RW
CRUMP, Caty Brown d/o Benjamin & Susanna Crump
    b.d. 17 Mar 1772; SPPR
CRUMP, Charles s/o Richard Crump b.d. 2 Feb bap 26
    Feb 1709; SPPR
CRUMP, Christian s/o Benjamin & Elizabeth Crump
    b.d. 27 Aug 1763 d.d. 20 Mar 1764; SPPR
CRUMP, Edmund P. Dr. POR New Kent & **WILKINSON**,
    Judith S POR New Kent; DOM 27 Mar 1806 by
    John Saunders; RE
CRUMP, Elizabeth d/o William Crump bap 24 Apr
    1690; SPPR
CRUMP, Elizabeth w/o Benjamin Crump d.d. 21 Jul
    1770 age 26; SPPR
CRUMP, Gutrick s/o Stephen & Anne Crump b.d. 22
    May 1709; SPPR
CRUMP, James & **BOSTICK**, Venicia; DOM 14 Jul 1709;
    SPPR
CRUMP, John Parke s/o Benjamin & Susanna Crump
    b.d. 28 Mar d.d. 5 Apr 179_; SPPR
CRUMP, Joseph s/o Robert Crump bap 17 Jul 1706;
    SPPR
CRUMP, Judith d/o William Crump bap 9 Mar 1715;
    SPPR
CRUMP, Julius s/o James Crump b.d. 5 Nov 1715;
    SPPR
CRUMP, Lucy d/o Robert Crump bap 25 Mar 1711; SPPR
CRUMP, Mary d/o James Crump bap 13 May 1711; SPPR
CRUMP, Mary d/o William Crump b.d. 30 Apr bap 8
    May 1709; SPPR
CRUMP, Mary d/o William Crump bap 9 Jun 1___ ;SPPR
CRUMP, Nannie d/o Beverley Parke Crump & Ann Lewis
    b.d. 2 Mar 1860 POB New Kent; KK1

CRUMP, Parthenia p.m. POR New Kent d.d. issue
dated 18 Feb 1833; RW

CRUMP, Richard s/o Richard Crump b.d. 12 Oct bap
11 Nov 1711; SPPR

CRUMP, Robert & POWELL, Martha; DOM 20 Jan 1700/1;
SPPR

CRUMP, Sarah twin d/o Stephen Crump b.d. 14 Feb
1713; SPPR

CRUMP, Stephen s/o William Crump bap 3 Nov ___;
SPPR

CRUMP, Susana d/o Robert Crump bap 23 Mar ____;
SPPR

CRUMP, Susannah d/o Stephen Crump bap 4 Sep 168_;
SPPR

CRUMP, Thomas POR New Kent & FRAYSER, Rebecca S
POR New Kent; DOM 2 Jun 1808 by Rev. Willis;
VA

CRUMP, Thomas twin s/o Stephen Crump b.d.14 Feb
1713; SPPR

CRUMP, Winfield s/o Christopher & Mildred W. Crump
b.d. Nov 1853 POB King & Queen father's POB
King & Queen fathers occupation, carpenter
birth reported by Agnes Anderson,
grandmother; KQBR

CRUMPSTON, Jane d/o Henry Crumpston bap 15 Mar
___; SPPR

CRUMPTON, Elizabeth d/o Henry Crumpton bap 2 Oct
169_; SPPR

CUMBO, Elizabeth buried by 30 Oct 1775; BP

CURLE, Richard d.d. by 29 Nov 1773; BP

CURLE, Suckey buried by 8 Nov 1785; BP

DABNEY, Benjamin d.d 13 Dec 1826 age 38 POR POD
King William; KWC

DABNEY, Diana p.m. POR King William d.d issue
dated 24 Aug 1824; RE

DABNEY, Diana w/o Col. Richard Dabney si/o Major
Joseph Gwathmey d.d. 14 ___ 1824 age 68 y 9
mo 13 days; KWC

DABNEY, Eliz. d/o George Dabney bap 11 Nov 1698;
SPPR

DABNEY, George H. POR King William d.d. issue
dated 23 Sep 1834; RW

DABNEY, George major d.d. 31 Dec 1827 age 57 POD
Greenville; KWC

DABNEY, George major POR King William d.d.issue
dated 9 Jan 1828; RE

DABNEY, George POR King William & TIBBS, Martha
E. d/o Capt.Foushee G.Tibbs POM Paradise,
Essex DOM 3 Mar 1824; VG

DABNEY, George POR King William & TIBBS, Martha E.
d/o Cap.Foushee G. Tibbs; DOM 3 Mar 1824 POM
Paradise, Essex; KWC

DABNEY, Henry T. only s/o George H. Dabney d.d. 19
Sep 1829; KWC

DABNEY, Henry T. POR King William d.d. issue dated 23 Sep 1829; RW

DABNEY, James POR King & Queen adjoined land of his sister Sarah DABNEY by 25 Apr 1701; C&P3

DABNEY, Mordecai B. POR Richmond & **HOOMES**, Martha P. POR King & Queen s DOM 15 Nov 1821; VG

DABNEY, Mordecai B. POR Richmond & **HOOMES**, Martha P. POR Point of View, King & Queen; DOM 15 Nov 1821 by Rev. Philip Courtney; KWC

DABNEY, Nelthan d/o James Dabney bap 8 Jan 1698/9; SPPR

DABNEY, Richard Col. POR King William age 50 d.d. 24 May 1800; KWC

DABNEY, Susan L. p.m. POR King William d.d. issue dated 27 Apr 1827; RW

DABNEY, Susan L. w/o Major George Dabney POR King William d.d. 15 Apr 1827 age 42; KWC

DABNEY, Susan S. p.m. POR King William d.d. issue dated 1 May 1827; RE

DABNEY, Thomas (Major) & **TOMPKINS**, Mary E. youngest d/o Col.Christopher Tompkins, (dec) POR King William POM Smyrna DOM 26 Dec 1826; VG

DABNEY, Thomas Gregory Smith s/o Benjamin Dabney & Sarah Smith POB King & Queen b.d.4 Jan 1798; BKQCHS

DABNEY, Thomas maj. & **TOMPKINS**, Mary E. youngest d/o Col.Christopher Tompkins (dec) POR King William; DOM 26 Dec 1826 POM Smyrna by Rev. D. Atkinson; KWC

DABNEY, Thomas POR King William & **TOMPKINS**, Mary E.; POM before Sep 1827; KWC

DABNEY, William d.d. 1 Dec 1828 age 60 POD Brookfield; KWC

DABNEY, William W. POR Richmond & **BOSHER**, Martha Ann d/o William Bosher S POR King William; issue date 2 Oct 1837; RW

DABNEY, William W. POR Richmond & **BOSHER**, Martha Ann d/o William Bosher POR King William s; DOM 28 Sep 1837 by Rev. G.W.Trice; KWC

DAINGERFIELD, Edward capt. & **BASSETT**, Mary d/o William Bassett POR New Kent b.d. 7 Aug 1716; KK2

DAINGERFIELD, Edwin d.d. between 8 Oct 1746 and 14 Oct 1748; BP

DAINGERFIELD, William & **BATHURST**, Elizabeth d/o Lancelot Bathurst of New Kent; DOM 1709; KK2

DANCE, Mary d.d. 1762; SMP

DANDRIDGE, Bartholomew d.d. between 28 Mar and 7 May 1785;BP

DEMETRIUS, Emanuel d.d. between 13 Oct 1725 and 24 Jun 1726; BP

DANDRIDGE, Bartholomew POR New Kent d.d. issue dated 18 Jan 1827; RE

38

DANDRIDGE, Bolling POR Goochland Co & **DUDLEY**,
    Laura E. POR New Kent s ML New Kent DOM 19
    Nov 1835; CTR
DANDRIDGE, Robert F. Dr. d.d. 7 Feb 1829 POD King
    William; KWC
DANDRIDGE, Robert s/o Nathaniel West Dandridge &
    Dorothea Spotswood b.d. 21 Jun 1760 & **ALLEN**,
    Mildred d/o Richard Allen & Elizabeth Terrell
    b.d. 7 Feb 1752 POB New Kent; DOM 11 May
    1783; FB
DANDRIDGE, William POR King William POB England
    d.d.1743 in VA; CVR
DANDRIDGE, William POR King William & **WEST**, Unity
    d/o Nathaniel West; DOM 18 Mar 1719; EHR
DANIEL, Richardson bap 14 Feb 1789; VBHS
DARELL, Sampson POR King & Queen & **HANFORD**,
    Elizabeth d/o (and heir of) Tobias Handford
    by 21 Oct 1699; C&P3
DARRUM, James s/o James Darrum bap 23 May 1703;
    SPPR
DARRUM, Susannah d/o James & Elliz. Darrum bap 19
    Mar 1698/9; SPPR
DAVENPORT, Anne bastard d/o Anne Davenport bound
    to Dr. John Strachey 10 Oct 1741; SMP
DAVENPORT, Emmanuel s/o Emmanuel Capman age 27 S
    waterman FPOC POB POR King & Queen & **LOCKLEY**,
    Nancy d/o Daniel Lockney age 21 S POC POB POR
    King & Queen; DOM 15 Sep 1860 POM King &
    Queen; KQMR
DAVENPORT, George mulatto illegitimate s/o Ann
    Davenport bound 8 Jul 1757; SMP
DAVIS, _____ s/o Albert & Welentina Davis (Albert
    is a farmer) b.d. 4 Dec 1853; KQBR
DAVIS, Ann E. d/o James M. & Louisa Davis (James
    was a farmer) b.d. May 1853; KQBR
DAVIS, Catherine bap 25 Nov 1788; VBHS
DAVIS, Grace d/o John Davis bap 3 Jun 17__; SPPR
DAVIS, Joseph R.E. s/o Stage & Sarah Elizabeth
    Davis (Stage was a farmer) b.d. 29 Apr 1853;
    KQBR
DAVIS, Olive C. d/o Henry C. & Susan Ann Davis
    (Henry was a farmer) b.d. 29 Jan 1853; KQBR
DAVIS, Peggy p.m. POR King & Queen d.d. issue
    dated 11 Feb 1832; RW
DAVIS, Richard (?) s/o Richard A. & Elizabeth B.
    Davis age 27 S farmer POB Northumberland POR
    Middlesex & **BROACHE** (?), Sarah P.(?) d/o
    Peter & Harriett Braoch(?) age 19 S POR King
    & Queen; DOM 21 Dec 1857 POM King & Queen by
    R.A.Christian; KQMR
DAVIS, Sarah T. d/o William B. & Evalina O. Davis
    b.d. 27 Feb 1853; KQBR
DAVIS, Thomas E. POR New Kent d.d. issue dated 8
    Mar 1838; RW

DAY, Edward s/o Francis & Elizabeth Day b.d. 1 Oct
1708; SPPR

DAY, Eliz. d/o Francis Day bap 20 Jan 1699; SPPR

DAY, Elizabeth d/o Francis Day bap 12 Mar ___
(this is included among early 1700 baptisms);
SPPR

DAY, Francis s/o Francis & Elizabeth Day b.d. 20
Feb (this is included among early 1700
baptisms); SPPR

DAY, Richard s/o Francis Day bap 9 May 168_; SPPR

DAY, Sally d/o Benjamin Day POR Fredericskburg
d.d.23 Sep 1823; KWC

DEANS, Josiah Lily d.d. 28 Aug 1812 & BASSETT,
Anna Maria d/o John Bassett & Elizabeth
Carter Browne b.d. 15 Mar 1789 POB "Elsing
Green" King William; DOM 15 Mar 1808; KK2

DENNETT, Eliza d/o John Dennett b.d. 13 Jun 1698;
SPPR

DENNETT, John s/o john Dennett b.d. 21 Oct 1702;
SPPR

DENNETT, Perthenia d/o John Dennett b.d. 27 Nov
1690; SPPR

DENNETT, Thomas s/o John Dennett b.d. 11 Feb 1699;
SPPR

DENOTT, Eliz. d/o John & Eliz. Denott bap 14 Aug
1698; SPPR

DEPRESS, Mary d/o Robert Depress bap 9 Nov 169_;
SPPR

DEPRESS, Sarah d/o Robert & mary Depress bap 4 Sep
1698; SPPR

DEPRESS, William s/o RObert Depress bap 24 Oct
168_; SPPR

DEPREST, Elizabeth d/o Robert Deprest bap 19 Jul
1702; SPPR

DESIGN, Elizabeth d/o Daniel & Mary Design bap 26
Oct ____ (this is included among early 1700
baptisms); SPPR

DEVENPORT, Amey mulatto illigetimate d/o Ann
Devenport bound to Dr. John Strachey 10 Oct
1743; SMP

DEVENPORT, Anne illegitimate d/o Anne Devenport
bound to Dr. Strachey 9 Oct 1738; SMP

DEVENPORT, William mulatto illegitimate s/o Ann
Devenport bound 9 Oct 1747; SMP

DEVONPORT, Amey molatto[sic] bastard of Ann
Devonport bound to Dr. John Strachey 10 Oct
1744; SMP

DEW, Benjamin Franklin s/o Thomas R. Dew & Lucy
Gatewood b.d. 1820 d.d. 1877 POR King &
Queen; SAR

DEW, Thomas Roderick s/o William Dew b.d.1765 d.d.
1849 POR King & Queen; SAR

DEW, Thomas s/o William Dew POB [probably MD] POR
King & Queen & GATEWOOD, Lucy d/o Chaney

Gatewood POR Newtown; DOM 1793; taken from
OLD HOUSES OF KING & QUEEN COUNTY,VA
DICKS, Henry s/o Henry Dicks bap 25 Feb 17__; SPPR
DICKS, Mary d/o Henry Dicks b.d. 5 Nov 170_; SPPR
DIDLAKE, Ethelbert A. & **HART**, Mary S.; DOM 1857
POM King & Queen; KQMR
DIDLAKE, Henry P. s/o Royaten & Catherine Didlake
age 24 carpenter S POB Middlesex POR King &
Queen & **CAUTHORN**, Tabithy A. E. d/o William &
Sarah Cauthorn age 17 S POB POR King & Queen;
DOM 11 May 1854 POM King & Queen by Archer
Bland; KQMR
DIGGS, R. Dudley s/o Rev.Isaac & Ann Elizabeth
Diggs b.d. 24 Jul 1845 POB King & Queen; HMBC
DIKE, John s/o Henry Dike b.d. 26 Mar 1716; SPPR
DILLAN, Margaret d/o Henry Dillan bap 15 Mar
1690/1; SPPR
DILLAN, Nitt s/o Henry & Elinor Dillan bap 1 Aug
168_; SPPR
DINSMOORE, David cap. POR King William &
HEMINGWAY, Elizabeth POR Richmond; DOM 15 Oct
1831 by Rev. Mr. Armstrong; KWC
DINSMORE, David captain POR King William &
HEMINGWAY, Elizabeth POR Richmond S; DOM 15
Oct 1831; RW
DIX, Mary Agnes w/o William Sheppard Dix b.d. 22
May 1840 d.d. 21 Mar 1887; MBC
DIX, William Sheppard b.d. 5 Nov 1829 d.d. 4 Jul
1896; MBC
DIXON, James POR New Kent & **BARKER**, Lucy POR
Hanover Co 30 Oct 1823 ML New Kent; CTR
DIXON, John R. s/o John & Elizabeth S. Dixon age
30 W POB POR New Kent farmer & **ATKINSON**, Lucy
A.C. d/o William A. & Elizabeth Atkinson age
24 S POB POR New Kent; DOM 26 Sep 1855 POM
New Kent by Lloyde Moore; NKMR
DIXON, Julius C. POR New Kent & **ATKINSON**, Mary C.
d/o William A. Atkinson & Elizabeth Moore;
DOM issue date 21 Jun 1849 POM New Kent by
Thomas S. Morris; KK1
DOBSON, Richard b.d. 10 Mar 1763 POB New Kent;
Rev. Pension file S9386
DOE, Rachel d/o Alice Doe bap 15 Mar 1690/1; SPPR
DOLLARD, Francis s/o William & Margaret Dollard
bap 13 Mar 1708/9; SPPR
DOLLARD, James s/o James Dollard bap 15 Apr 171_;
SPPR
DOLLARD, William s/o William Dollard bap 19 Mar
1703; SPPR
DOLLER, Elizabeth d/o James Doller bap 170_; SPPR
DORAN, John d.d. between 18 Oct 1743 and 15 Oct
1744; BP
DORMER, David buried by 21 Oct 1765; BP

41

DOSWELL, Paul G. POR Hanover & **GWATHMEY**, Frances S
    POR King & Queen; DOM 5 Dec 1816 by Rev.
    Hatchet; RE
DOUGLAS, George s/o Robert Douglas bap 9 Apr 168_;
    SPPR
DOUGLAS, Robert s/o Robert Douglas bap 15 Feb 168_
    ; SPPR
DOUGLASS, William POR New Kent d.d. issue dated 31
    Jan 1826; RE
DOWE, William s/o Nitte. Dowe bap 2 Jul 1699; SPPR
DREWRY, George & **POWELL**, Elizabeth N. POR King
    William   24 Dec 1823 ML King William; CTR
DUDLEY, Ann H. p.m. POR King William d.d. issue
    dated 8 Oct 1824; RE
DUDLEY, Peter A. POR New Kent d.d. issue dated 14
    Apr 1835; RW
DUDLEY, Robert POR King & Queen d.d. between 9 Oct
    1747 and 14 Apr 1748; SMP
DUDLEY, Thomas & **CURTIS**, Mary p.m.; DOM 13 May
    1775 POM King & Queen; VM
DUDLEY, William J. or I. s/o Thomas V.W.Dudley &
    Patsy Pillsberry age 22 s POB King & Queen
    farmer & **PITTS**, Elenor d/o Levi Pitts & Mary
    Walden age 19 POB King & Queen Co; DOM 9 Apr
    1853 POM King & Queen by Archer Bland; KQMR
DUGAR, Thomas buried by 19 Oct 1761; BP
DULING, Thomas L. s/o Isaac Duling & Frances
    Harpen age 27 S miller POB POR King & Queen &
    WATKINS, Martha d/o John Watkins & Lucy Minor
    age 28 S POB POR King & Queen; DOM 15 Dec
    1859 POM King & Queen by Howard W. Montague;
    KQMR
DUMAS, Mathen d/o Jeremiah Dumas bap 10 Oct 1703;
    SPPR
DUNCAN, Silas S. capt. in U.S.Navy & **AYLETT**,
    Martha Dandridge eldest d/o Philip Aylett POR
    King William; POM Montville issue date 11 Feb
    1831; RW
DUNCAN, Silas S. of the U.S.Navy & **AYLETT**, Martha
    Dandridge eldest d/o Philip Aylett POR King
    William; DOM issue dated 11 Feb 1831 POM
    Montville; KWC
DUNCAN, William captain POR King William d.d.
    issue dated 21 Oct 1836; RW
DUNGEE, _____ s/o John Dungee & Lucy Arnold FPOC
    (John is a farmer) POB POR King William b.d.
    Jan 1853; ROBKW
DUNGEE, Cornelius s/o Joe & Becca Dungee FPOC (Joe
    is a farmer) POB POR King William b.d. 1853;
    ROBKW
DUNGEE, Frances E. d/o Spotswood & Francis [sic]
    Dungee FPOC POB POR King William b.d. May
    1853; ROBKW

DUNGEE, Scott s/o Jesee & Mary Dungee FPOC (Jesee is a shoemaker) POB POR King William b.d. Sep 1853; ROBKW

DUNGY, Alexander s/o Richard C. & Kittura Dungy (Richard is a woodcutter) FPOC b.d. Feb 1853 d.d. Feb 1853 (born dead); KQBR

DUNKERTON, Elizabeth buried by 21 Oct 1765; BP

DURHAM, William s/o Jacob Durham & Catherine W. Greenwood age 25 S farmer & **COURTNEY**, Mary C. d/o Conway & Ann Courtney age 21 S POB King & Queen; DOM Dec 1856 POM King & Queen by Steward Montague; KQMR

DUVAL, Clarissa J. d/o John & Harriet Duval (John is a farmer) b.d. Aug 1853; KQBR

DUVAL, John Dr. POR King & Queen & **PENDLETON**, Mary Ann S POR King & Queen; DOM 4 Nov 1819 by Robert B. Semple; VP

DUVAL, Louis Philip s/o Philip P. & Betty Duval (Philip is a physician) POB POR King William b.d. Oct 1853; ROBKW

EACHO, John buried by 15 Oct 1755; BP

EARNEST, George L. widower POR King William & **HUGHES**, Agnes POR Hanover Co s ML Hanover Co DOM 1 Aug 1839; CTR

EASTHAM, Edward & **TAYLOR**, Ann d/o James Taylor POR King & Queen; DOM deed found 1750; Essex Deed Book 25

EASTWOOD, Alexander G. s/o William & Susan Eastwood age 23 S mechanic POB Gloucester & **WRIGHT**, Virginia d/o John & Rachel Wright age 16 S POB King & Queen Co; DOM 31 Jul 1853 POM King & Queen by Lis.Roler; KQMR

EDWARDS, Ambrose & **FINCH**, Barbary; DOM 22 Dec 1800 POM King William; VM

EDWARDS, Ambrose 3rd s/o Ambrose Edwards b.d. 3 Mar 1757 POB "Cherry Grove", King William d.d. 19 Jul 1829; KWH

EDWARDS, Ambrose Jr. POR King William & **EDWARDS**, Janet S POR King William; DOM 19 Dec 1816 by John Mill; RE

EDWARDS, Ambrose POR "Cherry Grove" King William wi/o Wealthean Butler & **FINCH**, Barbara wi/o Henry Finch POR King William; DOM 1800; KWH

EDWARDS, Ambrose POR King William & **EDWARDS**, Janet POR King William DOM 19 Dec 1816; VG

EDWARDS, Ambrose POR King William & **EDWARDS**, Janet s POR King William; DOM 19 Dec 1816 by Rev.John Mill; KWC

EDWARDS, Ambrose s/o Ambrose Edwards POB "Cherry Grove" King William & **SLAUGHTER**, Elizabeth Anne; DOM Feb 1775; KWH

EDWARDS, Ambrose Sr. POR King William d.d. 22 Jan 1811; KWC

EDWARDS, Austin & **THORNTON**, Jane Pemberton d/o
    James R. & Judith C. Thornton; DOM Feb 1836;
    KWH
EDWARDS, Charles L. POR King William & **BUTLER**,
    Maria Elleanor POR King William s DOM 23 Mar
    1825; VG
EDWARDS, Charles L. POR King William & **BUTLER**,
    Maria Elleanor s POR King William; DOM 23 Mar
    1825 by Rev. Mr. Todd; KWC
EDWARDS, Eleanor d.d. 14 Oct 1825 POD King
    William; KWC
EDWARDS, Eleanor p.m. POR King William d.d. issue
    dated 21 Oct 1825; RE
EDWARDS, Elizabeth p.m. POR King William d.d.
    issue dated 9 Jan 1828; RW
EDWARDS, George s/o Ambrose Edwards b.d. 3 Oct
    1795 POB "Cherry Grove" King William; KWH
EDWARDS, George s/o Ambrose Edwards POB King
    William & **EDWARDS**, Mary Anne; DOM 1827 POM
    "Forest Villa"; KWH
EDWARDS, Jacob & **GARRETT**, Margarett E.; DOM 21 Feb
    1857 POM King & Queen; KQMR
EDWARDS, James B. POR King William d.d. issue
    dated 19 Sep 1834; RW
EDWARDS, James Coleman s/o Butler Edwards b.d. 9
    Jan 1792 POR "Winchester" King William d.d. 6
    May 1834; KWH
EDWARDS, James Coleman s/o Butler Edwards POR King
    William & **GREGORY**, Elizabeth b.d.17 Feb 1791
    d.d.8 Dec 1827; DOM 3 Mar 1814; KWH
EDWARDS, James Coleman s/o Butler Edwards POR King
    William & **GARY**, Nancy wi/o Pleasants Dabney
    Ellett b.d. 28 Jul 1798; DOM 4 Aug 1830; KWH
EDWARDS, James Fendall s/o James Coleman Edwards
    POR King William b.d. 12 Dec 1823; KWH
EDWARDS, Judith d/o Ambrose Edwards b.d. 1790 d.d.
    11 Sep 1847 POR King William; KWH
EDWARDS, Julien T. s/o Dr. Lemuel Edwards b.d. 14
    Nov 1841 POB Lanesville, King William; KWH
EDWARDS, Lemuel s/o James Coleman Edwards b.d. 11
    Oct 1817 POB "Winchester" King William; KWH
EDWARDS, Mary d/o Samuel Edwards b.d. 7 Mar 1786;
    KWH
EDWARDS, Presley Coleman s/o Dr. Lemuel Edwards
    b.d. 23 Sep 1843 POR King William; KWH
EDWARDS, Samuel eldest s/o Ambrose Edwards b.d.
    abt 1750 POB "Cherry Grove" King William
    (married Jane Pemberton d/o John Pemberton &
    Jane Coleman); KHW
EDWARDS, Warner & **THORNTON**, Elizabeth d/o James R.
    & Judith C. Thornton; DOM 2 Mar 1826; KWH
EDWARDS, Wealthean d/o Ambrose Edwards b.d. abt
    1765 POB "Cherry Grove"; KWH

EDWARDS, William s/o George Edwards b.d. 22 May
1831 POR "Cherry Grove" King William; KWH

ELLETT, Nina d/o William & Louisa Ellett (William
is a farmer) b.d. Sep 1853; ROBKW

ELLETT, Sarah p.m. POR King William d.d. issue
dated 9 Jan 1828 RW 9 Jan 1828; RW

ELLETT, Temple POR New Kent & **ACREE**, Mary D. POR
New Kent ML New Kent DOM 13 Mar 1828; CTR

ELLETT, William s/o Capt. Daniel Ellet &
PEMBERTON, Louisa H. d/o Wilson Coleman
Pemberton [and probably Louisa C. Hilliard];
DOM 28 Nov 1844; KWH

ELLIOTT, Mary d/o Thomas Elliott bap 23 Nov 16__;
SPPR

ELLIOTT, William & **LIPSCOMB**, Sarah d/o James
Lipscomb (dec) ; DOM bond 31 Jan 1786 POM
bond King William; VCA

ELLIOTT, William E. POR King William & **BULLINGTON**,
Sarah T. d/o Harwood Bullington POR
Williamsburg; DOM 3 Dec 1829; RH

ELLIOTT, William E. POR King William & **BULLINGTON**,
Sarah T. second d/o Harwood Bullington; DOM 3
Dec 1829 by Rev. Mr. Armstrong; KWC

ELLIOTT/ELLETT, Robert s/o James Ellett POR King
William will dated 8 Mar 1804; SAR

ELLIS, William L. & **SAUNDERS**, Mildred C.; DOM 27
Jan 1857 POM King & Queen; KQMR

ELLIS, William T. POR Essex & **SAUNDERS**, Mildred C.
POR King & Queen; DOM 27 Jan 1857 POM Cedar
Plains, King & Queen; WA

ELLISON, John s/o Sirilla Ellison bap 17 Feb 168_;
SPPR

ELLYSON, Daniel POR New Kent & **WADE**, Martha A. POR
Hanover Co ML Hanover Co DOM 20 Dec 1827; CTR

ELLYSON, Havilah POR New Kent & **ACREE**, Elizabeth
POR New Kent ML New Kent DOM 4 Jun 1829; CTR

ELMOR, John s/o Thomas & Mary Elmor bap 10 Jul
1698; SPPR

ELMOR, Peter s/o Peter & Rebecca Elmor bap 9 Jun
1700; SPPR

ELMOR, Thomas s/o Thomas Elmor bap 29 Mar 170_;
SPPR

ELMOR, Will s/o Peter & Rebecca Elmor bap 10 Jul
1698; SPPR

ELMORE, Bathiah d/o Peter Elmore bap 11 May 1707;
SPPR

ELMORE, Elizabeth d/o Peter Elmore bap 17 Sep
1704; SPPR

ELMORE, Harris s/o Peter Elmor b.d. 5 Jul 170_;
SPPR

ELMORE, Mary d/o Peter Elmore b.d. 17 Oct 1715;
SPPR

ELMORE, Mary d/o Thomas Elmore bap 20 Aug 170_
;SPPR

ENGLAND, Elizabeth d/o William England bap 22 Nov
1702; SPPR

ENGLAND, John s/o Will England bap 29 Sep 170_;
SPPR

EPECEN, Francis s/o John Epecen bap 17 Apr 168_;
SPPR

EPERSON, Pall s/o John Eperson bap 23 Feb 1699–
1700; SPPR

EPPERSON, Elizabeth d/o John Epperson bap 13 Jun
1708; SPPR

EPPERSON, William s/o Thomas & Elizabeth Epperson
bap 20 Jun 1708; SPPR

EPPES, John T. POR Hanover Co & **FOX**, Sarah Ann POR
King William   ML King William   DOM 8 May
1828; CTR

EPPES, John T. POR King William d.d. 11 Nov 1834;
RW

EPPESON, John s/o William Eppeson bap 19 Sep 1703;
SPPR

ESROTT, An [sic] d/o Hugh Esrott b.d. 17 Oct 168_;
SPPR

ESROTT, Jane d/o Hugh Esrott bap 29 Jun 169_; SPPR

EUBANK, Betty bap 14 Feb 1789; VBHS

EUBANK, Marius s/o Benjamin F. & Mary C. Eubank
b.d. Apr 1853; KQBR

EUBANK, William s/o Philip & Susan Eubank age 21 S
farmer POB King & Queen & **CARLTON**, Catherine
d/o Humphrey Carlton age 18 S POB King &
Queen Co; DOM 25 Dec 1853 POM King & Queen by
Isaac Digge; KQMR

EVANS, _____ illegitimate s/o Maria C. Evans b.d.
May 1853 POB Poor House King & Queen; KQBR

EVANS, Andrew Briscom s/o Thomas B. Evans & Sarah
W. Brown age 26 S lawyer POB POR King & Queen
& **DEW**, Mary Emma d/o John W. Dew & Catherine
G. Pendleton age 19 S POB POR King & Queen;
DOM 2 Jul 1856 POM King & Queen by Thomas B.
Evans; KQMR

EVANS, Eliz. buried by 15 Oct 1741; BP

EVANS, John M. s/o Thomas B. Evans & S.W.Brown age
25 S POB POR Middlesex & **BAGBY**, Ellen d/o
Richard Bagby & D.A.Fleet age 19 S POB King &
Queen POR Middlesex; DOM 26 Dec 1854 POM King
& Queen by Thomas B. Evans; KQMR

EVANS, Mary d/o John & Mary Evans bap 20 Aug 169_;
SPPR

EVANS, Mary d/o Richard Evans bap 28 Mar 1702/03;
SPPR

EVANS, Mary p.m. POR King William d.d.issue dated
29 Oct 1819; RE

EVANS, Mary w/o Thomas R. Evans POR Frazer's
Ferry, King William d.d. 13 Oct 1819 age 54;
KWC

EVANS, Sarah W. p.m. POR King & Queen d.d. issue dated 28 Jun 1833; RW

EVANS, Thomas R. POR King William d.d. issue dated 26 Mar 1824; RW

EVANS, William Thomas s/o Lafayette & Maria E. Evans (Lafayette is a farmer and merchant) b.d. 29 Apr 1853 POB King & Queen; KQBR

FAIRFAX, Thomas POR Fairfax Co & **AYLETT**, Mary d/o Col.William Aylett (dec) S POR King William Co; DOM 20 Oct 1795 POM Evelington, Charles City; VGGA

FAKIRE, Sarah d/o Mathew Fakire both of whom were imported to New Kent by Thomas Scott and John Drummond before 29 Oct 1696; C&P3

FALL, Philip S. & **BACON**, Anna A. d/o John Bacon & Elizabeth Ware POR New Kent; DOM 1 May 1821; KK2

FARINHOLT, Jesse merchant & **JONES**, Emma d/o Thomas Jones POR Kennington, King William; DOM 6 Mar 1827 by Rev. Dudley Atkinson; KWC

FARINHOLTZ, Richard L. POR Gloucester Co & **PEIRCE**, Anna Martha V. POR New Kent DOM 1 Dec 1836 by Rev.S W.Jones; VCS

FARRAR, Robert POR Greensboro, N.C. & **GARY**, Elizabeth POR King William; DOM 14 Aug 1829; VG

FARRAR, Robert POR Greensboro, NC & **GARY**, Elizabeth s POR King William; DOM 14 Aug 1829; KWC

FARY, James P. s/o Jesse Fary & Sarah Padget age 20 S farmer POB Gloucester POR King & Queen & **MILBY**, Maria d/o William Milby & Jemima Padget age 18 S POB POR King & Queen; DOM20 Feb 1856 POM King & Queen; KQMR

FAULKNER, Richard C. & **LEE**, Frances; DOM 27 Jan 1812 POM King & Queen; VM

FAUNTELROY, Moore G. POR King & Queen & **DILLARD**, Flora POR Greensboro, Alabama S; DOM 7 Mar 1854; VH

FAUNTLEROY, A.R.C. wi/o Moore G. Fauntleroy b.d. 31 Oct 1789 d.d. 18 Nov 1868; VCA

FAUNTLEROY, Moore G. b.d. 2 Mar 1789 d.d. 28 Apr 1858; VCA

FAUNTLEROY, Sally ne Sarah **LOWREY** POR Caroline Co d.d. 24 Nov 1840 age 74; BKQCHS

FAUNTLEROY, Samuel G. & **COCKE**, Lucy E.; DOM 2 Jan 1816 POM King & Queen; VM

FAUNTLEROY, Samuel G. b.d. 11 May 1791 d.d. 9 Jun 1857; VCA

FAUNTLEROY, Samuel G. d.d. 8 Dec 1826; VCA

FAUNTLEROY, Samuel G. POR King & Queen d.d. issue dated 23 Dec 1826; RE

FAUNTLEROY, Samuel Griffin s/o Samuel Griffin Fauntleroy & Elizabeth Payne Todd Dr. & **COOKE**

Lucy Elizabeth (1800-1821) POR Gloucester Co
DOM 1816; BKQCHS

FAUNTLEROY, Samuel Griffin Jr. s/o Samuel Griffin
Fauntleroy & Lucy Elizabeth Cooke & **JONES**,
Elizabeth Pope d/o"Yankee" Jones POR
Middlesex Co DOM 1844; BKQCHS

FAUNTLEROY, Samuel Griffin Jr. s/o Samuel Griffin
Fauntleroy & Lucy Elizabeth Cooke Dr. &
CLAYBROOK, Frances Elizabeth (1830-1912) d/o
Rev. Richard Claybrook & Martha Lewis POR
Middlesex Co DOM Oct 1848; BKQCHS

FAUNTLEROY, Samuel Griffin Jr. s/o Samuel Griffin
Fauntleroy & Lucy Elizabeth Cooke POB King &
Queen b.d. 1818; BKQCHS

FAUNTLEROY, Samuel Griffin s/o Moore Fauntleroy &
LOWREY, Sarah POR Caroline Co DOM 1796;
BKQCHS

FAUNTLEROY, Samuel Griffin s/o Moore Fauntleroy
b.d. 1759; BKQCHS

FAUNTLEROY, Samuel Griffin s/o Moore Fauntleroy
POR Northern Neck & **TODD**, Elizabeth Payne DOM
1782; BKQCHS

FAUNTLEROY, Samuel Griffin s/o Moore Fauntleroy
POR Northern Neck d.d. 8 Dec 1826; BKQCHS

FAUNTLEROY, Samuel Griffin s/o Samuel Griffin
Fauntleroy & Elizabeth Payne Todd POB King &
Queen b.d. 1791; BKQCHS

FAUNTLEROY, Samuel Griffin s/o Samuel Griffin
Fauntleroy & Elizabeth Payne Todd d.d. 1858;
BKQCHS

FAUNTLEROY, Sarah Elizabeth w/o Samuel G.
Fauntleroy d.d. 22 Sep 1842; VCA

FAUNTLEROY, Thomas & **LORIMER**, Isabella; DOM 22 Aug
1796 POM King & Queen; VM

FEARE, Hamner d.d. by 28 Apr 1777; BP

FENNELL, Elizabeth d/o John Fennell bap 3 Mar
170_; SPPR

FENNELL, Sarah d/o John Fennell b.d Apr 1715; SPPR

FERGISON, Hannah d/o William Fergison bap 3 Mar
1704/05; SPPR

FINALL, James s/o John Finall bap 17 Feb 1702;
SPPR

FINCH, Henry s/o Edward Finch bap 15 Feb 169_;
SPPR

FINCH, John s/o Edward Finch b.d. 20 Mar 1699;
SPPR

FINCH, Mary d/o Edward Finch bap 1 Apr 168_; SPPR

FLEET, Alexander col.s/o William & Sarah Fleet
b.d. 26 Apr 1798 d.d. 23 Sep 1877; VCA

FLEET, Ann Temple d.d. 7 May 1754; ONKH

FLEET, Benjamin s/o Benjamin Fleet & Maria Wacker
b.d. 1 Oct 1846 POB Green Mount, King & Queen
Co; BKQCHS

FLEET, Benjamin s/o Benjamin Fleet & Maria Wacker
d.d. 2 Mar 1864 POD King William ; BKQCHS

FLEET, Betsy w/o Alexander Fleet d/o Robert
Pollard d.d. 26 Jun 1841 age 41y 21 days; VCA

FLEET, Catherine P. eldest d/o James R. & Martha
J. Fleet b.d. 2 Sep 1834 d.d. 4 Apr 1852; VCA

FLEET, Christopher B. POR King & Queen & **MCKIM**,
Mary Ann only d/o Andrew McKim (dec) S POR
Richmond; DOM 26 Sep 1820; RCC

FLEET, Christopher B. POR KIng & Queen & **MCKIM**,
Mary Ann d/o Andrew McKim (dec); DOM 26 Sep
1820; VCA

FLEET, Christopher POR King & Queen Dr. & **MCKIM**,
Mary Ann only d/o Andrew McKim (dec) POR
Richmond; DOM 26 Sep 1820 by Robert B.
Semple; RE

FLEET, Edwin br/o William Fleet d.d. between Apr &
Jul 1778 POR King & Queen; ONKH

FLEET, Henry s/o William Fleet & Ann Temple POR
King & Queen & **PIERCE**, Mildred d/o John
Pierce of Hanover Co; DOM 1775; EHR

FLEET, James Robert s/o William & Sarah Fleet b.d.
3 Jan 1812 d.d. 18 Jun 1882; VCA

FLEET, Martha Ann 2nd w/o Alexander Fleet d/o
Robert Baylor Hill & Catherine Pollard b.d. 2
Oct 1819 d.d. 23 May 1895; VCA

FLEET, Martha Jane w/o James R. Fleet d/o Josiah &
Catherine Peachy Ryland b.d. 22 Aug 1810 d.d.
11 Apr 1894; VCA

FLEET, Martha w/o Robert Myrick d.d. 1857; FB

FLEET, Sarah w/o William Fleet d/o Bennett Browne
of Essex d.d. 27 Jan 1818 age 42; VCA

FLEET, William d.d. 11 Apr 1833 age 76; VCA

FLEET, William s/o William Fleet & Ann Jones POR
King & Queen & **WALKER**, Susanna d/o John &
Elizabeth Baylor Walker POR Walkerton, King &
Queen; DOM 9 Nov 1755; ONKH

FLEET, William s/o William Fleet & Anne Jones
b.d.1726 POR King & Queen & **TEMPLE**, Ann; DOM
1744; ONKH

FLEMING, Carter; DOM 1 Jan 1778 POM King & Queen;
VM

FLEMING, Elizabeth d/o Charles & Susanna Fleming
bap 28 Oct 168_; SPPR

FLOYD, Gideon & **POWEL**, Lucy Ann eldest d/o George
N. Powel; POM Woodberry, King William DOM 20
Dec 1838; RW

FLOYD, Gideon & **POWELL**, Lucy Ann eldest d/o George
N. Powell s ; DOM 20 Dec 1838 POM Woodberry,
King William; KWC

FOGG, James H. s/o Thomas & Catherine Fogg age 23
S farmer POB King & Queen & **OWENS**, Elizabeth
d/o Thomas & Nancy Owens age 25 S POB King &

Queen Co; DOM 6 Jun 1853 POM King & Queen by
E.Peysan Waller; KQMR

FOGG, Mary Lewis d/o Tazwell U. & Mary Hill Fogg
(Tazwell is a harness maker) b.d. 1 Mar 1853
POB King & Queen; KQBR

FORD, Daniel POR Richmond & **JONES,** Mildred B. p.m.
POR New Kent; DOM 24 Oct 1816 by R. Ford; RC

FORD, John & his wife Margaret imported to King &
Queen by John Thomson before 25 Apr 1701;
C&P3

FORGESON, James s/o Robert F_____ bap 8 Mar 168_
;SPPR

FORGESON, Judith d/o William Forgeson bap 4 Jul
1708; SPPR

FORTUNE, Hezekiah s/o Washington & Ely Fortune
FPOC (Washington is a waterman) POR King
William b.d. 1853; ROBKW

FOSTER, Elizabeth d/o Joseph & Elizabeth Foster
b.d.1 Sep 1689 bap 27 Sep 1689; SPPR

FOSTER, John H. POR Richmond & **CLOPTON,** Sarah
A.E.C. s POR New Kent; 6 Apr 1824; CTR

FOSTER, Joseph s/o Coll. Joseph & Elizabeth Foster
b.d. 29 Oct 169_; SPPR

FOSTER, Joseph s/o Joseph & Elizabeth Foster bap 8
Apr 168_; SPPR

FOSTER, Luce d/o Joseph & Elizabeth Foster b.d.5
Oct 1697; SPPR

FOSTER, William POR Hanover Co & **BURTON,** Frances
T. POR New Kent ML New Kent DOM 5 May 1831;
CTR

FOSTER, William POR King William & **WHITE,** Susan
POR Hanover Co; 12 Feb 1824 ML Hanover Co;
CTR

FOX, Frederick s/o Edward C. & Ellen C. Fox
(Edward was a farmer) b.d. 28 Feb 1853 POB
King & Queen; KQBR

FOX, Isaac buried by 28 Apr 1777 with his daughter
(unnamed in this record); BP

FOX, John captain POR King William d.d. issue
dated 7 Jan 1815; RE

FOX, Joseph d.d. by 21 Oct 1765; BP

FOX, Joseph POR Locust Hill, King William d.d. 13
Mar 1831 age 44 POR Cool Spring; KWC

FOX, Sarah sister of Isaac Fox buried by 19 Oct
1772; BP

FRANSES, John s/o Thomas & Mary Franses imported
to New Kent by Thomas Scott and John Drummond
before 29 Oct 1696; C&P3

FRANSES, Margaret d/o Thomas & Mary Franses
imported to New Kent by Thomas Scott and John
Drummond before 29 Oct 1696; C&P3

FRANSES, Mary d/o Thomas & Mary Franses imported
to New Kent by Thomas Scott and John Drummond
before 29 Oct 1696; C&P3

FRANSES, Susan d/o Thomas & Mary Franses imported to New Kent by Thomas Scott and John Drummond before 29 Oct 1696; C&P3

FRANSES, Thomas & Mary his wife imported to New Kent by Thomas Scott and John Drummond before 29 Oct 1696; C&P3

FRANSES, Thomas s/o Thomas & Mary Franses imported to New Kent by Thomas Scott and John Drummond before 29 Oct 1696; C&P3

FREEMAN, Anderson s/o Daniel & Patsy Freeman age 39 W ditcher POB King & Queen & **GILMORE**, Betsy d/o Ben & Lucy Gilmore age 25 S POB King & Queen; DOM 4 Dec 1856 POM King & Queen by Isaac Digges; KQMR

FREEMAN, Barbary d/o William Freeman bap 5 Jul 170_; SPPR

FULLILOE, Thomas & his wife Anne imported to King & Queen by Mary Herbert before 25 Apr 1701; C&P3

FURTIN, Elizabeth bap 25 Nov 1788; VBHS

FUZELL, Sarah d/o Thomas Fuzell bap 10 Apr 17__; SPPR

FUZZELL, Elizabeth d/o Thomas Fuzzell bap 17 Jul 1708; SPPR

GADBERRY, William d.d. by 21 Oct 1765; BP

GADDEY, John d.d. between 3 Oct 1752 and 9 Oct 1753; BP

GAINES, Elizabeth p.m. POR King & Queen d.d. issue dated 17 Mar 1837; RW

GAINES, Francis d.d. between 7 Oct 1774 and 7 Jul 1775; SMP

GAINES, Harry POR "Providence", King & Queen w.p. 8 Jun 1789; VCA

GAINES, Harry POR King William d.d. 1767; issue dated 16 Jul 1767; VG

GAINES, Harry representative in Assembly POR King William d.d. issue dated 16 Jul 1767; KWC

GAINES, Henrietta E. d/o Alex & Eliza A. Gaines (Alex is a farmer) b.d. Sep 1853; KQBR

GAINES, Henry & **MUSE**, Mirenda; DOM 9 Sep 1803 POM King & Queen; VM

GAINES, Henry B. merchant POR Lynchburg & **GWATHMEY**, Agnes eldest d/o Joseph Gwathmey POR King William; DOM 16 May 1817 by Rev. Mr.Hatchett; KWC

GAINES, Henry B. POR Lynchburg & **GWATHMEY**, Agnes d/o Joseph **GWATHMEY** POR King William DOM 16 May 1817; VG

GAINES, John s/o Harry Gaines lawyer POR "Providence", King & Queen d.d. 1848 age 61; VCA

GAINES, Robert A. s/o Alexander Gaines age 27 S oysterman POB POR King & Queen & **HALL**, Laura

T. d/o Charles Hall age 29 S POB POR King &
   Queen; DOM 5 Jun 1860 POM King & Queen; KQMR
GALING, Anne d/o John Galing bap 4 Feb 170_; SPPR
GALING, Matthew d/o [sic] John Galing bap 9 Feb
   170_; SPPR
GARDNER, Anthony Dr. POR King & Queen d.d. issue
   dated 19 Oct 1824; RE
GARDNER, Betty bap 25 Nov 1788; VBHS
GARDNER, William F. Jr. POR Hanover & FOX,
   Elizabeth Lipscomb d/o Jeremiah Fox (dec) POR
   King William S; DOM 4 Apr 1833 by George W.
   Trice; RE
GARDNER, William F. Jr. s/o William & Drucilla
   Crutchfield Gardner & POR Hanover & FOX,
   Elizabeth Lipscomb d/o Jeremiah Fox (dec) POR
   King William; DOM 4 Apr 1833 by Rev. George
   W. Trice; KWC
GARDNER, William F. s/o William Gardner & Drucilla
   Crutchfield POR Hanover & FOX, Elizabeth
   Lipscomb d/o Jeremiah Fox (dec) S POR King
   William; DOM 4 Apr 1833; RW
GARLAND, Edward s/o Edward Garland b.d. 20 May
   1700 bap 8 Jul 1700; SPPR
GARLAND, William d.d. by 10 Nov 1760; BP
GARLICK, Braxton POR King William & WEBB, Mary
   adopted d/o Henry Webb POR Maringo, New Kent;
   DOM 22 Oct 1834 by J. Silliman; RW
GARLICK, Braxton POR King William & WEBB, Mary C.
   adopted d/o Henry Webb POR Maringo, New Kent;
   DOM 22 Oct 1834; RW
GARLICK, Braxton s/o Samuel Garlick & Mary Carter
   Braxton & HILL, Elizabeth d/o William Hill;
   DOM before 7 Feb 1837; KWC
GARLICK, Camm POR King William & TALIAFERRO, Mary
   S POR King William; DOM 19 Jan 1810; RE
GARLICK, Edward & GWATHMEY, Mary Hill d/o Joseph
   Gwathmey & Mary Hill; DOM 11 Apr 1820;
   Garlick Bible Records
GARLICK, Edward & WALKER, Fanny Hill d/o Thomas
   Walker DOM 20 Dec 1805; Garlick Bible Records
GARLICK, Edward & WALKER, Frances d/o Thomas
   Walker & Frances Hill; DOM 20 Dec 1805; EHR
GARLICK, Edward s/o John Garlick & Nancy Pollard
   b.d. 3 Mar 1779 d.d. 30 Aug 1829; Garlick
   Bible Records
GARLICK, Edward s/o John Garlick & Nancy Pollard
   POR King & Queen & King William b.d. 3 Mar
   1779 d.d. 30 Aug 1839 POD King & Queen; EHR
GARLICK, John William s/o Edward Garlick & Frances
   Walker b.d. 27 Feb 1823 d.d. 18 Apr 1866 POD
   "Leeds" King William; EHR
GARLICK, Joseph Robert s/o Edward Garlick & Mary
   Hill Gwathmey b.d. 30 Dec 1825; EHR

GARLICK, Richard Henry s/o Edward Garlick & Mary Hill Gwathmey b.d. 19 Feb 1828 d.d. 17 Oct 1830; EHR

GARLICK, Robert P. POR King William d.d. issue dated 8 Jun 1838; RW

GARNETT, Ann Maria p.m. POR King & Queen d.d. issue dated 11 Jul 1828; RE

GARNETT, Ann p.m. POR King & Queen d.d. issue dated 25 Jul 1828; RE

GARNETT, Anna Maria w/o Col. William Garnett POR Essex Co d/o Richard Brooke of Mantipike, King & Queen d.d. 8 May 1854 age 68 POD Lexington, VA; ONKH

GARNETT, Henry T. POR King & Queen & **WARING**, Eliza C. d/o Stuart Bankhead (dec) p.m. POR Westmoreland; DOM 17 Oct 1822 POM Westmoreland by Josias Clapman; RE

GARNETT, John J. POR Essex & **CARTER**, Lucy L. grand d/o Col. William Lyne POR King & Queen; DOM 21 Sep 1809; RE

GARNETT, Lewis & **BANKS**, Frances B. S POR King William; DOM 6 Feb 1806 by Robert S. Semple; RA

GARNETT, Mary Susan d/o Reuben Meriwether Garnett (1780-1846) b.d.1821 d.d. 1855 POR King & Queen; SAR

GARRARD, Joseph s/o James Garrard bap 24 Nov 1700; SPPR

GARRARD, Judith d/o Judith Garrard bap 24 Nov 1700; SPPR

GARRAT, Tyler s/o Thomas Garrat bap 14 Feb 1713; SPPR

GARRETSON, Isaac & **BASSETT**, Anna Maria Dandridge d/o John Bassett & Elizabeth Carter Browne b.d. 15 Mar 1789 POB "Elsing Green", King William; DOM 11 Aug 1815; KK2

GARRETT James W. s/o James Garrett & Elizabeth Greadman (?) age 26 s POB King & Queen farmer & **CLAYTON**, Sandal d/o William H. Clayton & Patsy Collins age 17 s POB King & Queen Co; DOM 27 May 1853 POM King & Queen by William B. Todd; KQMR

GARRETT, James s/o James Garrett bap 15 Jul 1690; SPPR

GARRETT, Joseph W. s/o Robert & Sallie Garrett age 36 S farmer POB POR King & Queen & **DUNN**, Mary A. d/o Thomas J. Dunn & Maria L.? Dunn age 20 S POB POR King & Queen; DOM 17 Apr 1856 POM King & Queen by Alfred Bagby; KQMR

GARRETT, Richard H. POR King & Queen & **BOULWARE**, Elizabeth L. d/o Muscoe Boulware POR Caroline; DOM 14 May 1836; RE

GARRETT, Robert L. & **CORR**, Juliet Ann d/o Thomas
R. Corr POR King & Queen; DOM 4 Oct 1821 by
Philip Montague; RE
GARRETT, Robert L. & **CORR**, Juliett Ann d/o Thomas
R. Corr POR King & Queen; DOM 4 Oct 1821 by
Philip Montague; RCC
GARRETT, Sallie Collins b.d. 9 Nov 1838 POB King &
Queen; IR Waters
GARRETT, Samuel former POR Middlesex & **GARDNER**,
Elizabeth Ann POR King & Queen; DOM 20 Oct
1836 POM Retreat by John Bird; RE
GARRETT, Sarah p.m. POR King & Queen d.d. issue
dated 18 Jun 1824; RE
GARRETT, Sarah w/o Edward Garrett POR King & Queen
age 48 d.d. 29 May 1824; RE
GARRETT, Silas S. POPR Caroline & **BATES**, Rosa Ann
youngest d/o William Bates (dec) POR King &
Queen; DOM 10 Mar 1836 by G.W.Trice of King
William; RE
GARRETT, William W. POR King & Queen & **GARRETT**,
Ann Roy d/o Larkin Garrett POR King WIlliam;
DOM 25 Nov 1835 POM Willow Green by Mr.
Acree; RE
GARY, Charles C. s/o William M. & Maria Gary age
23 S merchant POB open & **WALKER**, Lucy F. d/o
Temple & Jane Walker age 20 S POB King &
Queen Co; DOM 27 Dec 1853 POM King & Queen by
R.Y. Henly; KQMR
GATEWOOD, Chaney age 82 d.d. 10 Dec 1821 married
52 years, had 6 children survive him POR POD
King & Queen; VCA
GATEWOOD, Chany age 82 POR upper King & Queen d.d.
10 Nov 1821; RE
GATEWOOD, Elizabeth wi/o Chaney Gatewood age 80
d.d. 25 Jul 1830 POR POD King & Queen member
of Upper King & Queen Baptist Ch; VCA
GATEWOOD, Philip POD Travelers Rest, King & Queen
d.d. 23 Sep 1829; RE
GATEWOOD, Philip POR King & Queen & **PENDLETON**,
Mary M. S POR King & Queen; DOM 5 Apr 1804;
RA
GATEWOOD, Samuel S. & **HOWERTON**, Catherine Ann d/o
Robert G. Howerton POR King & Queen; DOM 15
Nov 1838; RE
GATEWOOD, Samuel S. d.d. 21 Sep 1840 POD King &
Queen; RW
GAUTERIE, James K. s/o Thomas Gauterie age 31 S
farmer POB POR King & Queen & **MILBY**, Mary Ann
d/o George Damm [or Darum] age 30 W POB POR
King & Queen; DOM 17 Jan 1860 POM King &
Queen; KQMR
GAYLE, William C. s/o John Gayle & Mary Hall age
23 S oysterman POB Gloucester POR King &
Queen & **ADAMS**, Maria F. d/o Henry Adams &

Maria Criter? age 16 POB POR King & Queen;
DOM 21 Dec 1854 POM King & Queen by William
Eastwood KQMR
GEDDY, Ann w/o Ed B. Geddy POR New Kent age 38
d.d. 4 Nov 1823; RE
GENTRY, Andrew I. or J. s/o Susan Gentry age 26 S
overseer POB POR King & Queen & COOK, Mahala
d/o Henry & Polley Cooke age 23 S POB POR
King & Queen; DOM 12 Dec 1857 POM King &
Queen by R.H.Bagby KQMR
GENTRY, Elizabeth d/o Nicholas Gentry bap 20 Aug
1689 SPPR
GENTRY, Henry POR King & Queen & KERBY, Joanna POR
Hanover Co; ML Hanover Co DOM 23 Mar 1826;
CTR
GENTRY, Mabell d/o Nicholas Gentry bap 13 Dec
1702; SPPR
GENTRY, Nicholas s/o Nicholas Gentry bap 30 May
1699; SPPR
GENTRY, Peter s/o Samuel Gentry bap 10 Apr 1687;
SPPR
GEROW, James major POR King & Queen d.d. issue
dated 22 Jan 1822; RE
GIBSON, George s/o Edwin Gibson age 24 W farmer
POB POR King & Queen & HART, Matilda d/o
Thomas Wyatt age 28 W POB POR King & Queen;
DOM 28 Jun 1860 POM King & Queen KQMR
GIBSON, Philip s/o Basillis & Frances Gibson age
26 S merchant POB POR King & Queen & GUTHRIE,
Jane d/o James & Matilda Guthrie age 18(?) S
POR King & Queen; DOM 12 Jan 1857 POM King &
Queen by Isaac Digges KQMR
GILL, John s/o Patient Gill bound 9 Oct 1747 SMP
GILL, John s/o Patient Gill bound to Richard
Kelley 9 OCt 1747 SMP
GILLAM, Elizabeth d/o Richard Gillam bap 5 Oct
1690 SPPR
GILLAM, John s/o Richard Gilliam bap 25 Aug 168_
SPPR
GILLAM, Richard s/o Richard Gillam bap 1 Apr 1705
SPPR
GILLUM, Margaret d/o Richard Gillum bap 2 Nov 1701
SPPR
GILLUM, William s/o Richard & Margaret Gillum bap
26 Mar 1699 SPPR
GILMAN, John buried by 9 Oct 1753; BP
GLASEBROOK, Sarah buried by 23 Feb 1784; BP
GLASS, Robert s/o Thomas Glass Jr. bap 25 May 1701
SPPR
GOALDER, Richard s/o James A. & Clanda Goalder
b.d.Oct 1853; KQBR
GODDIN, Avery POR New Kent d.d. issue dated 3 Sep
1822 RE

GODDIN, Isaac d.d. between 15 Oct 1755 and 19 Oct 1761; BP

GOLDMAN, Elijah s/o Rob__ Wilson & Sally G. Goldman age 26 S lumber getter POB Middlesex & **COLLINS**, Cordelia d/o Thomas Collins & Nancy Going age 26 S POB King & Queen Co; DOM 14 May 1853 POM King & Queen by Thomas B. Evans KQMR

GOLEMAN, Mary J. d/o Wormley & Elton Goleman FPOC b.d.Dec 1853; KQBR

GOODIN, Charles s/o Alexander Goodin bap 28 May 17__ SPPR

GOODIN, James d.d. by 21 Oct 1765; BP

GOODIN, Thomas s/o Alexander Goodin bap 8 Jun 1712 SPPR

GOODING, Robert POR Blishland Parish New Kent dd before 28 Oct 1697 leaving widow Mary C&P3

GOODINGS, Martha d.d. between 24 Apr 1725 and 13 Oct 1725; BP

GOODMAN, Samuel s/o Benjamin Goodman bap 27 Apr 1700/01 SPPR

GOODWIN, Elizabeth d/o Peter Goodwin bap 2 Feb 1700 SPPR

GOODWIN, John s/o Peter Goodwin bap 25 Dec 1698 SPPR

GOOGER, Frances d/o John Googer b.d. 8 Sep 1697 SPPR

GOOGER, Jacob s/o John Googer b.d. 10 Oct 1700 SPPR

GOOGER, Lucy d/o John Googer b.d. 8 Sep 1705 SPPR

GORDON, Elizabeth p.m. POR King & Queen d.d. issue dated 22 Oct 1822 RE

GOUGH, William s/o John Gough POR King & Queen by 26 Oct 1697 C&P3

GOULDMAN, Ann Catherine b.d. 15 Oct 1832 FB VSA #34117

GOULDMAN, John Musker b.d. 30 Dec 1843 FB VSA #34117

GOULDMAN, Louisa Etta b.d. 19 May 1850 FB VSA #34117

GOULDMAN, Maria F. b.d. 13 Oct 1830 FB VSA #34117

GOULDMAN, Mary Susan b.d. 15 Aug 1841 FB VSA #34117

GOULDMAN, Mary Susan d.d. 1895 FB VSA #34117

GOULDMAN, Phebealis b.d. 29 Jun 1852 FB VSA #34117

GOULDMAN, Richard & **SCHOOLS**, Sarah; DOM 24 Dec 1827 FB VSA #34117

GOULDMAN, Richard b.d. 19 Jan 1811 FB VSA #34117

GOULDMAN, Richard d.d. 24 Jan 1874 FB VSA #34117

GOULDMAN, Richard Henry b.d. 7 Oct 1837 FB VSA #34117

GOULDMAN, Robert Alpheius b.d. 31 Aug 1845 FB VSA #34117

GOULDMAN, Sarah Ann b.d. 21 Sep 1839 FB VSA #34117

GOULDMAN, Sarah w/o Richard Gouldman b.d. 7 Nov
  1812 FB VSA # 34117
GOULDMAN, Saslly Schools d.d. 1893 FB VSA #34117
GOULDMAN, Thomas b.d. 30 Jul 1835 FB VSA #34117
GOULDMAN, William Banum b.d. 15 May 1848 FB VSA
  #34117
GOULDMAN, William Baynliam d.d. 15 Dec 1923 FB VSA
  #34117
GOVAN, Elizabeth d/o Samuel & Mary Garlick w/o
  James Govan d.d. 15 Oct 1822 POD "White Hall"
  King & Queen; EHR
GOVAN, Elizabeth w/o James Govan POR Hanover POD
  Whitehall, King & Queen d.d. 15 Oct 1822; VCA
GOVAN, James d.d. Apr 1852; VCA
GOVAN, James merchant POR Aylett's Warehouse, King
  William & GARLICK, Elizabeth s; DOM 25 Nov
  1788 KWC
GOVAN, James POR Aylett's Warehouse & GARLICK,
  Elizabeth S; DOM 25 Nov 1788 VG
GOVAN, James POR Aylette's Warehouse & GARLICK,
  Elizabeth s; DOM 25 Nov 1788; VG
GOVAN, Lucy Garrett b.d. 25 Jan 1799 d.d. 3 May
  1836; VCA
GRANGER, Elizabeth d/o Thomas Granger bap 21 Jan
  1699-1700 SPPR
GRANTLAND, John POR Richmond & ACREE, Miss POR New
  Kent ML Henrico Co DOM 3 Jul 1828; CTR
GRAVES, David T. s/o Thomas Graves age 27 S
  overseer POB Essex Co POR King & Queen &
  GRAVES, Dorothy S. d/o John Graves age 25 S
  POB Essex Co POR King & Queen; DOM 8 Jan 1860
  POM King & Queen KQMR
GRAVES, Matthew s/o John Graves bap Oct 1710 SPPR
GRAVES, Richard Col. POR New Kent d.d. issue dated
  7 Apr 1835 RW
GRAVES, Robert s/o Robert Graves bound to Thomas
  Collier 10 Oct 1733 SMP
GRAVES, Susanna d/o John & Elizabeth Graves b.d.
  17 Dec 170_ SPPR
GRAY, Gabriel POR Culpeper & DABNEY, Emily A. S
  POR Greenville, King William; DOM 9 Oct 1828
  POM Orange C.H. VG
GRAY, Gabriel POR Culpeper & DABNEY, Emily A. s
  POR Greenville, King William; DOM 9 Oct 1828
  POM Orange C.H.; KWC
GRAY, Margaret buried by 9 Oct 1750; BP
GRAY, William POR Surry & CHAMBERLAYNE, Elizabeth
  w/o William Chamberlayne POR New Kent; DOM 9
  Apr 1738 VG
GREEN, Isaac buried by 30 Oct 1784; BP
GREEN, James s/o Edward Green bap 23 Sep 1705 SPPR
GREEN, James s/o William Green bap 13 Feb 1710
  SPPR
GREEN, John s/o William Green bap 13 Feb 1710 SPPR

GREEN, Mary d/o Edward Green bap 11 Aug 1700 SPPR

GREENE, Forrist s/o Edward & Jane Greene bap 17 Jul 1698 SPPR

GREGORY, John F. POR King William & POWELL, Lucy N. POR King William; DOM 31 Mar 1831 RW

GREGORY, John F. POR King William & POWELL, Lucy N. s POR King William; DOM 31 Mar 1831 by Rev. Samuel T. Moorman; KWC

GREGORY, Mary Ann Sutherland POR King William d.d. issue dated 4 Oct 1825 RE

GREGORY, Mary w/o Roger Gregory POR POD King William d.d. 10 Nov 1771; KWC

GREGORY, Nannie Sidney d/o William N. Gregory & Wealthean Thornton b.d. 17 Nov 1845 KWH

GREGORY, Nathaniel s/o Roger Gregory POR King William b.d. 11 Mar 1763; EHR

GREGORY, Roger s/o Richard & Agnes Gregory & CLAIBORNE, Mary Cole d/o Nathaniel Claiborne & Jane Cole; DOM 2 Sep 1756; EHR

GREGORY, Roger s/o Richard Gregory & Agnes West POR King William b.d. 1 May 1729 d.d. 2 Oct 1803; EHR

GREGORY, Roger s/o Roger Gregory & Maria Elliot age 22 S lawyer POB King William & BROOKES, Ann M. d/o William Brookes & Evalina Garrott age 17 S POB King & Queen Co; DOM 20 Dec POM King & Queen by Samuel Edwards KQMR

GREGORY, William N. s/o Thomas West Sidney Gregory & THORNTON, Wealthean d/o James R. Thornton & Judith C. Pemberton; DOM 11 Jan 1845 KWH

GREGORY, William s/o Roger Gregory POR "Elsing Green" King William b.d. 12 May 1767 d.d. 1840; EHR

GRESHAM, Anderson B. s/o Benjamin & Ann C. Gresham b.d. 5 Jan 1853; KQBR

GRESHAM, Bonnie d/o E. & I. Gresham b.d. 29 Aug 1851 d.d. 14 Oct 1873; MBC

GRESHAM, Charles s/o James & Mary E. Gresham age 25 S Dr. no POB or POR & CAMPBELL, Columbia d/o William & Priscilla Campbell age 22 S POB King & Queen; DOM 25 Mar 1856 POM King & Queen by Alford Bagby SPPR

GRESHAM, Clarence s/o Edwin J. Gresham & Maria Josephine Lumpkin POR Newtown, King & Queen b.d. 1853 BKQCHS

GRESHAM, Edward b.d. 22 Sep 1818 d.d. 9 Mar 1873; MBC

GRESHAM, Edward Mann s/o E. & I. Gresham b.d. 22 Sep 1860 d.d. 9 Oct 1885; MBC

GRESHAM, George POR Prince Edward & WATTS, Betty d/o Thomas Watts POR King & Queen; DOM deed found 1781 POM found Essex; Essex Deed Book 32

GRESHAM, Henry POR King & Queen & **OLIVER**,
Elizabeth s POR King & Queen; DOM 17 Dec 1816
by Philip Montague; RE
GRESHAM, Isabella w/o Edward Gresham b.d. 5 Nov
1818 d.d. 23 Aug 1892; MBC
GRESHAM, Mary G. b.d. 8 Sep 1855 d.d. 8 May 1907;
MBC
GRESHAM, Philip Dr. b.d. 1 Feb 1843 d.d. 22 Mar
1882 buried in Galveston, TX; MBC
GRESHAM, Philip s/o E. & I. Gresham b.d. 1 Feb
1843 d.d. 17 Mar 1882; MBC
GRESHAM, Uriah POD Rock Castle River, KY (native
of King William Co.) issue date 17 Sep 1859;
WA
GRESHEM, Sally bap 25 Nov 1788; VBHS
GRIFFIN, Elizabeth d/o Leroy Griffin & Mary Anne
Bertrand b.d. abt 1738 d.d. 23 Dec 1800; KK1
GRIFFIN, Thomas & **MILLS**, Elizabeth; DOM 22 Sep
1783 POM King & Queen VM
GRIFFITH, John s/o Thomas & Milly **GRIFFITH** b.d.20
Dec 1778; FB
GRIFFITH, Joseph; DOM 1 Apr 1778 POM King & Queen
VM
GRIFFITH, Virginia T. d/o Richard I. & Adaline
Griffith b.d. 12 May 1853 POB King & Queen;
KQBR
GRIGGS, Robert Lear illegitimate s/o Mary Griggs
b.d. Jun 1853 POB Poor House, King & Queen
KQBR
GRINDLEY, Anne d/o Christopher Grindley bound to
Sarah Gramshill 30 Nov 1759; SMP
GRINDLEY, Mary & Ann Grindley illegitimate
children of Chris. Grindley cared for using
vestry funds from 8 Jul 1757 SMP
GRISLEY, Jeffrey POR King William d.d. issue dated
14 Oct 1775; KWC
GROOM, Alexander s/o Beverley & Kittura Groom b.d.
Feb 1853; KQBR
GROOM, Benjamin & **MUIR**, Mary A. S POM King & Queen
DOM 16 Jan 1847 by Rev. W.J.Norfleet; RCA
GROOM, Mary d/o Richard N. & Sarah Groom b.d. Jun
1853; KQBR
GUILLAM, Agnes d/o John Guillam b.d. 20 Feb 1713
bap 21 Mar 1713 SPPR
GUILLAM, James s/o John Guillam b.d. 11 Dec 1711
bap 27 Jan 1711 SPPR
GUNN, Ann Eliza p.m. POR New Kent d.d. issue dated
10 Sep 1819 RE
GUNNELL, Ann d/o William Gunnell bap 12 Oct 1701
SPPR
GUNNELL, Judith d/o Will Gunnell bap 5 Feb 1699
SPPR
GUTHERIE, Buckner E. s/o James Gutherie & Matila ?
Eubank abe 28 S farmer POB POR King & Queen &

DIDLAKE, Matilda A.S. d/o Thomas R. Didlake &
    Juliza Newcomb age 20 S POB POR King & Queen
    Co; DOM 7 Mar 1853 by Archer Bland KQMR
GUTHRIE, Ann d/o John Guthrie Jr. cared for by
    others by 19 Nov 1756; SMP
GUTHRIE, Elizabeth buried by 12 Nov 1772; SMP
GUTHRIE, Major & Ann Guthrie children of John
    Guthrie Jr. kept using vestry funds 7 Oct
    1754 SMP
GUTHRIE, Major s/o John Guthrie Jr. cared for by
    others by 19 Nov 1756; SMP
GWATHMEY, Ann d/o Temple Gwathmey & Ann Baylor
    b.d. 5 Feb 1780 d.d. 7 Sep 1795; Gwathmey FB
GWATHMEY, Ann w/o Richard Gwathmey POR King
    William d.d. issued dated 21 Apr 1837 RW
GWATHMEY, Anna Maria w/o Temple Gwathmey age 26
    d.d. 29 Sep 1819; VCA
GWATHMEY, Elizabeth Brooke d/o Temple Gwathmey &
    Ann Baylor b.d. 25 Jul 1788; Gwathmey FB
GWATHMEY, Frances d/o Temple Gwathmey & Ann Baylor
    b.d. 31 Jan 1790; Gwathmey FB
GWATHMEY, George Dr. POR King & Queen & IRVINE,
    Anne d/o Cap. William Irvine POR Locust
    Grove, Bedford Co.; DOM 28 Nov 1811 by Mr.
    Mitchell; RE
GWATHMEY, George s/o Temple Gwathmey & Ann Baylor
    b.d. 24 Feb 1785; Gwathmey FB
GWATHMEY, Hannah Temple d/o Temple Gwathmey & Ann
    Baylor b.d. 29 Dec 1791; Gwathmey FB
GWATHMEY, Humphrey Brooke s/o Temple Gwathmey &
    Ann Baylor b.d. 29 May 1793; Gwathmey FB
GWATHMEY, John Baylor s/o Temple Gwathmey & Ann
    Baylor b.d. 25 Jul 1781; Gwathmey FB
GWATHMEY, Joseph major d.d. 13 Feb 1824 age 67 POR
    POD King William; KWC
GWATHMEY, Joseph major POR King William d.d. issue
    dated 19 Feb 1824 RE
GWATHMEY, Lucy Ann d/o Temple Gwathmey & Ann
    Baylor b.d. 26 Apr 1796 d.d. 26 Dec 1811 POD
    Richmond; Gwathmey FB
GWATHMEY, Lucy d/o Temple Gwathmey & Ann Baylor
    b.d. 26 Nov 1786 d.d. 17 Feb 1790; Gwathmey
    FB
GWATHMEY, Mary Hill b.d. 2 Sep 1785; EHR
GWATHMEY, Mary Hill d/o Joseph & Mary Gwathmey
    b.d. 2 Sep 1785 d.d. 29 Oct 1838; Garlick
    Bible Records
GWATHMEY, Mollie d/o Temple Gwathmey & Ann Baylor
    b.d. 10 Jan 1777; Gwathmey FB
GWATHMEY, Owen s/o Temple Gwathmey & Ann Baylor
    b.d. 19 Jun 1775; Gwathmey FB
GWATHMEY, Robert s/o Temple Gwathmey & Ann Baylor
    b.d. 10 Sep 1778; Gwathmey FB

GWATHMEY, Robert T. POR King & Queen & **BROWN**,
Evelyn C. d/o Archie Brown POR North Point,
King WIlliam; DOM 6 Nov 1835 by Eli Ball; RW

GWATHMEY, Temple & **BAYLOR**, Ann; DOM 30 Sep 1774 by
Hancock Dunbar; Gwathmey FB

GWATHMEY, Temple POR King & Queen d.d. issue dated
26 Mar 1831 RW

GWATHMEY, Temple s/o Temple Gwathmey & Ann Baylor
b.d. 1 May 1783; Gwathmey FB

GWYN, Ethaline d/o Charles E. & Cordelia Ann Gwyn
b.d. 15 Oct 1853; KQBR

HAGERTY, Daniel R. s/o Patrick & Elizabeth Hagerty
age 30 S bricklayer POB London, England POR
New Kent & **BOND**, Emily A. d/o William & Mary
Bond age 21 S POB King William POR New Kent;
DOM 23 Sep 1858 POM Olivet Presbyterian Ch,
New Kent by Isaac O. Sloan; NKMR

HALL, Franklin B. b.d. 9 Apr 1835 d.d. 11 Oct
1913; MBC

HALL, Franklin s/o Warner & Mary Hall age 25 S
painter POR King & Queen & **WALTON**, Susan
d/o John C. & Sarah Walton age 22 S POB
King & Queen; DOM 9 May 1860 POM King & Queen
KQMR

HALL, John buried by 14 Oct 1735; BP

HALLYBURTON, Ann C. w/o James D. Hallyburton POR
New Kent d.d. issue dated 24 Feb 1837 RW

HANNA, Mary d/o Peter Hanna bap 29 Jul 169- SPPR

HARDCASTLE, Hannah d/o William Hardcastle bap 7
Sep 1711 SPPR

HARDCASTLE, John s/o William Hardcastle bap 3 Mar
1707 SPPR

HARDCASTLE, William s/o William Hardcastle b.d. 21
Jun 1714 SPPR

HARDDEN, Anne d/o Matthew Hardden bap 14 Jan 1710
SPPR

HARFIELD, Michael & **ALFORD**, Grace; DOM 14 Feb
1726/7; SPPR

HARGROVE, William K. POR King William d.d. issue
dated 5 OCt 1829 RW

HARMAN, Robert s/o Robert Harman bap 20 Jun 168_
SPPR

HARPER, Mary d/o Robert Harper b.d. 7 Aug 1714
SPPR

HARPER, Richard s/o Robert Harper bap 4 May 1701
SPPR

HARRIS, Anne d/o Edward Harris bap 24 Nov 1700
SPPR

HARRIS, Benjamin s/o John & Ann Harris b.d. 5 Jun
170_ SPPR

HARRIS, Benjamin s/o Street & Chuny Harris FPOC
b.d. Nov 1853 POB King & Queen; KQBR

HARRIS, Elizabeth d/o Thomas Harris bap 14 May
170_ SPPR

HARRIS, Elizabeth d/o William Harris bap 27 Nov 1698 SPPR

HARRIS, George s/o William Harris bap 13 Apr 1701 SPPR

HARRIS, John s/o William Harris bap 28 Mar 170_ SPPR

HARRIS, Julia Ann d/o Cesar & Lucy Ann Harris FPOC (Cesar is a laborer) b.d. Dec 1853 POB King & Queen; KQBR

HARRIS, Richard s/o Robert Harris b.d. 21 Jan 1709 SPPR

HARRIS, Robert & **TURNER**, Elizabeth; DOM Oct 1699; SPPR

HARRIS, Thomas POR Richmond & **MEAUX**, Fanny POR New Kent; DOM 24 Dec 1800 RA

HARRIS, William s/o Frances Harris age 23 S free POC farmer POB POR King & Queen & **TWOPENCE**, Julia d/o Mary Twopence age 23 S free POC POB King William POR King & Queen; DOM 21 Dec 1859 POM King & Queen by Isaac Digges KQMR

HARRISON, William L. POR Caroline & **LUMPKIN**, Laura d/o Capt.Lumpkin (dec) POR King William; DOM 5 Jun 1855 POM Dover VH

HARRISON, William POR Caroline & **GATEWOOD**, Martha S POR King & Queen; DOM 19 Dec 1816 by Robert B. Semple RE

HARRISON, William POR Caroline & **GREGORY**, Mary d/o Gregory Baylor POR Drysdale Parish, King & Queen; DOM 1779; EHR

HARRISON, William POR Caroline & **LUMPKIN**, Laura d/o Capt. Lumpkin (dec) POR King William; POM Dover POM 5 Jun 1855 VH

HART, John s/o Thomas Hart b.d. 1 Oct 1689 bap 24 Oct 1689 SPPR

HART, Joseph W. Rev. b.d. 19 Feb 1842 d.d. 11 Aug 1914; MBC

HART, Mary C. w/o Rev. J.W. Hart b.d. 26 Jul 1850 d.d. 10 May 1883; MBC

HART, Robert O. s/o Jeremiah & Harriet Hart age 23 W farmer POB King & Queen & **SPENCER**, Mary E. d/o William W. & Sarah Spencer age 27 S POB King & Queen Co; DOM 26 Jul 1853 POM King & Queen by A.F.Scott KQMR

HART, Sudie M. w/o Rev. J.W. Hart b.d. 31 Jan 1850 d.d. 2 Jan 1901; MBC

HART, Thomas s/o Thomas Hart bap 6 May 1694 SPPR

HARWOOD, Archibald R. Col. POR King & Queen d.d. issue dated 26 Sep 1837 RW

HARWOOD, Christopher & **CRANE**, Eleanor; DOM 23 Aug 1795 POM King & Queen VM

HASELWOOD, Benjamin d.d. by 29 Nov 1773; BP

HASELWOOD, Joseph d.d. by 9 Oct 1753; BP

HASEWELL, Frances illiigetimate d/o Mary Hasewell cared for by Dr. William Levengston 5 Oct 1724 d.d. before 22 Dec 1725; BP

HASKIN, Benjamin & **EVANS**, Mariah B.; DOM 5 Feb 1857 POM King & Queen KQMR

HAWES, Aylett physican POR Kentucky & **HAWES**, Mary d/o Walker Hawes s POR King William; DOM 6 Jul 1827 by Rev. William Hill; KWC

HAWES, Aylett POR Kentucky & **HAWES**, Mary d/o Walker Hawes S POR King William; DOM 6 Jul 1827 VG

HAWKINS, Mourning d.d. between 23 Feb 1784 and 8 Nov 1785; BP

HAY, James s/o Gideon Mesila Hay b.d. 8 Sep 1803; VCA

HAY, John s/o Gideon Mesila Hay b.d. 27 Jul 1797; VCA

HAY, Priscilla wi/o Gideon Hay former wi/o James Sheppard d.d. 18 Mar 1844 POD King William; VCA

HAY, Richard s/o Gideon Mesila Hay b.d. 8 Feb 1801; VCA

HAY, Robert s/o Gideon Mesila Hay b.d. 10 Jan 1805; VCA

HAY, Saley d/o Gideon Mesila Hay b.d.2 Sep 1808; VCA

HAY, Thomas s/o Gideon Mesila Hay b.d. 2 Oct 1799; VCA

HAYES, Mary F. b.d. 1840- d.d.1933 GN VSA #34327

HAYFIELD, James & Mary his wife imported to King & Queen Co by 25 Apr 1701 C&P3

HAYNES, David s/o William Haynes bap 20 Dec 170_ SPPR

HAYNES, William & **CADE**, Letitia; DOM 8 Aug 1703; SPPR

HAYNSWORTH, Elizabeth d/o Richard Haysworth bap 11 Aug 170_ SPPR

HAYNSWORTH, John s/o Richard Haynsworth b.d. 9 Jan bap 27 Jul 1712 SPPR

HAYNSWORTH, Richard & **DYND**, Margaret p.m. 19 Jan 169_ SPPR

HAYNSWORTH, Richard s/o Richard Haynsworth bap 17 Oct 1703 SPPR

HAZELWOOD, widow buried by Dec 1724; BP

HEATH, George & **OAKLEY**, Mary; DOM 14 Apr 172-; SPPR

HEATH, James E. Auditor of Public Accounts & **MACON**, Elizabeth Ann d/o Col. William H. Macon POR New Kent; DOM 21 Sep 1820 POM Fairfield, Hanover Co. by Bishop Moore; RE

HELTON, Francis d/o John Helton bap 24 Apr b.d.18 Mar 1715 SPPR

HELTON, John s/o John Helton b.d. 29 Aug 1709 SPPR

HELTON, Mary d/o John Helton b.d. 1 Jun 1712 SPPR

HELTON, Mary d/o John Helton b.d. 2 Feb 1691 SPPR
HENDERSON, James & KING, Jone; DOM 19 Mar 1714;
    SPPR
HENDERSON, Thomas & WILKESON, Sarah; DOM 10 Nov
    1698; SPPR
HENDERSON, Thomas s/o James Henderson b.d. 17 Jan
    1715 SPPR
HENDESON, Jane d/o Thomas Hendeson bap 5 Mar 1708-
    9 SPPR
HENDRICK, Hance & Jane his wife imported to King &
    Queen by 25 Apr 1701 C&P3
HENLEY, Leonard d.d. between 9 Oct 1759 and 19 Oct
    1761; BP
HENLEY, Sally ne YATES w/o Thomas M. Henley d.d.
    1812; FB
HENLEY, Thomas M. & YATES, Sally; DOM 1806 FB
HENLEY, Thomas M. b.d. 6 Jan 1783; FB
HENLEY, Thomas M. d.d.1846; FB
HENLY, Thomas M. s/o Robert & Maria S. Henly age
    21 S no occupation POB Brook Co,VA & BAGBY,
    Parmelia B. d/o Richard & F.A.Bagby age 18 S
    POB King & Queen Co; DOM 20 Sep 1853 POM King
    & Queen by R.Y.Henly KQMR
HENRY, Bryan d.d. between 12 Oct 1726 and Dec 1727
    leaves a widow, Dorothy; BP
HENSON, Elizabeth d/o Philip Henson bap 25 Dec
    1701 SPPR
HENSON, Philip & Sarah his wife imported by
    Phillip Williams to King William before 24
    Apr 1703 C&P3
HERBERT, Mary d/o Thomas Herbert (dec) POR King &
    Queen by 25 Apr 1701 C&P3
HESTER, Mary d/o Fran. Hester bap 1 Maar 1689 SPPR
HESTER, Robert s/o Frances Hester (father) bap 10
    Oct 1686 SPPR
HICKMAN, Daniel S. POR King William & ANDERSON,
    Mary C. POR Goochland; DOM 10 Dec 1834 RW
HICKMAN, Daniel S. POR King William & ANDERSON,
    Mary C. s POR Goochland; DOM 10 Dec 1834 by
    Rev. Webber; KWC
HICKMAN, William P. POR King William d.d. issue
    dated 26 Aug 1825 RW
HIGGINS, Foster POR New Kent & BAILEY, Rebecca POR
    New Kent; ML Henrico DOM 24 Dec 1827 CTR
HIGHT, John s/o John Hight bap 16 Sep 1688 SPPR
HIGHT, John s/o John Hight bap 3 Spe 168_ SPPR
HIGHT, Mary d/o William Hight bap 6 Dec 1711 SPPR
HIGHT, Robert s/o John Hight bap 20 Aug 1699 SPPR
HIGHT, William s/o John Hight bap 28 Oct 1686 SPPR
HILL Brook POR King & Queen & GAINES, Sarah d/o
    Cap. William F. Gaines POR King William; DOM
    20 Dec 1810 by J.D.Blair; RE
HILL, Agnes d/o Fra. Hill Jr. bap 13 Aug 17__ SPPR

HILL, Baylor s/o Humphrey Hill of King & Queeen Co
    & Frances Baylor 1760-1804; SAR
HILL, Brooke POR King & Queen d.d. issue dated 31
    Oct 1834 RW
HILL, Catherine Gaines d/o Robert Baylor Hill &
    Martha Fleming Gaines b.d. 9 Oct 1804 POR
    King & Queen d.d. 15 Mar 1881; VCA
HILL, Edward s/o Humphrey Hill & Frances Baylor
    POR Hillsborough, King & Queen d.d. about 15
    Jan 1816 at age 70; VMHB
HILL, Edward POR "Frenchtown" King William &
    GOVAN, Elizabeth Tucker d/o James Govan &
    Elizabeth Garlick; DOM 12 Jan 1826; EHR
HILL, Edward POR King & Queen d.d. issue dated 23
    Jan 1816 RE
HILL, Edward POR King William & **GOVAN**, Elizabeth
    d/o James **GOVAN** POR Hanover Co; DOM 12 Jan
    1826 ML 9 Jan 1826 parish register, St.John's
    Church, Richmond
HILL, Edward POR King William & **GOVAN**, Elizabeth
    d/o James Govan POR Powhite, Hanover; DOM 12
    Jan 1826 ML 9 Jan 1826; KWC
HILL, Eliz. d/o Francis Hill bap 3 Jun 1688 SPPR
HILL, Elizabeth w/o Major Thomas Hill d.d. 13 Dec
    1820 POD Oak Grove, King William age 54; KWC
HILL, Emily Brooke p.m. POR King William d.d.
    issue dated 15 Aug 1834 RW
HILL, Francis s/o Fr.Hill JR. bap 12 Jan 1709 SPPR
HILL, George s/o William & Elizabeth Hill b.d. 24
    Sep 1782 d.d. 14 Sep 1855; VCA
HILL, Humphrey s/o Thomas Hill (of London) & Edith
    Bell will dated 8 Feb 1774; VCA; will
    probated 13 Mar 1776; VMHB
HILL, Humphrey s/o Thomas Hill of London & Edith
    Bell b.d.1706; VMHB
HILL, John Jr. & Jane his wife owned land in King
    William by 28 Oct 1702 C&P3
HILL, Mary w/o George Hill d/o Major H. & F.
    Walker b.d. 23 Dec 1786 d.d. 18 May 1851; VCA
HILL, Park POR New Kent & **RAWLEIGH**, Mildred p.m.
    POR Richmond; DOM 14 Jan 1813 by J. Bryce; RE
HILL, Peter s/o Francis Hill bap 1 Mar 1712 SPPR
HILL, Richard POR Spotsylvania & **GOVAN**, Mary d/o
    James Govan POR Hanover, former POR King
    William; DOM 11 Dec 1828; KWC
HILL, Richard s/o Robert & Hannah Hill & **GOVAN**,
    Mary d/o James Govan & Elizabeth Garlick; DOM
    11 Dec 1828; EHR
HILL, Robert B. POR King & Queen & **POLLARD**,
    Catherine d/o Robert **POLLARD** POR King
    William; DOM 15 Mar 1810 VG
HILL, Robert B. POR King & Queen & **POLLARD**,
    Catherine d/o Robert Pollard s POR King
    William; DOM 15 Mar 1810; RE

HILL, Robert B. s/o Robert & Hannah ne Garlick
    Hill POR King & Queen & **POLLARD**, Catherine
    d/o Robert Pollard POR King William; DOM 15
    Mar 1810; KWC
HILL, Robert Baylor s/o Robert Hill & Hannah
    Garlick POR "The Vineyard", King & Queen &
    GAINES, Martha Fleming d/o Harry Gaines &
    Elizabeth Herndon; DOM 22 Dec 1803; VCA
HILL, Robert s/o John & Mary (Elliott) Hill POR
    POD Woodroofe, King William d.d. 23 Dec 1815;
    KWC
HILL, Robert W. POR New Kent & **WRIGHT**, Martha POR
    Hanover S; ML Hanover Co DOM 27 Dec 1834 CTR
HILL, Thomas POR King William & **WALKER**, Elizabeth
    G. POR New Kent; ML New Kent DOM 19 Apr 1832
    CTR
HILL, Wiliam s/o John Hill bap 25 Apr 17__ SPPR
HILL, William s/o Humphrey Hill & **BAYLOR**,
    Elizabeth; DOM 23 Feb 1776 FB
HILLIARD, John H. POR King William & **DABNEY**,
    Catherine s POR King William; DOM 28 Oct 1814
    POM King William; VP
HILLIARD, Louisa C. b.d. 19 Mar 1794 d.d.2 Jan
    1858; KWH
HILTON, Anne d/o John Hilton bap 14 Jun 170_ SPPR
HILTON, Bridgett d/o John Hilton bap 20 Dec 170_
    SPPR
HILTON, Elizabeth d/o John Hilton b.d. 25 Jun 1696
    SPPR
HILTON, George s/o John & Elizabeth Hilton bap 27
    Aug 1699 SPPR
HILTON, George s/o John Hilton b.d. 30 Jul no year
    SPPR
HILTON, Ruth d/o John Hilton bap 11 Aug no year
    SPPR
HILYARD, Allen s/o John W. Hilyard & Ann Richerson
    age 30 S POB King & Queen farmer & **ALEXANDER**,
    Catharine d/o Thomas Walton & Lucy Pynes age
    35 W POB King & Queen; DOM 10 Jan 1853 POM
    King & Queen by Isaac Digge KQMR
HINSON, John s/o Philip Hinson b.d. 3 Jun 1708
    SPPR
HITCHCOCK, William s/o John Hitchcock b.d.10 Feb
    bap 15 Mar 1712 SPPR
HIX, Nathan d.d. by 23 Feb 1784; BP
HIX, Preston d.d. by 20 Dec 1780; BP
HIX, Sarah d.d. by 23 Feb 1784; BP
HOCKADAY, John POR James City & **HOWLE**, Elizabeth
    W. S POR New Kent; DOM 2 Mar 1847 by Rev.
    William E.Lee RCA
HOCKADAY, William major d.d. between 12 Oct 1756
    and 6 Oct 1757; BP

HOGG, James W. s/o William & Juliett Ann Hogg (William is a laborer by day) b.d. Jul 1853 POB King & Queen; KQBR

HOGG, William d.d. between 16 Oct 1758 and 19 Oct 1761; BP

HOLDCROFT, Thomas d.d. between 8 Oct 1745 and 8 Oct 1746; BP

HOLLAWAY, Phebe d/o John Holloway bap 16 May 1697 SPPR

HOLMES, Benjamin P. d.d. 16 Aug 1821 POD King & Queen age 38 RCC

HOLT, Mary d/o "a white woman and a mulatto man" b.d. 10 Jan 1698 SPPR

HOLT, Mary mulatto owned by Mr. Allin d.d. 24 Dec 1718; SPPR

HOOD, Robert s/o Richard & Elizabeth Hood b.d. 14 Feb 1698 bap 10 Jul 1698 SPPR

HOOK, Michael s/o James Hook bap 24 Apr 1714 SPPR

HOOMES, Benjamin P. POR Dunkirk, King & Queen & **DABNEY**, Eleanor d/o Maj. George Dabney POR King William; DOM 21 Nov 1816 VG

HOOMES, Benjamin P. POR Dunkirk, King & Queen & **DABNEY**, Elenor d/o Maj. Geo Dabney s POR King William; DOM 21 Nov 1816 by Robert B. Semple; RE

HOOMES, Thomas C. POR King & Queen & **POLLARD**, Betsy d/o Robert Pollard POR King & Queen; DOM 16 Dec 1817 by Robert B. Semple; RE

HOOMES, Thomas C. POR Melrose, King & Queen d.d. 5 Feb 1821 RCC

HOOMES, Thomas Claiborne POR Melrose, King & Queen d.d. 5 Feb 1821; ONKH

HOPE, William; DOM 1 Mar 1778 POM King & Queen VM

HOPKINS, John S. POR New Kent d.d. issue dated 20 Apr 1831 RW

HORNE, Ralph d.d 21 Sep 1829 age 73; KWC

HOSKINS, Catherine M. POR King & Queen d.d. issue dated 1 Jun 1838 RW

HOSKINS, John Dr. POR King & Queen & **RUFFIN**, Lucy s POR King William; DOM 18 May 1809; RE

HOSKINS, John POR King & Queen & **CHEANEY**, Elizabeth d/o John Cheaney; DOM deed found 1782; Essex Co. Deed Book 33

HOSKINS, John POR King & Queen d.d. issue dated 26 Nov 1813 RE

HOSKINS, Polly p.m. POR King & Queen d.d. issue dated 22 Nov 1825 RE

HOULE, Will s/o Will Houle bap 4 Mar 1687/8 SPPR

HOUSMAN, George s/o Stephen Housman b.d. 29 Jan 1715 SPPR

HOWARD, John POR St.Paul's Parish [probably Hanover] & **HOWLE**, Jane; DOM 11 Jul 1711; SPPR

HOWARD, John s/o Luke Howard bap 13 Feb 1686/7 SPPR

HOWCHENS, Charles s/o Edward Howchens bap 17 Aug 1690 SPPR

HOWELL, William; DOM 1 Aug 1778 POM King & Queen VM

HOWLE, Ann p.m. POR New Kent d.d issue dated 9 Jun 1826 RE

HOWLE, Anne d/o John Howle bap 23 Jul 1710 SPPR

HOWLE, Eliz. d/o William Howle bap 28 Jun 1691 SPPR

HOWLE, Gidion N. POR New Kent & **GATHWRIGHT,** Orina POR Hanover; ML Hanover Co DOM 22 Dec 1825 CTR

HOWLE, Judith d/o John & Elizabeth Howle b.d. 24 Oct 1714 SPPR

HOWLE, Robert & **BASSETT,** Francis; DOM 9 Dec 1708; SPPR

HOWLE, Robert s/o John Howle b.d. 14 Apr bap 11 May 1712 SPPR

HOWLE, Thomas s/o Epaphoditus & Ann Howle b.d. "middle of the summer at break of day"; SPPR

HUBARD, James Jr. POR Gloucester & **WHITING,** Molly POR King & Queen S; DOM issue date 7 Jul 1775 VG

HUBBARD, Christopher POR Richmond & **COTTRELL,** Catherine s POR King William; DOM 29 Jun 1813 by Rev. Mills; VA

HUBBARD, James Jr. POR Gloucester & **WHITING,** Molly S POR King & Queen Co; 7 Jul 1775 VG

HUBERT, Elizabeth d/o John Hubert bap 20 Nov 1709 SPPR

HUCHENS, Rachel d/o Edward & Rebecca Huchens bap 24 Oct 1686 SPPR

HUGHES, Charles s/o William Hughes bap 18 Oct 1691 SPPR

HUGHES, Elinor d/o John Hughes bap 6 Aug 1710 SPPR

HUGHES, Eliz. d/o John Hughes bap 21 Mar 17__ SPPR

HUGHES, Eliz. d/o William Hughes bap 19 Oct 1691 SPPR

HUGHES, Jane d/o John Hughes bap 25 Mar 1708 SPPR

HUGHES, John s/o Will Hughes bap 23 Apr 1689 SPPR

HUGHES, Will s/o Will Hughes bap 18 Sep 1687 SPPR

HUGHES, William s/o John & Sarah Hughes b.d.1 Jan 1711 SPPR

HULETT, Augustin & **LANE,** Hannah; DOM 10 Jan 1685/6; SPPR

HUNDLEY, _____ d/o William C. & Sarah B. Hundley (William was a farmer) b.d. Aug 1853 POB King & Queen; KQBR

HUNDLEY, Henry L. s/o Arthur J. & Mary Ann Hundley (Arthur was a carpenter) b.d. Oct 1853 POB King & Queen; KQBR

HUNDLEY, John T.T. POR King & Queen & **GARNETT,** Sarah E.; DOM 4 May 1859; Essex Co Marriage Register

HUNDLEY, William Clark s/o John P. Hundley & Pattie Clark POR King & Queen & **THOMAS**, Sarah Branch wi/o Philip Lipscomb POR King William; DOM 1845 HMBC

HUNDLEY, William Thomas s/o William Clark Hundley & Sarah Branch Thomas b.d. 24 Aug 1851 POB Pleasant Retreat, King & Queen; HMBC

HUNT, George & **POINDEXTER**, Elizabeth; DOM 24 [probably Aug] 1709; SPPR

HUNT, William d.d. between 20 Sep 1773 and 21 Dec 1775; SMP

HURT, Eliz. buried by 15 Oct 1741; BP

HURT, John b.d. 1655 POR King William d.d. 1723 POD King William IR

HUTCHINGS, Burton & **ALLEN**, Judith d/o William & Hannah Allen b.d. 1715 POB New Kent; DOM 16 Mar 1742 POM Goochland; KK1

HUTSON, William; DOM 1 Jun 1778 POM King & Queen VM

Indian Will POC owned by Ebenezer Adams d.d. 18 Oct 1723; SPPR

JACKSON, Anne d/o John Jackson bap 4 Oct 1713; SPPR

JACKSON, Anne d/o William Jackson bap 18 Feb 1714; SPPR

JACKSON, Eliz. d/o Thomas Jackson bap 9 Dec 1694; SPPR

JACKSON, Frances d/o William Jackson bap 15 Oct 1710; SPPR

JACKSON, Job buried by 19 Nov 1756; SMP

JACKSON, John s/o John Jackson b.d. 14 Jun 1715; SPPR

JACKSON, Mary d/o John Jackson bap 9 Feb 1709; SPPR

JACKSON, Sarah d/o John Jackson bap 3 Dec 1711; SPPR

JACKSON, Sarah d/o Thomas Jackson bap 14 Nov 1703; SPPR

JACKSON, Thomas s/o Thomas & Mary Jackson b.d. 1 Jun 1699; SPPR

JACKSON, Thomas s/o William & Anne Jackson bap 3 May 1713; SPPR

JAMES, John d.d. between 13 Oct and 22 Dec 1725; BP

JAMES, William W. s/o Henry James age 22 S overseer POB Caroline POR King & Queen & **MAHON**, Ellen d/o Abram Mahon age 19 S POB POR King & Queen; DOM 22 Dec 1859 POM King & Queen by R.H.Bagby; KQMR

JARRATT, Devereux s/o Robert Jarratt & Sarah Bradley minister b.d. 6 Jan 1732/3 POB New Kent d.d. 1800 or 1801; autobiographical letter to Rev. John Coleman

JARRATT, Robert s/o Robert & Mary Jarratt bap 16
Aug 1698; SPPR
JEFFERD, John d.d. by 12 Nov 1762; BP
JEFFERS, Richmond buried by 28 Apr 1777; BP
JEFFRIES, James M. b.d. 25 Jun 1809 POB "within
sight of this spot" (Mattaponi Baptist
Church, King & Queen) d.d. 6 Apr 1890 POD
West Point, VA judge of the 9th Circuit
Court; MBC
JEFFRIES, Juliet d/o James M. & Malvina M.
Jeffries d.d. 3 Oct 1857 age 15; MBC
JEFFRIES, Mrs. M.F. d.d. Dec 1851; MBC
JEFFRIES, Mrs. M.F. d.d. Dec 1851; VCA
JEFFRIES, Thomas H. s/o George & Susan Jeffries
age 36 S farmer POB Gloucester POR King &
Queen & **DIGGS**, Mary M. d/o Dudley & Catherine
Diggs age 16 S POB POR King & Queen; DOM 18
Apr 1854 POM King & Queen by Isaac Diggs;
KQMR
JEFFRIES, Thomas M. d.d. 15 Mar 1855 age 61; MBC
JEFFRIES, Thomas M. d.d. 15 Mar 1855 age 61; VCA
JEFFRIES, William POR King & Queen & **GRAHAM**, Lucy
s POR King & Queen; DOM 16 Nov 1820 by
William Todd; RE
JENINGS, John s/o Robert Jenings b.d.2 Sep bap 16
Aug 1698; SPPR
JENINGS, William s/o Robert Jenings bap 5 Jul
1702; SPPR
JENKINS, Elizabeth d/o John & Hanna Jenkins bap 7
May 1699; SPPR
JENNINGS, George d.d. by 23 Feb 1779; BP
JENNINGS, Robert b.d. abt 1665 POR New Kent d.d.
1716 POD New Kent; EHR
JENNINGS, Robert POR New Kent abt 1692 POD Hanover
d.d. 1758; EHR
JERDONE, Francis POR New Kent d.d. issue dated 10
May 1836; RW
JERDONE, James POR New Kent d.d. issue dated 16
Sep 1836; RW
JOANES, Eliz. d/o John Joanes bap 30 May 1688;
SPPR
JOANES, Eliz. d/o Richard & Debora Joanes bap 15
Mar 1680; SPPR
JOANES, George s/o George & Jane Joanes bap 5 Dec
1689 SPPR
JOANES, John s/o Richard & Debora Joanes bap 15
Jan 1683 SPPR
JOANES, Mary d/o Richard & Debora Joanes bap 16
Jan 1685 SPPR
JOHNSON, Agnes d/o Michael Johnson bap 2 Apr 1708;
SPPR
JOHNSON, Ammon POR King William & **LITTLEPAGE**, Ann
s POR King William; DOM 26 Dec 1816 by John
Mill; RE

JOHNSON, Ammon s/o James Johnson & Lucy Ammon &
    LITTLEPAGE, Ann S DOM 26 Dec 1816 VG
JOHNSON, Ammon s/o James Johnson & Lucy Ammon POR
    Old Town, King William & **LITTLEPAGE**, Ann s;
    DOM 26 Dec 1816 by Rev. John Mill; KWC
JOHNSON, Ann d/o James & Lucy Johnson b.d. 25 Dec
    1781 gravestone at "Old Town", New Kent
JOHNSON, Anne d/o Michael Johnson bap 12 Feb 1705;
    SPPR
JOHNSON, Anne d/o William & Sarah Johnson bap 16
    Apr 1699; SPPR
JOHNSON, Benjamin s/o Edward Johnson b.d. 17 Aug
    1701; SPPR
JOHNSON, Benjamin s/o William Johnson bap 18 Apr
    1705; SPPR
JOHNSON, Christopher s/o James Johnson & Lucy
    Ammons b.d. 1780 POR King William; KK1
JOHNSON, Cicely d/o William Johnson bap 3 Dec
    1711; SPPR
JOHNSON, Collins s/o William Johnson bap 4 Feb
    170_; SPPR
JOHNSON, Daniel s/o Michael Johnson bap 16 May
    169_ (probably 9); SPPR
JOHNSON, David & Jane his wife imported by
    Nicholas Rodes to King William before 24 Apr
    1703 C&P3
JOHNSON, Eliz. d/o Edward Johnson b.d. 7 Jul bap 6
    Aug 1682 SPPR
JOHNSON, Jacob s/o Alex Johnson b.d. Sep 1708;
    SPPR
JOHNSON, James H. POR King & Queen & **LANE**, Martha
    T. S POR Hanover Co; DOM 17 Feb 1848 by Rev.
    A.MacDowell RCA held by Randolph Macon
    College
JOHNSON, James s/o Christopher Johnson & Elizabeth
    Hawes POR King William & **HAWES**, Elizabeth POR
    King William; DOM 1 Dec 1831 by Rev. William
    Hill; KWC
JOHNSON, James s/o Christopher Johnson POR "Old
    Town" & **HAWES**, Elizabeth d/o Walker Hawes &
    Mary Martin POR King William; DOM 1 Dec 1831
    RW
JOHNSON, Jane p.m. POR King William d.d. issue
    dated 11 Dec 1835
JOHNSON, John s/o John Johnson bap 22 Nov 1702;
    SPPR
JOHNSON, Lucy d/o Christopher Ammon w/o James
    Johnson POR New Kent d.d. 1826 SPPR
JOHNSON, Lucy p.m. POR King William d.d. issue
    dated 11 Apr 1826 RW
JOHNSON, Massie s/o John Johnson bap 5 Feb 1705;
    SPPR
JOHNSON, Miranda p.m. d.d. issue dated 13 Nov 1832
    RW

JOHNSON, Penelope d/o Edward Johnson b.d.4 Aug bap
17 Aug 1684 SPPR
JOHNSON, Rachell d/o Edward & Elizabeth Johnson
b.d. 8 Dec bap 2 Jan 1686/87 SPPR
JOHNSON, Rebecka d/o Edward Johnson b.d. 8 ___ bap
11 Nov 1698; SPPR
JOHNSON, Richard POR King & Queeen Co POB England
d.d. abt 1698 POD Virginia CVR
JOHNSON, Richman s/o Alex. Johnson bap 27 Apr
1712; SPPR
JOHNSON, Robert W. s/o Henry Johnson & Mary
Montague age 29 W farmer POB open & **LUMPKIN**,
Mary G. d/o William Lumpkin & Sally Marshall
age 24 S POB King & Queen Co; DOM 17 Dec 1853
POM King & Queen by Thomas Durham KQMR
JOHNSON, Sarah d/o Michael Johnson bap 12 Oct
1707; SPPR
JOHNSON, Thomas POR King William & **TURNER**,
Temperance POR Hanover S; ML Henrico DOM 12
Apr 1834 CTR
JOHNSON, Thomas s/o Anthony Johnson bap 9 Dec
1694; SPPR
JOHNSON, Thomas s/o Edward Johnson b.d. 5 May bap
30 May 1680 SPPR
JOHNSON, Thomas s/o John Johnson b.d.11 Sep 1714;
SPPR
JOHNSON, William d.d. 13 Aug 1832 age 48; KWC
JOHNSON, William s/o William Johnson bap 31 Aug
1701 ;SPPR
JONES, Agnes d/o John Jones b.d 13 Oct 170_; SPPR
JONES, Catesby (Major) POR Gloucester Co &
TALIAFERRO, Mary B. youngest d/o John
Taliaferro POR King William; DOM 29 Apr 1822
VG
JONES, Catesby POR Gloucester & **TALIAFERRO**, Mary
B. youngest d/o John Taliaferro s POR King
William; DOM 29 Apr 1822; KWC
JONES, Evan buried by 10 Oct 1737; BP
JONES, Francis d/o Orlando & Martha Jones b.d. 6
Aug 1710; SPPR
JONES, Jane Chandler d/o Richard Reins of King
William & Jane Frances Worthain of Caroline
b.d. 6 Jan 1824; Jones FB
JONES, John illegitimate s/o Mary Jones cared for
by Job Jackson 1742; SMP
JONES, John Robert s/o Mortimer Jones age 28 S
farmer POB POR King & Queen & **COX**, Elizabeth
F. d/o William W. Cox age 27 S POB POR King &
Queen; DOM 27 Sep 1860 POM King & Queen; KQMR
JONES, John s/o John Jones Jr. bap 30 May 1706;
SPPR
JONES, John s/o Mary Jones kept by Job Jackson 10
Oct 1743 SMP

JONES, John W. POR New Kent & **JONES**, Martha
Recelia d/o William M. Jones s; DOM 10 Dec
1840 POM James City Co. by James Clopton; RW

JONES, Lane s/o Orlando & Martha Jones b.d. 15 Jun
1707; SPPR

JONES, Mary d/o Evan Jones is under age in 13 Nov
1728; BP

JONES, Richard s/o John Jones b.d. 6 Mar 17__;
SPPR

KATTLE, William POR King & Queen d.d.before 8 Oct
1750; SMP

KAUFFMAN, Jeremiah s/o George & Polly Kauffman age
21 S free POC farmer POB POR King & Queen &
ROBINSON, Pinkey d/o Lorenzo & Betsy Robinson
age 16 S free POC POB POR King & Queen; DOM 6
Mar 1856 POM King & Queen by John Bird; KQMR

KEEBLE, Elleoner d/o Henry Keeble bap 30 Oct 1689;
SPPR

KEEBLE, Henery s/o Henry Keeble bap 11 Jan 1701/2;
SPPR

KEMP, Mathew POR Gloucester age 63 & **LYNE**,
Elizabeth POR King & Queen age 58 s; DOM 20
Oct 1821 by Thomas Henley; RE

KEMP, Peter W. b.d. 15 Feb 1840 d.d. 11 Apr 1921;
MBC

KENNEY, William d.d. by 8 Oct 1745; BP

KENNON, Beverley capt. USN & **CLAIBORNE**, Elizabeth
D. s; DOM 1 Jul 1829 POM King William; RE

KENNON, Beverley captain, U.S.Navy & **CLAIBORNE**,
Elizabeth D. S POR King William; DOM 1 Jul
1829; VG

KERNUTE, James bound to Richard Maples on 13 Mar
1730 until he is 21; BP

KIDD, Thomas bap 25 Nov 1788; VBHS

KILLEY, Susey bap 14 Feb 1789; VBHS

KILLY, Joseph a bastard child b.d.beginning of Mar
1706/7; SPPR

KIMBRIELL, Bulkley s/o John & Margaret Kimbriell
Sr. b.d. 19 Nov 1699; SPPR

KIMBRIELL, Rebecka d/o John & Eliz. Kimbriell Jr.
b.d. 10 Aug 1699; SPPR

KIMBURROW, John s/o John Kimborow Jr. bap 21 Dec
1701; SPPR

KIMBURROW, Major s/o John Kimburrow bap 29 _____
1703/4; SPPR

KIMBURROW, Mary d/o John Kimburrow Jr. b.d. or bap
30 Jan 1703/4; SPPR

KING, Alexander s/o Robert King bap 19 Dec 1689;
SPPR

KING, John POR King & Queen d.d. before 28 Oct
1702; C&P3

KING, John POR Richmond & **LIPSCOMB**, Sally Ann only
d/o Reuben Lipscomb former POR King William;
DOM 27 Dec 1837 by Rev. Philip Courtney

(pastor of First Baptist Church, Richmond);
KWC

KING, John POR Richmond & **LIPSCOMBE**, Sally Ann
only d/o Capt. Reuben Lipscombe former POR
King William; DOM 27 Dec 1837 by Philip
Courtney; RE

KING, Mary d/o Thomas & Mary King bap 11 Jun 1689;
SPPR

KING, Peter s/o Thomas King bap 7 Oct 1694; SPPR

KING, Robert s/o Robert King bap 11 Mar 1687/8;
SPPR

KIRBY, Joseph s/o Henry & Susan Milby [Kirby] age
61 farmer POB Middlesex POR King & Queen &
MILBY, Lucy Ann d/o Thomas Milby age 30 W POB
POR King & Queen; DOM 14 Jan 1860 POM King &
Queen; KQMR

KITSON, Betty buried in 1763; BP

LACY, David Richeson POR Charlottesville & **MERRY**,
Joice Clopton eldest d/o Capt. John Merry POR
New Kent; DOM 27 Apr 1826 POM Richmond Hill,
Henrico by William H. Hart; RE

LACY, Edmund B. POR New Kent & **VAUGHAN**, Harriett
H. S POR New Kent; DOM 21 Apr 1836 by Rev.
S.W.Jones; VCS

LACY, Richard B. s/o Bartholomew & Eliza Lacy age
26 S farmer POB POR New Kent & **ANDERSON**,
Ellen d/o Samuel & Eliza Lacy age 16 S POB
POR New Kent; DOM 6 Jun 1860 POM New Kent by
William S. Briggs; NKMR

LACY, Richmond T. POR New Kent & **LANE**, Ellen d/o
Mrs. Sarah Lane; DOM 30 Apr 1835 POM
Vancluse, Amelia by Parke Farley Berkley; RE

LACY, Theophilus A. POR New Kent & **PEAKE**, Mary E.
POR Westmoreland s; DOM 26 Mar 1828 by S.
Templeton; RE

LADD, William b.d. 8 Feb 1760 POB New Kent d.d. 9
May 1843 & _____, Mary; DOM 17 Dec 1778 POM
New Kent by Parson Semple; Rev. Pension File
W8079

LAKE, Mary d/o William & Mary Lake bap 16 Apr
1699; SPPR

LAKE, Peter s/o William Lake bap 19 Sep 1697; SPPR

LAMB, Jane d/o Richard Lamb bap 8 Jan 1687/8; SPPR

LANCESTER, Richard s/o Robert Lancester bap 15 Mar
1690/1; SPPR

LANE, Horace s/o Horace & Lucy Lane age 40 W
blacksmith POB King & Queen & **SHELTON**, Nancy
d/o Ben & Mildred Shelton age 21 S POB King &
Queen Co; DOM 18 Aug 1853 POM King & Queen by
J.W.Shackford; KQMR

LANEFORD, Martha d/o John Laneford bap 9 Aug 1688;
SPPR

LANKFORD, Elinor d/o _____ Lankford bound to her
grandfather William Morris 13 Oct 1729; SMP

LARUS, Philip Dr. POR Richmond & **FRANCIS**, Polly
   POR New Kent; DOM 26 Nov 1805; VGGA
LARUS, Philip Dr. POR Richmond & **FRAYSER**, Mary
   eldest d/o Thomas Frayser POR New Kent; DOM
   26 Nov 1805; VA
LAWSON, Elenor d/o John & Judith Lawson bap 10 Jul
   1698; SPPR
LAWSON, John s/o John Lawson bap 8 May 1690; SPPR
LEAKE, Jane d/o William Leake b.d. 11 Jan 1700/1;
   SPPR
LEAKE, Mary d/o William & Mary Leake bap 16 Apr
   1699; SPPR
LEAKE, Peter s/o William Leake bap 16 Apr 1699;
   SPPR
LEAKE, Richard s/o William Leake bap 13 Dec 17--;
   SPPR
LEAVER, Anne illegitimate d/o Mary Leaver (dec) is
   too young to determine if she is mulatto.
   She is bound to Roger Williams 24 Apr 1725;
   BP
LEE, William P. s/o Courtney Lee age 23 S farmer
   POB Essex & **BALL**, Penelope A. age 22 S POB
   King & Queen; DOM Dec 1855 POM King & Queen
   by John W. Shackelford; KQMR
LEE, William P. s/o Courtney Lee age 23 S POB
   Essex POR King & Queen & **BALL**, Penelope A.
   age 22 S POB King & Queen ; DOM 19 Dec 1855
   POM King & Queen by John W. Shackleford; KQMR
LEEKE, Will s/o William Leeke bap 15 Jul 1694;
   SPPR
LEIGH, Col. William d.d. 1703 POR King & Queen;
   ONKH
LEWES, John s/o John Lewes bap 27 Feb 1686/7; SPPR
LEWIS, Abraham s/o John Lewis, planter bap 27 Nov
   1698; SPPR
LEWIS, Angelico d/o Nicholas Lewis b.d.20 Mar bap
   27 Apr 1712; SPPR
LEWIS, Ann buried by 7 Oct 1754; SMP
LEWIS, Ann d/o Owin Lewis b.d. 19 Mar bap 25 Apr
   17__; SPPR
LEWIS, Ann w/o George Lewis d.d. 11/6/1754; SMP
LEWIS, Ann w/o George Lewis kept by William Ware 8
   Oct 1750; SMP
LEWIS, David s/o John Lewis bap 5 May 1695; SPPR
LEWIS, Edward s/o Nicholas Lewis bap 29 Oct 1___;
   SPPR
LEWIS, Elisabeth d/o Owin Lewis b.d. 6 Feb 1715;
   SPPR
LEWIS, John POB Munmoth Shire d.d. 21 Aug 1657 age
   63; ONKH
LEWIS, Maria Louisa Adelaid w/o Zachary Lewis d.d.
   30 Jan 1869; Lewis FB
LEWIS, Martha Rosalie d/o Zachariah & M.L.A.Lewis
   b.d. 27 Aug 1837; Lewis FB

LEWIS, Mary d/o Nicholas Lewis bap 16 Jan 1708/9; SPPR

LEWIS, Robert nephew & Aide de Camp to the Pres. of the U.S. & **BROWN**, Judith Walker d/o William Burnet Brown; DOM 15 Mar 1791 POM Elsing Green, King William; VGGA

LEWIS, Sarah G. d/o Z. & A.C. Lewis POR King William d.d. 31 Aug 1840; Lewis FB

LEWIS, William B. Dr. former POR King William & **HENRY**, Maria Rosalie eldest d/o Edward W. Henry POR Charlotte ; DOM 11 Jan 1840 POM Presby.Ch, Charlotte C.H. by Samuel J. Price; RW

LEWIS, William POR Middlesex & **DAME**, POR King & Queen; DOM 14 Dec 1839; RE

LEWIS, William s/o Nicholas & Elisabeth Lewis b.d. 22 Mar 1715; SPPR

LEWIS, Zachary & **CLOPTON**, Maria Louisa Adelaid d/o John Clopton of New Kent; DOM 4 May 1831; Lewis FB

LIGHT, George POR King & Queen d.d. before 24 Apr 1700; C&P3

LIGHTFOOT, Alice d/o John & Anne Lightfoot b.d. 25 Sep 1698; SPPR

LIGHTFOOT, Anne d/o Goodrich Lightfoot b.d. 22 Sep 1708; SPPR

LIGHTFOOT, Frances d/o Sherwood Lightfoot b.d. 31 Oct 1708; SPPR

LIGHTFOOT, Goodrich s/o Goodrich Lightfoot bap 14 Feb 171-; SPPR

LIGHTFOOT, John s/o Goodrich Lightfoot b.d. 13 Nov 1711; SPPR

LIGHTFOOT, John POB England POR New Kent d.d.28 May 1707 in Virginia; CVR

LIGHTFOOT, Mary d/o Sherwood Lightfoot b.d. 9 Sep 1707; SPPR

LIGHTFOOT, Sherwood s/o Sherwood Lightfoot b.d. 1 May 17__; SPPR

LINSEY, Ann buried by 20 Oct 1766; BP

LIPSCOMB, Ann d/o James & Lucy Johnson w/o W.B.Lipscomb d.d. 25 Sep 1819 gravestone at "Old Town", New Kent

LIPSCOMB, Bernard A. s/o Austin & Mildred Lipscomb age 27 S farmer POB King William & **BRUMBRY**, Fanny A. d/o Robert & Mary M. Brumbry age 21 S POB King & Queen Co; DOM 4 Sep 1853 POM King & Queen by William B. Todd; KQMR

LIPSCOMB, Chamberlaine & **CROW**, Susan S POR King William; DOM 21 Dec 1832; RW

LIPSCOMB, Chamberlaine & **CROW**, Susan s POR King William; DOM 21 Dec 1832; KWC

LIPSCOMB, Corbin s/o Temple & Margaret Lipscomb b.d. 2 Mar _____; He is recorded between

Reuben and William Temple Lipscomb in the
Lipscomb FB

LIPSCOMB, Daniel & **FRAZER**, Jane 3 Nov 1792 POM
King William; VM

LIPSCOMB, George & **LIPSCOMB**, Ann; DOM 26 Oct 1785
POM King William; VM

LIPSCOMB, James H. POR King William & **HILL**, Eliza
C. d/o James Hill POR Hanover; DOM 3 Dec 1829
by Philip Courtney; RC

LIPSCOMB, Lucy wi/o Pemberton Lipscomb d.d. 17 Aug
1811 age 57; KWC

LIPSCOMB, Preston s/o Temple & Margaret Lipscomb
b.d. 19 Dec____; he is recorded after William
Temple Lipscomb in the Lipscomb FB

LIPSCOMB, Reuben s/o Temple & Margaret Lipscomb
b.d. 12 May 1818 d.d. 17 Sep 1830; Lipscomb
FB

LIPSCOMB, Sterling & **JOHNSON**, Elizabeth youngest
d/o James Johnson POR Oldtown, King William;
DOM 13 May 1813 by John Mill; VA

LIPSCOMB, Temple d.d. Sep 1835; Lipscomb FB

LIPSCOMB, William Temple s/o Temple & Margaret
Lipscomb b.d. 19 Dec 1821 d.d. 14 Oct 183_;
Lipscomb FB

LITTLEPAGE, Alice d/o Capt. Richard Littlepage
b.d. 14 Jan 1707/8; SPPR

LITTLEPAGE, Edmund s/o Richard & Frances
Littlepage POR King William b.d. 16 May
1712; VCA & SPPR

LITTLEPAGE, Elisabeth d/o Capt. Richard Littlepage
b.d. 11 Dec 1703; SPPR

LITTLEPAGE, Frances d/o Capt. Richard Littlepage
b.d. 2 Oct 1705; SPPR

LITTLEPAGE, James s/o Richard & Francis Littlepage
b.d. 14 Jul 1714; SPPR

LITTLEPAGE, John s/o Richard & Francis Littlepage
b.d. 14 Jul 1714; SPPR

LITTLEPAGE, Judith d/o Richard Littlepage b.d. 31
Jul 1715; SPPR

LITTLEPAGE, Richard s/o Richard Littlepage 21 Mar
1709/10/ SPPR

LITTLEPAGE, Richard POR King William d.d.20 Mar
1717; VCA

LITTLEPAGE, Richard s/o Richard & Frances
Littlepage POB New Kent b.d.21 Mar 1710; VCA

LIVINGSTON, John d.d. between 24 Nov 1760 and 22
Feb 1762; SMP

LOCKLEY, William s/o Daniel & Rachel Lockley age
30 W free POC miller POB POR King & Queen &
BLUEFORD, Caty d/o William & Elizabeth
Blueford age 22 S free POC POB POR King &
Queen; DOM 3 Jan 1856 POM King & Queen by
Thomas Bivens; KQMR

LONGEST, Richard POR King & Queen & **CLAYTON**,
Martha s POR King & Queen; DOM 5 Dec 1816 by
William Todd; RE
LONGWORTHY, John POR New Kent d.d. before 24 Apr
1703; C&P3
LOWILL, Charles s/o George Lowill bap 16 Feb 1700;
SPPR
LOWILL, John s/o George & Eliz. Lowill bap 15 Oct
1699; SPPR
LOVILL, Sarah d/o George Lovill bap 31 Jan 1___;
SPPR
LUCAS, Thomas s/o Thomas & Virginia Lucas age 25 S
waterman POB Gloucester POR King & Queen &
PILSBERRY, Ann E. d/o George & Lucy Pilsberry
age 27 S POB POR King & Queen; DOM 3 Jan
1856 POM King & Queen by William Eastwood;
KQMR
LUCK, Mary d/o John Luck bap 14 Sep 1707; SPPR
LUCK, Richard s/o John Luck bap 24 Sep 1699; SPPR
LUCK, Samuel s/o John Luck bap 18 Sep 1709; SPPR
LUMPKIN, Anthony bap 16 Jun 1775; VBHS
LUMPKIN, Christoper s/o Robert Lumpkin age 28 S
pinter POB POR King & Queen & **JONES**, Sarah E.
d/o Mortimer Jones age 26 S POB POR King &
Queen; DOM 16 Oct 1860 POM King & Queen; KQMR
LUMPKIN, Elizabeth d/o Robert & Lucy Lumpkin
b.d.1797; GN
LUMPKIN, Henry 1 Jan 1741 POB King & Queen Co; GN
LUMPKIN, Henry Jr. s/o Henry Lumpkin b.d.2 Aug
1768; GN
LUMPKIN, Henry POB King & Queen d.d.1823; GN
LUMPKIN, Henry s/o Henry Lumpkin d.d.7 May 1846;
GN
LUMPKIN, Jacob d.d. 14 Sep 1708 age 64 years POR
Newington, King & Queen; HMBC
LUMPKIN, John & **DABNEY**, Ann W. p.m.; POM The
Dorrell, King William DOM 6 Aug 1835; RW
LUMPKIN, John capt. & **DABNEY**, Anne W. p.m.; DOM 11
Aug 1835 POM Dorrels, King William; RE
LUMPKIN, John Roane Jr. s/o John Roane Lumpkin &
Catherine Wyatt Garrett b.d. 1836 d.d.1920;
GN
LUMPKIN, John Roane s/o Robert Lumpkin & Lucy
Roane b.1799; GN
LUMPKIN, John Roane s/o Robert Lumpkin & Lucy
Roane d.d. 1842; GN
LUMPKIN, Molley bap 25 Nov 1788; VBHS
LUMPKIN, Patsey bap 25 Nov 1788; VBHS
LUMPKIN, Patsy d.d. 25 Nov 1789; VBHS
LUMPKIN, Polly b.d.1790; FB
LUMPKIN, Sara d.d. 17 Jun 1777; VBHS
LUMPKIN, William d.d. 19 Jul 1782; VBHS
LUMPKIN. Richardson POR King & Queen & **PENDLETON**,
Priscilla d/o Benjamin Pendleton s POR King &

Queen; DOM 4 Nov 1828 POM Green Meadow by
Andrew Broaddus; RE

LUMPKINS, Rach__ bap 25 Nov 1788; VBHS

LUMPKINS, Thomas bap 14 Feb 1789; VBHS

LYON, Daniel d.d. between 1774 and 29 Jul 1776; BP

LYDDALL, George Col. d.d. Jan 1705; tombstone
found in St. Peter's Churchyard, New Kent

LYDE, Cornelius major s/o Lionel Lyde POD King
William d.d. issue dated 27 Jan 1737; VG

LYDE, Cornelius s/o Lionel Lyde of Bristol POR POD
King William d.d. issue dated 27 Jan 1737;
KWC

LYNE, Robert Dr. POR King & Queen & **EDWARDS**, Mary
Ann POR King William s ; DOM 24 Apr 1834 by
Dr. Duval; RE

LYNE, Robert Dr. POR King & Queen & **EDWARDS**, Mary
Ann s POR King William; DOM 24 Apr 1834 by
Dr. Duvall; KWC & RW

LYNE, William d.d. between 30 Nov 1759 and 24 Nov
1760; SMP

LYONS, John POR Hanover & **CARTER**, Ann POR King
William; DOM 24 Jul 1789; VIC

M'CARTY, John POR King William & **MOORE**, Polly POR
King William DOM 12 Dec 1816; VG

M'CARTY, John POR King WIlliam & **MOORE**, Polly s
POR King William; DOM 12 Dec 1816 by Rev.
John Mill; KWC

M'CARTY, John POR King William & **MOORE**, Polly s
POR King William; DOM 12 Dec 1816 by John
Mill; RE

M'COMICK, Mary buried by 29 Nov 1773; BP

M'GARY, Thomas d.d. between 10 Oct 1768 and 23 Oct
1769; BP

M'HONE, Sackville d.d. by 21 Oct 1765; BP

MACHIN, Thomas s/o Edmond & Anne Machin bap 5 Nov
169_ (probably 9); SPPR

MACKAIN, William d.d. between 8 Oct 1739 and 29
Sep 1740; BP

MACKEKE, Will s/o Thomas Mackeke bap 10 Oct 1689;
SPPR

MACON, Ann d/o Gedeon & Martha Macon b.d. 15 Dec
bap 2 Feb 1685; SPPR

MACON, Gedeon s/o Gedeon & Martha Macon b.d. 20
Jun bap 22 Jun 1682; SPPR

MACON, James s/o Gideon & Martha Macon b.d. 28 Oct
1701; SPPR

MACON, John s/o Gideon & Martha Macon b.d. 17 Dec
1695; SPPR

MACON, Thomas POR New Kent & **SAVAGE**, Virginia s;
DOM 1 Dec 1825; RE

MACON, William d.d. between 21 Nov 1763 and 20 Oct
1766; BP

MACON, William Hartwell s/o William Macon POR
Hanover & Lucy Scott b.d. 1759 POR New Kent
d.d. 1843; SAR

MACON, William s/o Gideon Macon & Martha Woodward
POR New Kent b.d. 1693 d.d. 1773; SAR

MACON, William s/o Gideon Macon b.d. 12 Nov 169_;
SPPR

MACON, William s/o Gideon & Martha Macon b.d. 11
Nov 1693; SPPR

MACON, William s/o William Macon & Mary Hartwell
b.d. 1725 POR New Kent d.d. 1813; SAR

MACEY, Mark s/o John Macey bap 7 Dec 1690; SPPR

MACKGERT, Sarah d/o Daniel Mackgert bap 3 May
1702; SPPR

MACKHANY, William s/o Daniel Mackhany b.d. 15 Jul
1712; SPPR

MADDOX, Robert s/o John Maddox bap 25 Feb 1704/5;
SPPR

MADDOX, Susanna d/o John Maddox bap 19 Oct 1707;
SPPR

MADISON, John d.d. 1689 POD King & Queen; ONKH

MADLIN, Richard Nicholas (Richard has been
scratched through) s/o Richard & Susana
Madlin bap 16 Apr 1699; SPPR

MADOX, Michael d/o John Madox bap 31 May 1713;
SPPR

MADOX, Sarah d/o John Madox bap 27 Sep 1702; SPPR

MAHON, Mr. POR King & Queen & EUBANK, Emily POR
King & Queen; DOM issue dated 4 Feb 1831 POM
King & Queen by Rev. Mr. Clark; RW

MAIDLIN, Richard s/o Richard Maidlin bap 5 Jul
1702; SPPR

MAJOR, Frances d/o William Major bap 19 Nov 169_
(probably 9); SPPR

MAJOR, John s/o William Major bap 17 May 1702;
SPPR

MAJOR, Thomas s/o William Major bap 28 Nov 1703;
SPPR

MALLORY, Edward T. POR Gloucester & COLLIER,
Elizabeth T. POR King & Queen; DOM 13 Nov
1839; RE

MANN, John late POR King & Queen & EASLEY, Sarah
C. d/o Edward Easley s POR Perry Co.,
Alabama; DOM 9 Aug 1838 by Rev. Baptist; RW

MANN, William deputy marshall & GATEWOOD, Frances
d/o Chany Gatewood POR King & Queen; DOM 9
Mar 1809; RE

MANNING, Ann buried by 3 Nov 1781; BP

MARCEY, Elizabeth d/o Thomas Marcey bap 6 Nov
1702; SPPR

MARETON, Oliver J. s/o Allen & S. Mareton age 38 W
merchant POB James City & SPENCER, Margaret
A. d/o William W. Spencer & Sally Spencer

age 18 S POB King & Queen Co; DOM 19 Dec 1853
POM King & Queen by A. F. Scott; KQMR

MARR, George s/o George Marr bap 18 Mar 1701/2;
SPPR

MARR, George & **MILLS**, Jane; DOM 27 Sep 1699; SPPR

MARR, Nicholas s/o George Marr bap 21 Jul 170_;
SPPR

MARSHALL, Francis POR New Kent & **HOWLE**, Eliza S
POR New Kent; DOM 3 Mar 1814; RE

MARSHALL, William & **ADAMS**, Alice d/o Richard Adams
& Elizabeth Griffin b.d. 20 Feb 1768 POR New
Kent; DOM 28 Jun 1788; KK1

MARTIN, Ames__a d/o Martin Martin bap 6 Apr 1706;
SPPR

MARTIN, Anne d/o James & Rebecca Martin bap 18 Aug
1708; SPPR

MARTIN, Anne d/o Martin & Sarah Martin bap 9 Aug
1708; SPPR

MARTIN, Bethia d/o James Martin bap 27 Feb 1703/4;
SPPR

MARTIN, David s/o William Martin bap 6 Mar 1708/8;
SPPR

MARTIN, Elizabeth d/o William Martin bap 21 May
1704; SPPR

MARTIN, George s/o John Martin bap 24 Mar 17__;
SPPR

MARTIN, Henry s/o John & Sarah Martin bap 18 Aug
1708; SPPR

MARTIN, James & **BELL**, Rebecca; DOM 16 Feb 1701/2;
SPPR

MARTIN, John s/o John Martin b.d. 8 Apr 1697 bap
10 Oct 1698; SPPR

MARTIN, John s/o Thomas Martin bap 18 Apr 1714;
SPPR

MARTIN, Josiah POR New Kent & **HOLLINS**, Mary POR
Hanover Co S; ML Hanover Co DOM 22 Feb 1834;
CTR

MARTIN, Martin & **HIX**, Sarah; DOM 10 Feb 1698/9;
SPPR

MARTIN, Mary d/o John Martin b.d. 19 Apr 1709;
SPPR

MARTIN, Mary d/o William Martin bap 9 Sep 169_
(probably 9); SPPR

MARTIN, Parke POR New Kent & **WADE**, Patsy POR New
Kent ML New Kent DOM 11 Feb 1828; CTR

MARTIN, Rebecca d/o John Martin b.d. 18 Aug 1713
bap 14 Feb 1713; SPPR

MARTIN, Richard & **TURNER**, Hannah; DOM 13 Aug 1718;
SPPR

MARTIN, Robert s/o William Martin bap 13 Apr 1701;
SPPR

MARTIN, Robert & **PYNES**, Catherine s late POR King
& Queen; DOM 22 Dec 1814 by John Courtney;
RCC

MARTIN, Susanna d/o John Martin b.d. 20 May 1711
  bap 27 Jul 1712; SPPR

MARTIN, Thomas s/o Richard Martin bap 10 Oct 1689;
  SPPR

MARTIN, Thomas s/o William & Mary Martin bap 10
  Jul 1698; SPPR

MARTIN, Thomas s/o Thomas Martin bap 13 Jan ____;
  SPPR

MARTIN, Thomas & **TUCKER**, Mary; DOM 1 Dec 1709;
  SPPR

MARTIN, Unity d/o James Martin bap 24 Mar ____:
  SPPR

MARTIN, Valentine s/o Martin Martin bap 18 Jun
  1710; SPPR

MASCY, Elizabeth d/o John Mascy bap 27 Sep 1691;
  SPPR

MASIE, Mary d/o Thomas Masie bap 6 Apr 1705; SPPR

MASK, Judeth d/o John Mask b.d. 14 Apr bap 10 Jul
  1698; SPPR

MASK, Mary d/o John Mask b.d. 14 Apr bap 10 Jul
  1698; SPPR

MASK, Timothy s/o John Mask b.d. 20 Jun 1702; SPPR

MASK, William s/o John Mask b.d. 6 May 1701; SPPR

MASON, Malvina w/o James M. Jeffries b.d. 3 Dec
  1814 d.d. 31 May 1883; MBC

MASSE, Peter s/o Thomas Masse bap 14 Apr 170_;
  SPPR

MASSE, Thomas & **WALKER**, Mary; DOM 23 Mar 1698/9;
  SPPR

MASSIE, Anne d/o Charles Massie bap 20 Apr 1707;
  SPPR

MASSIE, Charles s/o Charles Massie b.d. 13 Oct
  1712; SPPR

MASSIE, James s/o Thomas Massie bap 16 May 1708;
  SPPR

MATTHEWS, Matthew s/o Cornelius Matthews b.d. 5
  Oct 1711 bap 13 Apr 1712; SPPR

MCCARTY, Nathaniel br/o John McCarty d.d. between
  30 Nov 1759 and 24 Nov 1760; SMP

MCCARTY, William br/o Charles McCarty kept using
  vestry funds 9 Oct 1747; SMP

MCCARTY, William d.d.between 16 Nov 1757 and 21
  Nov 1758; SMP

MCCARTY, William to keep his brother Charles
  McCarty 9 Oct 1747; SMP

MCCRAE, Sherwin attorney & **JOHNSON**, Sarah Ann d/o
  Christopher Johnson POR King William; DOM 4
  Jan 1832 by Rev. Dudley Atkinson; KWC

MCFARLAND, Richard s/o James & Elizabeth McFarland
  age 37 S farmer POR King & Queen & **GOULDMAN**,
  Elizabeth d/o Thomas & Phebe Gouldman age 40
  S POR King & Queen; DOM 1 Mar 1856 POM King &
  Queen by Isaac Diggs; KQMR

MCGEORGE, Wiley R. POR King William & **CLARKSON**, Sarah Ann POR King & Queen; DOM 20 Mar 1835; RW

MCGEORGE, Wiley R. POR King William & **CLARKSON**, Sarah Ann POR King & Queen; DOM 20 Mar 1835; KWC

MCHOMES, Joseph POR King & Queen & **CLARK**, Hannah B. d/o Rev. John Clark s POR King & Queen; DOM 11 Oct 1832; RW

MCKENDREE, Jane w/o D. McKendree buried by 22 Feb 1762; SMP

MCKENDREE, Jane w/o D.McKendree d.d. about 22 Feb 1762 (under care using vestry funds from 10 Oct 1748); SMP

MCLAURIN, Lewis POR Powhatan & **TOMPKINS**, Rebecca s POR King William; DOM 25 Dec 1827 by Rev. Dudley Atkinson; RE

MCLELLAND, Hezekiah Methodist minister d.d. abt 1828; BKQCHS

MCRAE, Sherwin attorney & **JOHNSON**, Sarah Ann d/o Christopher Johnson S POR King William; DOM 4 Jan 1832; RW

MCRAE, Sherwin attorney POR King William & **JOHNSON**, Sarah Ann d/o Christopher Johnson POR King William; DOM 4 Jan 1832; RE

MCRAE, Sherwin POR Chesterfield & **JOHNSON**, Sarah Ann d/o Christopher Johnson POR King William; DOM 4 Jan 1832; KWC

MEANLY, Millinton s/o Richard Meanly bap 9 Feb 1709; SPPR

MEAUX, John s/o John Meaux b.d. 5 Jun 1707; SPPR

MEAUX, Lucy A. w/o William Meaux eldest d/o Col. William Nelson (dec) d.d. 16 Sep 1824 age 54 POD Fork Quarter, King William; KWC

MEAUX, Richard s/o John Meaux bap 31 Mar 1711; SPPR

MECHI, Robert s/o John & Mary Mechi bap 24 Oct 1686; SPPR

MEDLOCK, George s/o John Medlock Jr. bap 8 Jun 1701; SPPR

MEDLOCK, John & bride not mentioned; DOM 27 Apr 1701; SPPR

MEDLOCK, Thomas s/o John Medlock Jr bap 21 Nov 1703; SPPR

MEDLOCK, William s/o John Medlock bap 19 Jul 1702; SPPR

MEEKS, Thomas & **WATKINS**, Margery; DOM 24 Dec 1699; SPPR

MEENLY, Richard s/o Richard Meenly b.d. 17 Sep 1712; SPPR

MEGGS, Robert W. s/o Frank Meggs & Polly Collins age 26 s POB King & Queen lumber getter free POC & **SMITH**, Elizabeth T. d/o Robert Smith & Polly Davenport age 17 S POB King & Queen

free POC; DOM 24 Apr 1853 POM King & Queen by
Thomas B. Evans; KQMR

MELTON, Mary d/o Richard Melton bap 10 May 1702;
SPPR

MELTON, Thomas s/o Richard Melton bap 28 Apr 170_;
SPPR

MEREDITH, Edward D. POR New Kent & **POE**, Selina B.
d/o George Poe, (dec); DOM 16 Jan 1840 POM
Henrico by Rev. William S. Plumer; RW

MEREDITH, John D. & **LEWIS**, Martha Rosalie; POM
Croton, King & Queen DOM 6 Aug 1856; Lewis FB

MERIAM, George POR Richmond & **ATKINSON**, Mary Y.
POR New Kent s; DOM 1 Feb 1821 POM New Kent
by Rev. George Ratcliffe; RCA

MERIDETH, J.D. s/o P.W.& H.G.Merideth age 26 S
preacher POB Buckingham & **LEWIS**, Martha R.
d/o Z. & M.L.A.Lewis age 18 S POB King &
Queen; DOM 5 Aug 1856 POM King & Queen KQMR

MERIWETHER, Anne d/o Nicholas Meriwether bap 15
Jul 169_ (probably 9); SPPR

MERIWETHER, Elizabeth d/o Nicholas & Elizabeth
Meriwether b.d. 20 Jun bap 3 Jul (the
following year) 1703; SPPR

MERIWETHER, Nicholas s/o Nicholas & Elizabeth
Meriwether b.d. 11 Jul bap 6 Aug 1699; SPPR

MERRIDETH, William s/o George Merrideth bap 19 Dec
1703; SPPR

MERRIMAN, James d.d. by 23 Feb 1779; BP

MEUKS, Anne d/o John Meuks b.d. 15 Apr bap 14 May
1709; SPPR

MEYER, William H. s/o Henry & Louisa Meyer age 27
S farmer POB Germany & **DILLARD**, Emiline P.(?)
d/o Nicholas & Betsy Dillard age 23 S POB
King & Queen; DOM 23 Sep 1856 POM King &
Queen by R.Y.Henly; KQMR

MICHELL, Elizabeth d/o Stephen Michell Jr. b.d. 20
Feb 1702/3; SPPR

MICHELL, John s/o Stephen Michell Jr. b.d. 19 Dec
1698; SPPR

MICHELL, Stephen s/o Stephen Michell Jr. b.d. 24
Dec 1699; SPPR

MILBY, Hezekiah H. s/o Richard & Martha(?) Milby
age 25 S farmer POB King & Queen & **MILBY**,
Lucy A. d/o Thomas & Lucy Milby age 22 S POB
King & Queen; DOM 25 Oct 1856 POM King &
Queen by Isaac Digges; KQMR

MILL, James G. s/o James Mill age 22 S farmer POB
King William POR King & Queen & **SMITH**, Mary
A. d/o Mortimer Smith age 18 S POB POR King &
Queen; DOM 14 Jun 1860 POM King & Queen; KQMR

MILL, Thomas d.d. 1 Oct 1825 age 60 POD Lilly
Point, King William; KWC

MILLER, John G. attorney POR Goochland &
CHRISTIAN, Jannetta H. d/o Robert Christian

POR New Kent; DOM 6 Feb 1821 by Rev. John H.
Rice; RE

MILLER, Jones Dr. POR Kentucky & **CHRISTIAN**,
Minerva M. POR New Kent; DOM 16 Dec 1830; RE

MILLER, Nathaniel M. Miller Dr. POR Goochland &
CHRISTIAN, Mary E. d/o Robert Christian s POR
New Kent; DOM 15 Jan 1822 by Rev. Dr. Rice;
RE

MILLER, Thomas POR Powatan & **GAINES**, E.H. s POR
King & Queen; DOM 11 Sep 1828 by Edward
Baptsit; RE

MILLINGTON, Margaret d/o William Millington Jr.
bap 5 Nov 169_ (probably 9); SPPR

MILLS, Henery s/o Nicholis Mills bap 10 Apr 1687;
SPPR

MIMES, Sarah d/o Thomas Mimes b.d. 19 May 1712;
SPPR

MIMMS, Anne d/o Lionel Mimms bap 18 Jun 1710; SPPR

MIMMS, Benjamin s/o Thomas Mimms bap 18 Jun 1710;
SPPR

MIMS, John s/o Thomas Mims Jr. bap 3 May 1705;
SPPR

MIMS, Lineal & **MARTIN**, Anne; DOM 2 Jan 1706/7;
SPPR

MIMS, Thomas Jr. & **MARTIN**, Mellyan; DOM 10 Feb
1698/9; SPPR

MIMS, Thomas s/o Thomas b.d. 15 Feb 1707/8; SPPR

MIMS, William s/o William Mims bap (this is found
among the baptismal entries of 1705); SPPR

MINOR, George former POR King William & **DOWNEY**,
Sarah s former POR Richmond; DOM 28 Jan 1840
POM Petersburg; RE

MINOR, Jefferson Dr. POR Fredericksburg & **JONES**,
Virginia F. POR Essex; DOM 1 Jan 1829 POM
Kennington, King William; VG

MINOR, Jefferson Dr. POR Fredericksburg & **JONES**,
Virginia F. s POR Essex; 1 Jan 1829 POM
Kennington, King William; KWC

MINOR, Nancy B. w/o Archibald Minor POR Aylett's
Warehouse POD Caroline d.d. 21 Sep 1821; KWC

MITCHELL, Anne d/o Stephen Mitchell Jr.bap 20 Jan
1705; SPPR

MITCHELL, Archelus s/o Thomas Mitchell b.d. 9 Feb
1703; SPPR

MITCHELL, Evan s/o Stephen Mitchell b.d. 16 Jan
bap 18 Feb 1710/11; SPPR

MITCHELL, John & **WATTS**, Mary d/o Thomas Watts POR
King & Queen; DOM deed found 1781 POM deed
found Essex; Essex Deed Book 32

MITCHELL, Martha d/o Thomas & Mary Mitchell bap 17
Jul 1698; SPPR

MITCHELL, Mary d/o Stephen Jr. & Mary Mitchell
bap 22 Aug 1708; SPPR

MITCHELL, Thomas s/o Thomas Mitchell b.d. 3 Jan
    1701; SPPR
MITCHELL, Valentine s/o Stephen Mitchell Jr. bap
    27 Sep 1713; SPPR
MOIRE, Thacker minister POR King & Queen C.H. &
    TEMPLE, Ann s POR Boush Green, King & Queen;
    DOM 10 Jan 1826 by Rev. Hezekiah B. Lelliend;
    RE
MOON, Christopher s/o Jacob Moon (dec) POR Bedford
    Co & JOHNSON, Patsy 1st d/o James Johnson POR
    King William; DOM 25 Dec 1800; VA
MOON, Elisabeth d/o Peter Moon bap 14 Dec 1712;
    SPPR
MOON, John s/o Stephen Moon bap 13 Jan 1711/12;
    SPPR
MOON, Peter & SMITH, Elizabeth; DOM 24 Nov 1709;
    SPPR
MOON, Peter s/o Peter Moon bap 15 Oct 1710; SPPR
MOON, Peter s/o Stephen Moon b.d.24 Jan 1683; SPPR
MOON, Phillis d/o Stephen Moon Jr. bap 13 Jun
    1708; SPPR
MOON, Stephen s/o Sttephen Moon b.d. 12 Oct 1705;
    SPPR
MOOR, Pellom s/o Pellom Moor b.d. 7 Feb bap 13 Mar
    1689; SPPR
MOORE, A.L. d.d. 8 Mar 1828 POD Chelsea, King
    William; KWC
MOORE, Anne d/o John Moore bap 10 Oct 1703; SPPR
MOORE, Bernard POR King William & LEIPER, Lucy
    niece of Dr. Andrew Leiper of Richmond; DOM 3
    May 1788; VG
MOORE, Casandra d/o Pellham Moore bap 14 Apr 170_;
    SPPR
MOORE, Elizabeth d/o James Moore bap 2 Aug 1702;
    SPPR
MOORE, Elisabeth d/o John Moore b.d. 25 Aug 1690;
    SPPR
MOORE, Elisabeth d/o Thomas Moore bap 8 Jan 1710;
    SPPR
MOORE, Elizabeth b.d. 28 Feb 1801 d.d. 16 Jan
    1886; KK1
MOORE, Frances d/o Edward Moore bap 13 Dec 1702;
    SPPR
MOORE, James s/o John Moore b.d. 23 Mar 1693/4;
    SPPR
MOORE, James s/o Thomas & Elizabeth Moore b.d. 7
    Feb 1713; SPPR
MOORE, John s/o John Moore bap 13 Dec 169_
    (probably 9); SPPR
MOORE, John s/o John Moore b.d. 28 Sep 1706; SPPR
MOORE, Jude d/o Thomas Moore bap 23 May 1703; SPPR
MOORE, Marlmeduke [sic] s/o Pellham Moore bap 9
    Jun 169_ (probably 9); SPPR
MOORE, Lucy d̄/o Edward Moore b.d. 4 Feb 1712; SPPR

MOORE, Martha d/o John Moore b.d. 22 Sep 1697; SPPR

MOORE, Mary d/o James Moore bap 17 Mar 1699/1700; SPPR

MOORE, Mary d/o John Moore bap 11 Nov 1698; SPPR

MOORE, Rebeca d/o John Moore bap 2 Feb 1700/1; SPPR

MOORE, Robert s/o John Moore b.d. 17 Apr 1711; SPPR

MOORE, Sarah d/o John Moore b.d. 6 Feb 1713; SPPR

MOORE, Susana d/o Thomas Moore bap 25 Feb 1704/5' SPPR

MOORE, Turner s/ Mary Moore (dec) bound to Christopher Steadman 24 Sep 1762; SMP

MOORE, William s/o James Moore bap 17 Oct 169_ (probably 9); SPPR

MOORE, William s/o Pellham Moore b.d or bap 18 Mar 1701/2; SPPR

MOORMAN, Andrew s/o Thomas Moorman bap 4 Nov 1689; SPPR

MOORMAN, Samuel T. minister of the Virginia Conference & **GARNETT**, Emily C. formerly of King & Queen; DOM 29 Jun 1837 POM Greensborough, Alabama by Rev. Claiborne Pirtle; RE

MORE, Elizabeth d/o Pellom More bap 25 Dec 1687; SPPR

MOREMAN, Mary d/o Thomas & Eliz. Moreman bap 29 Aug 1686; SPPR

MORGAN, Amy d/o Edward Morgan bap 9 May 169_ (probably 9); SPPR

MORGAN, Robert s/o Edward Morgan bap 14 Jul 170_; SPPR

MORRIS, Charles s/o Robert & Eliz Morris bap 27 Aug 1699; SPPR

MORRIS, Edward s/o Joseph Morris b.d. 5 Oct 1708; SPPR

MORRIS, Elizabeth d/o Robert & Rebecca Morris bap 13 Dec 1685; SPPR

MORRIS, John bastard s/o Sarah Morris (dec) bound to Thomas & Elizabeth Burnet 10 Oct 1733; SMP

MORRIS, John illegitimate s/o Sarah Morris bound to Thomas Burnet 10 Oct 1733; SMP

MORRIS, Mary d/o Edward Morris bap 30 Jan 1689/90; SPPR

MORRIS, Robert s/o Robert Morris bap 9 Jun 169_ (probably 9); SPPR

MORRIS, Susanna d/o Edward Morris bap 8 Jan 1710; SPPR

MORRIS, Will s/o Robert Morris bap 1 Apr 1688; SPPR

MORRISE, Anne d/o John Morrise (dec) kept by Amey Adams 16 Nov 1757; SMP

MORRISE, Sally d/o John Morrise (dec) bound 16 Nov
    1757; SMP
MORRISE, Sally d/o John Morrise (dec) kept by
    William Richards 16 Nov 1757; SMP
MORRISS, Charles s/o John Morriss bap 13 Dec 1712;
    SPPR
MORRISS, William & WALKER, Tabitha; DOM 12 Feb
    1712; SPPR
MOSS, Joyce d/o Thomas Moss bap 4 Apr 1714; SPPR
MOSS, Robert H. POR Northumberland Co & TYREE,
    Elizabeth Ann Maria S POR New Kent DOM 5 May
    1836 by Rev. S.W.Jarvis; VCS
MOSS, Samuel s/o Samuel & Elizabeth Moss b.d. 23
    May 1764 POB New Kent; Rev. Pension File 8988
MOSS, Thomas s/o William Moss bap 4 Apr 1714; SPPR
MOSS, Will s/o Thomas Moss bap 17 Feb 1688/9; SPPR
MOSS, William & MARTIN, Elizabeth; DOM 20 Nov
    1711; SPPR
MOSSE, Anne d/o Samuel Mosse bap 7 Feb 1708/9;
    SPPR
MOSSE, James s/o Thomas Mosseb.d. 27 Jan bap 13
    Mar 1708/9; SPPR
MOSSE, Judith d/o Samuel Mosse bap 7 Feb 1708/9;
    SPPR
MOSSOM, David minister of St. Peter's Parish POR
    New Kent d.d. 4 Jan 1767; SPPR
MUIRE, Thacker & TEMPLE, Ann d/o Joseph Temple POR
    Chatham Hill age 58 (d.d. 1826); DOM Jan
    1826; BKQCHS
MUIRE, Thacker minister POR King & Queen & TEMPLE,
    Ann s POR Rose Green, King & Queen both
    members of M.E.Ch; DOM 12 Jan 1826; VCA
MUIRE, Thad.(?) D. Muire s/o Thacker Muire age 22
    S farmer POB POR King & Queen & POINTER, Lucy
    B. d/o Archer Pointer age 22 S POB POR King &
    Queen; DOM 6 Oct 1860 POM King & Queen; KQMR
MURFIELD, Daniel & COKER, Rachel POR St.Paul's
    Parish [probably Hanover]; DOM 22 Jul 1708;
    SPPR
MURROW, John s/o John Murrow bap 25 Jun 1699; SPPR
MURROW, Robert s/o John Murrow bap 18 Jul 1703;
    SPPR
MUSE, Charles H. POR Essex & HART, Maria Louisa
    POR King & Queen; issue date 18 Jun 1853; WA
MUSE, Elliott & CORBIN, Betty T. p.m.; DOM 3 May
    1800 POM King & Queen; VM
MUSE, Hudson & NEILSON, Agnes; DOM 28 Dec 1790 POM
    King & Queen; VM
MYRICK, Martha w/o Robert Myrick POR King & Queen
    d.d. 1858; ONKH
MYRICK, Robert & DIGGS, Frances A. DOM 1858; FB
MYRICK, Robert & FLEET, Martha d/o Henry Fleet POR
    Rural Felicity, King & Queen; DOM 1826; ONKH

MYRICK, Robert & **FLEET**, Martha POR Rural Felicity
DOM 1825; FB

NAPIER, Bouth s/o Robert & Mary Napier b.d. 1 Oct
1692; SPPR

NAPIER, Elizabeth d/o Robert & Mary Napier b.d. 25
Oct 1704; SPPR

NAPIER, Frances d/o Robert & Mary Napier b.d. 5
Feb 1694/5; SPPR

NAPIER, Katherin d/o Robert & Mary Napier b.d. 12
Oct 1700; SPPR

NAPIER, Robert s/o Robert & Mary Napier b.d. 16
Sep 1697; SPPR

NASH, Edward & **WILLIAMSON**, Mary; DOM 20 Jun
[probably 1685-1699]; SPPR

NASH, Mary d/o Edward Nash bap 24 Jun 1711; SPPR

NASH, Mary d/o Edward & Mary Nash b.d. 29 Jun
1715; SPPR

NASH, Michael s/o Michael Nash b.d. 17 Jun 1714;
SPPR

NASH, Michael & **RENN**, Catherine; DOM 1 Sep
[probably 1685-1699]; SPPR

NAYLER, William & **MIMES**, Sarah; DOM Oct [probably
1685-1699]; SPPR

NEALE, James Hill s/o William Neale & Judith Hill
b.d.1784 POR "Eggleston" King William d.d.
May 1823; KWH

NEALE, James Peyton s/o James Hill Neale & Judith
Edwards b.d. 11 Nov 1811 d.d. 7 Nov 1854 POD
King William; KWH

NEALE, Juan Stanley s/o James Peyton Neale b.d. 16
Nov 1844; KWH

NEAVES, Thomas s/o James Neaves b.d. 18 Mar
1704/5; SPPR

NEEVES, James s/o James Neeves bap 25 Sep 1698;
SPPR

NEEVES, William s/o James Neeves bap 4 Oct 1691;
SPPR

NELSON, George d.d. before 8 Jun 1686; C&P3

NELSON, Lucy wi/o Col. Wiliam Nelson POR King
William d.d. 13 Apr 1810 age 57; KWC

NELSON, Mary w/o George Nelson will recorded in
King & Queen 12 Mar 1696/7; C&P3

NELSON, Sally Cary d.d. 13 Jan 1779; KWC

NELSON, Sarah w/o Thomas C. Nelson d/o Benjamin
Day of Fredericksburg d.d. 29 Sep 1825 age 54
POD Bleak Hill, King William; KWC

NELSON, Thomas Cary POR King William & **DAY**, Sally
DOM 1803; KWC

NELSON, Thomas Cary s/o Capt. Thomas Nelson &
Sally Cary b.d. 4 Jan 1779; KWC

NELSON, Thomas Cary s/o Capt. Thomas Nelson &
Sally Cary d.d.2 Jan 1840 POD King William;
KWC

NELSON, Thomas Cary s/o Capt. Thomas Nelson & Sally Cary b.d. 4 Jan 1779; KWC

NELSON, Thomas d.d. 1805 POD King William; KWC

NELSON, William s/o Thomas Nelson & Judith Armistead b.d. 17 Jun 1746 POB Yorktown POR King William & **CHISWELL**, Lucy d.d. 13 Apr 1810; DOM 24 Nov 1770; KWC

NELSON, Wilson C. POR King William & **DABNEY**, Susan D. s POR King William; DOM 15 May 1828 POM Greenville by Rev. Andrew Broaddus; KWC

NELSON, Wilson C. POR King William & **DABNEY**, Susan D.; DOM 15 May 1828 POM Greenville, King William; VG

NEWTON, Alice buried by 24 Sep 1764; SMP

NICKS, Edward s/o James & Elizabeth Nicks bap 7 Nov 1686; SPPR

NORRIS, Mrs. Nathaniel buried by 10 Oct 1722; BP

NORRIS, Walter s/o William & Susanna Norris b.d. 21 Dec 1707; SPPR

NUCKLES, Isabell d/o James Nuckles bap 14 Nov 1697; SPPR

NUCKLES, James s/o James Nuckles bap 30 Jun 1695; SPPR

NUNN, Catharine d/o Thomas Nunn & Sarah Smith b.d. 7 May 1782 d.d. 1834 (married John de Shazo in King & Queen); IR Flores

NUNN, Elizabeth d/o Thomas Nunn & Sarah Smith b.d. 27 Apr 1792 (married Lewis Phillips in Newtown); IR Flores

NUNN, Emma Burgess 1836-1922 w/o Richard B. Nunn; GN VSA #34327

NUNN, George C. s/o F.or J. Nunn & Sarah Smith age 52 W farmer POB King & Queen & **WALKER**, Nancy d/o Philip Walker & Nancy Boughton age 50 S POB King & Queen Co; DOM 27 Nov 1853 POM Middlesex by _ B. Evans; KQMR

NUNN, George s/o Thomas Nunn & Sarah Smith b.d. 25 Mar 1803; IR Flores

NUNN, George s/o Thomas Nunn b.d. 25 Mar 1803 POR King & Queen; IR Flores

NUNN, Henrietta E. w/o Robert Alexander Nunn b.d. 1 Mar 1859 d.d. 1 Jan 1944; GN VSA #34327

NUNN, Jane Quarles d/o Thomas Nunn & Sarah Smith b.d. 11 Apr 1780 (married James Stewart); IR Flores

NUNN, John s/o Thomas Nunn & Sarah Smith b.d. 11 Aug 1778; IR Flores

NUNN, Joseph G. Sr. b.d. 3 Feb 1837 d.d. 19 Dec 1915; GN VSA #34327

NUNN, Joseph Goodman b.d. 3 Feb 1837 POB King & Queen IR Waters

NUNN, Lucy Ann Griffith w/o Robert Emmett Nunn b.d. 16 Jun 1849 d.d. 12 Jun 1915 GN VSA #34327

NUNN, Mary d/o Thomas Nunn & Sarah Smith b.d. 22 Apr 1798 d.d. 1868 (married Henry S. Nunn) IR Flores

NUNN, Moses d.d. 8 Jun 1821 age 63 POR POD King & Queen Rev. soldier RCC

NUNN, Nancy d/o Thomas Nunn & Sally Pendleton b.d. 23 Jan 1784 POB King & Queen GN VSA #34327

NUNN, Nancy d/o Thomas Nunn & Sarah Smith b.d. 23 Jan 1784 d.d. 29 Mar 1863 (married Lewis Brown) IR Flores

NUNN, Richard B. b.d. 2 Mar 1833 d.d. 3 May 1894 GN VSA #34327

NUNN, Richard B. s/o Robert S. & Eliza P. Nunn age 23 S farmer POB King & Queen & **BURGESS**, Emma d/o Roben & Sarah Burgess age 20 S POB England; DOM 30 Oct 1856 POM King & Queen by J.W.Shackford KQMR

NUNN, Robert Alexander "Darnie" b.d.21 Aug 1853 d.d. 4 May 1935 GN VSA #34327

NUNN, Sallie C. w/o Joseph G. Nunn Sr. b.d. 9 Nov 1838 d.d. 24 Jan 1919 GN VSA #34327

NUNN, Sally d/o Thomas Nunn & Sarah Smith b.d. 28 Mar 1796 IR Flores

NUNN, Thomas POR King & Queen will dated 8 Jan 1833 will probated 12 Jun 1837 names daughters Jane, Elizabeth,Catherine, Nancy, Mary & Lucinda W. sons John, William, George and Thomas; IR Flores

NUNN, Thomas b.d. 13 Mar 1753 d.d. 22 Apr 1837 & **SMITH**, Sarah (Sally) White b.d. 24 Apr 1761 POB Louisa; DOM 1777 IR Flores

NUNN, Thomas s/o Thomas Nunn & Sarah Smith b.d. 6 Dec 1789 (Married Sally Davis) IR Flores

NUNN, Thomas; DOM 1 Nov 1777 POM King & Queen VM

NUNN, William S. s/o Thomas Nunn & Sarah Smith b.d. 27 Mar 1787; IR Flores

OGILIVE, James POR Richmond & **WILKINSON**, Sally s POR New Kent; DOM 20 Dec 1803; VGGA

OGLESBY, George W. POR King & Queen & **HODGES**, Susan; DOM 23 Dec 1858; Essex Co Marriage Register

OLIVER, John L. s/o John & Martha Oliver age 40 W farmer POB POR King & Queen & **DAVIS**, Sarah d/o Peter & Sarah Davis age 20 S POB POR King & Queen; DOM Mar 1854 POM King & Queen by William B. Todd; KQMR

OMOONEE, James & Sarah his wife imported to New Kent by Thomas Scott & John Drummond before 29 Oct 1696; C&P3

OSLIN, Samuel s/o John Oslin bap 18 Oct 1691; SPPR

OSLIN, Will s/o john & An Oslin bap 18 Mar 1687/88; SPPR

OTEY, Charles Anna d/o Isaac Otey & Ann K.C.Binns
b.d. 4 Nov 1837 POB "Knotty Oak" New Kent;
KK2

OTEY, Isaac s/o James Otey & Mary Frances Graves &
BINNS, Ann Kidley Cooke d/o Daniel Binns &
Ann Kidley Cooke; DOM 2 Dec 1812 POM New
Kent; KK2

OTEY, Isaac s/o James Otey & Mary Frances Graves
b.d. 5 Feb 1787 POB POR New Kent d.d. 7 Feb
1859; KK2

OTEY, John Otway s/o Isaac Otey & Ann K.C.Binns
b.d. 13 Aug 1839 POB "Knotty Oak" New Kent;
KK2

OTEY, mary d/o John Otey b.d. 17 Jul 1715; SPPR

OTTEY, John s/o John Ottey b.d. 19 Jul 1713; SPPR

PAGE, Charles C. d.d.17 Oct 1822 POR POD King
William; KWC

PAGE, Elizabeth d/o Cap. Matthew & Mary Page b.d.
6 Jan bap 16 Jan 1689/90; SPPR

PAGE, Norborne T. POR King William & **JONES,** Maria
Louisa d/o George R. Jones (dec) S POR
Petersburg; DOM 7 Nov 1833 by Re. Plumer RW

PAGE, Robert Carter s/o Charles Carter Page &
Sallie Cary Nelson b.d. 18 Apr 1803 & **TEMPLE,**
Martha Ann; DOM 2 Sep 1829 VMHB

PAGE, Robert POR Hanover & **BRAXTON,** Molly d/o Col.
Carter Braxton s POR King William; DOM issue
date 14 Oct 1773; VG

PAGE, William B. Jr. POR Richmond & **SEGAR,** Lucy A.
s POR King William; DOM 28 Oct 1814 POM King
William; VP

PAINE, Americus W. Dr. POR Goochland & **DUDLEY,**
Jane Beverley s POR King William; DOM 15 Jun
1820 by Rev. Mills; RE

PAINE, Americus W. POR Goochland Co & **DUDLEY,** Jane
Beverley s POR King William DOM 15 Jun 1820;
VG

PAINE, Sarah w/o Daniel Paine of Westmoreland POD
Mount Pisgah, King William d.d.22 Jul 1824;
KWC

PAITE, Judeth d/o Jeremiah Paite bap 4 Jul 1703;
SPPR

PANNILL, Edward POR King William & **SLAUGHTER,**
Elizabeth A. POR King William; DOM 14 Aug
1834 by John Duval; RW

PANNILL, Thomas A. POR King William & **LACY,**
Elizabeth C. s POR New Kent; DOM 18 Nov 1824
by Rev. Mr. Sillman of New Kent; VG

PARISH, Anne d/o Humphrey & Mary Parish bap 4 Sep
1698; SPPR

PARISH Jane d/o Humphrey Parish b.d. 20 Dec 1699
bap 21 Jul 170_; SPPR

PARISH, Joseph s/o John Parish bap 20 Sep 1713;
SPPR

PARK, Frances d/o John Park Jr. bap 16 feb 1700/1; SPPR

PARKE, John s/o John Parke Jr. bap 19 Jul 1707; SPPR

PARKER, Bobinet b.d. 24 Apr 1865; FB VSA #34117

PARKER, Charlie B. b.d. 12 Aug 1869; FB VSA #34117

PARKER, Emma T. b.d. 17 Apr 1855; FB VSA #34117

PARKER, John B. b.d. 12 ___ 1867; FB VSA #34117

PARKER, John F. & **GOULDMAN**, Maria F.; DOM 26 Mar 1851; FB VSA #34117

PARKER, Richard H. b.d. 10 Apr 1863; FB VSA #34117

PARKER, Robin s/o Joseph Parker & Elizabeth Parker age 23 S farmer & **GATEWOOD**, Isabella d/o John Gatewood & Elizabeth Schooler age 21 S; DOM 1 Feb 1853 POM King & Queen by Howard W. Montague; KQMR

PARKER, Sarah F. b.d. 13 Feb 1858; FB VSA #34117

PARKER, Simon Peter s/o James & Sarah Parker age 23 S farmer POB King & Queen & **LEFTWICH**, Cordelia d/o William & Mary Leftwich age 23 S POB King & Queen; DOM 10 Dec 1856 POM King & Queen by Isaac Digges; KQMR

PARKER, Virgin A. b.d. 10 Dec 1853; FB VSA #34117

PARKS, Sara d/o John Parks Jr. bap 8 Apr 1688; SPPR

PARRISH, Henry s/o Humphrey Parrish bap 27 Apr 1701; SPPR

PARSONS, James POR Hanover Co & **WADE**, Elvira POR New Kent; ML New Kent DOM 24 Dec 1830; CTR

PASLEY, Aniss d/o Robert Pasley b.d. 17 Dec 1691; SPPR

PASLEY, Ellenor d/o Robert & Ellenor Pasley bap 26 Mar 1699; SPPR

PASLEY, Margaret d/o Robert Pasley b.d. 25 Jun 1706; SPPR

PASLEY, Mary d/o Robert Pasley b.d. 25 Oct 1693; SPPR

PASLEY, Robert s/o Robert Pasley b.d. 16 Oct 1701; SPPR

PASLEY, Solomon s/o Robert Pasley b.d. 4 Nov 1703; SPPR

PASLEY, William s/o Robert Pasley b.d. 26 Jul 1696; SPPR

PATTESON, William s/o Thomas Patteson bap 30 Jan 1689/90; SPPR

PATTISON, Anne d/o David Pattison bap 2 Nov 1701; SPPR

PATTISON, Charles s/o David Pattison b.d. 6 may 1711; SPPR

PATTISON, David s/o David Pattison b.d. 14 Oct 1703; SPPR

PATTISON, Edward s/o Thomas Pattison bap 13 Jun 1710; SPPR

PATISON, Elizabeth d/o Edward Pattison bap 21 Mar
    1713; SPPR
PATTISON, Frances d/o David Pattison b.d. 19 Dec
    1715; SPPR
PATTISON, Jane d/o Edward Pattison b.d. 12 May
    1716; SPPR
PATTISON, John s/o Edward Pattison bap 12 Nov
    1707; SPPR
PATTISON, Jonathan s/o David Pattison b.d. 6 Jun
    1713; SPPR
PATTISON, Sarah d/o David Pattison bap 24 Mar
    1699/1700; SPPR
PATTISON, Thomas s/o David Pattison bap 13 Jan
    1708/9; SPPR
PATTISON, Thomas s/o Thomas Pattison bap 4 Feb
    1707; SPPR
PAUL, Lydda d.d. between 6 Oct 1757 and 16 Oct
    1758; BP
PEACE, James R. s/o John & Elizabeth Peace age 25
    S shoemaker POB Orkney Isle, Scotland &
    HENDLEY, Mary L. d/o Lambeth Hendley & Mary
    Hendley age 29 S POB POR King & Queen; DOM 21
    Jul 1856 POM King & Queen by John Bagley;
    KQMR
PEACE, Joseph s/o John Peace bap 13 Oct 1700; SPPR
PEACE, Susannah d/o john Peace bap 31 Jan 170_;
    SPPR
PEACOCK, Jane buried 14 Nov 1770; SMP
PEARSON, Christopher s/o Thomas Pearson (dec) in
    King & Queen by 2 May 1705; C&P3
PEARSON, Frances d/o Charles & Rebecca Pearson
    b.d. 2 Jul 1739 POB New Kent bap 13 Aug 1739
    at St. Peter's Parish; KK2
PEASLEY, Anne d/o Robert Peasley bap 21 Nov 1708;
    SPPR
PEDLEY, John s/o Eliz Pedley bap 30 Jun 169_; SPPR
PEEKE, Roland s/o John & Jane Peeke bap 25 Jun
    1699; SPPR
PEIRSON, Francis d/o William Peirson bap 13 Dec
    1713; SPPR
PEMBERTON, Judith Coleman d/o Wilson Coleman
        Pemberton & Wealthean Edwards b.d.4 Oct 1786
        d.d. 22 Sep 1843; KWH
PEMBERTON, Wilson Coleman s/o John Pemberton &
        Jane Coleman & **EDWARDS**, Wealthean d/o Ambrose
        Edw ards; DOM 13 Nov 1785; KWH
PEMBERTON, Wilson Coleman s/o Wilson Coleman
        Pemberton & Wealthean Edwards b.d. 14 Oct
        1794 POR "Cool Springs", King William; KWH
PENDLETON, Benjamin POR King & Queen & **GATEWOOD**,
        Catherine POR King & Queen; RA issue dated 11
        Apr 1804

94

PENDLETON, Benjamin POR King & Queen & **GATEWOOD,**
Catherine s POR King & Queen; DOM 6 Apr 1804;
VA

PENDLETON, Catherine d/o Philip Pendleton POR King
& Queen & Old Rappahannock Co b.d. 1699 d.d.
1774; SAR

PENDLETON, Elizabeth d/o Whitaker Campbell &
Martha Deshazo POR King & Queen will dated 31
Aug 1847; VCA

PENDLETON, Philip 1650-1721 immigrated 1674 of
King & Queen & Essex married Isabella **HURT;**
SAR

PENDLETON, Philip b.d. 1650 POB England POR King &
Queen d.d. 1721; SAR

PENICK, William s/o Edward Penick bap 25 Aug 1694;
SPPR

PENNINGTON, Robert d.d. between 14 Oct 1747 and 14
Oct 1748; BP

PERKINS, Anne d/o William Perkins bap 4 May 1701;
SPPR

PERKINS, Anne d/o William Perkins b.d. 26 Jan
1708/8; SPPR

PERKINS, Anne d/o William & Elizabeth Perkins bap
12 Mar 1698/9; SPPR

PERKINS, Judith d/o William Perkins b.d. 15 Dec
bap 27 Jan 1711; SPPR

PERKINS, William s/o William Perkins bap 25 Aug
1706; SPPR

PERRY, Francis s/o James Perry bap 13 Jan 1705;
SPPR

PERRY, Robert s/o James Perry bap 30 Sep 1711;
SPPR

PERSON, Charles s/o George Person bap 7 Feb
1685/6; SPPR

PERSON, John s/o Charles Person bap 19 Sep 1703;
SPPR

PETERS, Rees carpenter former POR Philadelphia
d.d. 7 Aug 1829; KWC

PETHWOOD, John buried by Dec 1724; BP

PHILLIPS, James Aaron s/o James Nunn Phillips &
Emily Lewis Brown b.d. 11 Jan 1856 POB King &
Queen GN VSA #34327

PHILLIPS, James b.d. 1818 d.d. 1863 POD Camp Lee
VA & **BROWN,** Emily Lewis d/o Lewis Brown &
Nancy Nunn b.d. 10 Apr 1816 d.d. 10 Dec 1887;
IR Flores

PHILLIPS, James Nunn POB Newton, King & Queen d.d.
1863; GN VSA #34327

PICKRING, Eliz d/o Gabrill Pickring bap 13 Dec
1696; SPPR

PIERCE, Philip s/o Philip Pierce age 24 S farmer
POB Gloucester POR King & Queen & **BOWDEN,**
Mary E. d/o John Bowden age 30 W POB

Middlesex POR King & Queen; DOM 14 Jan 1858
POM King & Queen by James C. Hummer; KQMR

PIERCE, Philip s/o Philip Pierce age 24 S farmer
POB Gloucester POR King & Queen & **BREEDEN**,
Mary E. d/o John Breeden age 30 W POB
Middlesex(?) POR King & Queen; DOM 14 Jan
1858 POM King & Queen by Isaac Digges; KQMR

PILSBURY, William J. & **MADISON**, Agnes; DOM 1857
POM King & Queen; KQMR

PINES, Nathaiell s/o Susana Pines b.d. 22 Nov bap
30 Nov 1676 (also listed in 1682); SPPR

PINICK, Edward s/o Edward & Elizabeth Pinick bap
15 Aug 1686; SPPR

PIRAM, James s/o Susana Piram bap 24 Apr 1688;
SPPR

PIRANT, William s/o John Pirant bap 28 Mar 1703;
SPPR

PIRSON, Charles bap 8 Aug 1714; SPPR

PITMAN, Hipkins age 74 minister POR Caroline &
ADAMS, Phoebe p.m. age 72 POR King & Queen;
by Rev. Thomas H. Henley; RE issue date 8 Jun
1819

PITMAN, Hipkins Rev. POR Caroline Co age 74 &
ADAMS, Phoebe p.m. age 72 POR King & Queen
(her mother is still living having married
Mr. James Bates about 1725; DOM 13 May 1819
by Rev. Thomas M. Henly of Essex Co; RE

PITTS, Reuben s/o Younger & Nancy Pitts age 32 W
POB King & Queen overseer & **COOKE**, Rosa E.
d/o John & Lucy Cook age 22 S POB Caroline
Co; DOM 23 Apr 1853 POM King & Queen by A.
Broadous; KQMR

PLANT, Ann d/o William & Elizabeth Plant bap 3 Jan
1688/9; SPPR

PLANT, Mary d/o William & Eliz. Plant bap 11 Jul
1686; SPPR

PLANTINE, William s/o Peter Plantine bap 12 Oct
1701; SPPR

POINDEXTER, Armisstead s/o George B. & Frances
Poindexter b.d. 14 May 1775; SPPR

POINDEXTER, Edwin s/o George B. & Frances
Poindexter b.d. 10 Jan 1762; SPPR

POINDEXTER, Elizabeth d/o Thomas Poindexter b.d.
14 Jan 1699/1700; SPPR

POINDEXTER, Frances d/o George B. & Sarah
Poindexter b.d. 10 Sep 1781 d.d. 17 Sep 1785;
SPPR

POINDEXTER, George B. & **LIGHTFOOT**, Frances; DOM 17
Jul 1760; SPPR

POINDEXTER, George B. & **PARKE**, Sarah; DOM 20 Mar
1777; SPPR

POINDEXTER, George s/o George B. & Frances
Poindexter b.d. 29 Mar 1767; SPPR

POINDEXTER, James s/o George B. & Frances
Poindexter b.d. 7 Jan 1770; SPPR
POINDEXTER, Judith d/o George Poindexter b.d. 1
Jun bap 8 Jun 1706; SPPR
POINDEXTER, Lightfoot s/o George B. & Frances
Poindexter b.d. 20 Oct 1772; SPPR
POINDEXTER, Mary d/o George Poindexter Jr. b.d. 5
Sep 1715; SPPR
POINDEXTER, Parke s/o George B. & Sarah Poindexter
b.d. 12 Mar 1779; SPPR
POINDEXTER, Philip s/o George & Mary Poindexter
bap 26 Dec 1708; SPPR
POINDEXTER, Robert s/o George B. & Frances
Poindexter b.d. 23 Feb 1765; SPPR
POINDEXTER, Sarah d/o Thomas Poindexter b.d. 12
May 1702; SPPR
POINDEXTER, Susanna d/o Thomas Poindexter b.d. 6
Feb 1696/7; SPPR
POINDEXTER, Susannah d/o George B. & Sarah
Poindexter b.d. 3 May 1778; SPPR
POINDEXTER, Susana bureid 15 Jul 1698; SPPR
POLLARD, John b.d. 1803 POR King & Queen; HMBC
POLLARD, John d.d. 13 Sep 1877 age 75 deacon of
Mattaponi Church; MBC
POLLARD, John s/o Joseph & Catherine Pollard POR
King & Queen & JEFFRIES, Juliett d/o Maj.
Thomas Jeffries; DOM 1824; ONKH
POLLARD, Joseph d.d. 6 Oct 1836 POD King & Queen
age 79; ONKH
POLLARD, Juliet w/o Col John Pollard b.d. 10 Sep
1807 d.d. 4 Sep 1874 four surviving sons; MBC
POLLARD, Mary Ellen w/o John Camm Pollard d/o Byrd
& Elizabeth Dandridge Chamberlayne POR POD
King William d.d. 1817/18 age 23; KWC
POLLARD, Richard age 53 d.d. 4 Aug 1809 POD King &
Queen; VCA
POLLARD, Robert b.d. 12 Jan 1760 POB New Kent d.d.
17 Jul 1835 & HOWLE, Susanna; DOM 10 Feb 1804
ML 9 Feb 1804 New Kent; Rev. Pension File
W811
POLLARD, Robert Boyd POR King William &
PEMBERTON, Mary C. d/o Wilson C. PEMBERTON S
POR King William; DOM 22 Mar 1836 by
Rev.Atkinson; VCS held by Randolph Macon
College
POLLARD, Robert Jr. POR King William &
CHAMBERLAYNE, Eveline S POR Henrico; DOM 19
or 26 Jan 1809 by John D. Blair; VA
POLLARD, Robert Nelson s/o Robert Nelson Pollard
b.d. 8 Jun 1847 POB King & Queen; HMBC
POLLARD. Robert d.d. 30 Apr 1819 age 63 years;
Camm FB
POMFREY, Sarah Frances POR New Kent C.H. b.d.14
Jan 1861 d.d. 7 Aug 1934; FB VSA #34267

PONTIN, Thomas s/o Thomas Pontin bap 21 Jun 1691;
    SPPR
PONTON, William s/o Thomas Ponton bap 12 May 1700;
    SPPR
PORTER, Anne d/o Henry Porter bap 25 Feb 1710/11;
    SPPR
POWELL, E.T. s/o John & Mary Powell age 23 or 73
    merchant POB King William POR Ayletts, King
    William & CAVE, Mary A. d/o Robert P. &
    S.F.Cave age 18 POB Green Co POR Orange Co;
    DOM 15 Jan 1857 POM Orange Co; taken from
    Orange County Marriage License
POWELL, Nancy w/o John Powell wi/o Presley T.
    Atkinson d.d. 26 Jul 1826 age 30 POD near
    Mangohick Church; KWC
POWELL, William Sr. POB Gloucester POR King
    William carpenter d.d. 27 May 1827 age 77;
    KWC
PRICE, James C. s/o Carter & Elizabeth Price age
    32 W farmer POB POR King & Queen &
    WELLINGTON, Louisa M. d/o Elias & Elizabeth
    Wellington age 20 S POB POR King & Queen; DOM
    12 May 1856 POM King & Queen by John B.
    Laurens; KQMR
PRIOR, Anne bap 5 Jan 1706/7; SPPR
PROSSER, William POR Richmond & RING, Letitia POR
    Tuckomon, King William; DOM 19 Jan 1809; VA
PRYER, Elisabeth d/o William Pryer b.d. 7 May
    1716; SPPR
PULLAM, Anne d/o William Pullam bap 22 Nov 1702;
    SPPR
PULLAM William s/o William Pullam b.d. 3 Aug bap 3
    Sep 1690; SPPR
PULLER, William D. d.d. 18 Sep 1827 age abt 43;
    KWC
PULLUM, Benjamin s/o William Pullum bap 31 Mar
    1700; SPPR
PULLUM, James s/o William Pullum bap 2 May 169_;
    SPPR
PURDE, Elizabeth d/o Nicolas Purde bap 15 Mar
    1701/2; SPPR
PURDE, Mary d/o Nicolas Purde bap 15 Mar 1701/2;
    SPPR
PURDEY, Hannah d/o Nicholas Purdey bap 6 Apr 1707;
    SPPR
PURDIE, Susanna d/o Jane Purdie b.d. 25 Apr 1716;
    SPPR
PYRANT, James s/o James Pyrant bap 27 Apr 1701;
    SPPR
QUARLES, Francis W. POR Richmond & RICHESON, Mary
    E. W. only d/o Francis W. Richeson (dec) POR
    King William; DOM 17 Apr 1834 by Mr. Acree;
    KWC & RW

QUARLES, Mary w/o Francis West Quarles d.d. 6 Jan 1832 age 20; KWC

QUARLES, Mary West only d/o Francis West Quarles d.d. 4 Jan 1832 age 15 mo 20 days; KWC

RABINEAU, John E. s/o William T. Robineau & Harriet Batkins of New Kent b.d. 1859; KK2

RAGLIN, Isaac s/o Thomas Raglin bap 2 Aug 1713; SPPR

RAGLIN, Jacob s/o Thomas Raglin b.d. 22 Oct 1715; SPPR

RAGLING, John s/o Evan Ragling Jr. bap 18 Mar 1710; SPPR

RAGLING, William s/o Evan Ragling Jr. b.d. 1 May bap 29 May 1709; SPPR

RAMSEY, Bartholomew POR King & Queen Co married the relict of [John] Roberts by 6 Jun 1699; C&P3

RANDELL, Elizebeth d/o John Randell bap 13 Jun 1686; SPPR

RANDOLPH, Thomas POR Henrico & **FLEMING**, Judith; DOM 16 Oct 1712; SPPR

RAPIER, John & his wife Alice imported to King & Queen before 25 Apr 1701; C&P3

RATCLIFFE, Francis d.d. between 6 Mar and 9 Oct 1750; BP

RAWLEIGH, Walter d.d. by 23 Feb 1784; BP

RAXFORD, John s/o William Raxford bap 9 Dec 1694; SPPR

RAYLE, Elizabeth d/o John Rayle bap 17 May 1702; SPPR

RAYLEE, Alice d/o John Raylee bap 27 Nov 1687; SPPR

RAYMOND, Elisabeth d/o James Raymond b.d. 11 Sep 1714; SPPR

RAYMOND, John s/o James & Unity Raymond b.d. 10 Sep 1717; SPPR

RAYMOND, John s/o James & Unity Raymond b.d. 10 Jul 1720; SPPR

RAYMOND, Judith d/o James Raymond bap 9 Apr 1710; SPPR

RAYMOND, William s/o James & Unity Raymond b.d. 10 Oct 1719; SPPR

REABY, Thomas s/o Elinoor Reaby b.d. 26 Dec 1686; SPPR

READE, [John] minister of Stratton Major Parish POR King & Queen & **YATES**, Fanny d/o Rev. Bartholomew Yates POR Middlesex; DOM Feb 1737 issue date 17 Feb 1737; VG

READE, John s/o Thomas Reade & Mildred Gwyn of Gloucester minister of Stratton Major Parish. King & Queen & **YATES**, Frances s d/o Rev. Bartholomew Yates late minster of Christ Ch, Middlesex; DOM issue dated 17 Feb 1737/8; VG & VCA

REAMY, William A. s/o John N. & Jane Reamy age 22y
3mo S carpenter POB Westmoreland POR Richmond
& **BROADDUS**, Mary C. d/o John & Sophia (?)
Braoddus age 21 S POR King & Queen; DOM 24
Dec 1857 POM King & Queen by A. Bagby; KQMR

REDD, William & **FLOYD**, Mary d/o Thomas Floyd S POR
King William; DOM 13 Apr 1832; RW

REDD, William & **FLOYD**, Mary d/o Thomas Floyd s POR
King William; DOM 13 Apr 1832; KWC

REDDCOCK, Collin (Dr.) & **BEVERLEY**, Jane W. p.m.;
DOM 8 Oct 1785 POM King William; VM

REID, Joseph W. & **MITCHELL**, Martha A.; DOM 1857
POM King & Queen; KQMR

RENALL, Susana d/o Jonas Renall bap 21 Dec 1690;
SPPR

RENALL, Will s/o Thomas & Mary Renall bap 5 Dec
1686; SPPR

RENALLS, Elizabeth d/o Thomas Renalls bap 15 Mat
1690/1; SPPR

RENALLS, Judeth d/o Thomas Renalls bap 19 Jul
1688; SPPR

RENN, Edward & **CHAPPELL**, Catherine; DOM 1 Apr
1711; SPPR

REYNOLDS, Bathsheba d/o William Reynolds b.d. 12
Oct 1711; SPPR

REYNOLDS, Elisabeth d/o William Reynolds bap 7 Nov
1708; SPPR

REYNOLDS, Jane d/o Thomas Reynolds bap___ (entry
is included between entries of 1694 and
1697); SPPR

REYNOLDS, John & **WOODE**, Mary; DOM 30 Dec 1708;
SPPR

REYNOLDS, Leticia d/o Thomas Reynolds bap 4 Apr
1697; SPPR

REYNOLDS, Lucy d/o William Reynolds b.d. 17 Apr
1714; SPPR

REYNOLDS, Philip s/o Thomas & Mary Reynolds bap 15
Oct 1699; SPPR

REYNOLDS, William s/o William Reynolds bap 12 May
1706; SPPR

RHODES, Henery s/o George Rhodes bap 5 Jan 1700/1;
SPPR

RICE, Alice d/o Thomas Rice bap 29 Sep 1700; SPPR

RICE, Edward s/o Thomas Rice bap 17 Apr 1690; SPPR

RICE, James s/o Thomas & Marce Rice bap 4 Apr
1686; SPPR

RICE, John s/o Thomas & Marcey Rice bap 18 Sep
1698; SPPR

RICE, Marcy d/o Thomas Rice bap 5 Jul 1702; SPPR

RICE, Mary d/o Thomas Rice bap 15 Jul 1694; SPPR

RICE, Thomas s/o Thomas Rice bap 24 Jun 1688; SPPR

RICH, John s/o Daniel & Patsy Rich age 27 S FPOC
sailor POB Richmond City POR King & Queen &
TUPPENCE, Betsy d/o Randall & Maria Tuppence

age 21 S FPOC POB POR King & Queen; DOM 15
Mar 1856 POM King & Queen; KQMR
RICHARDS, Horace A. POR King William & **DOGGETT**,
Jemima L.S. S POR Caroline ; POM Caroline Co
DOM 18 May 1848 by Rev.Thos. Diggs; RCA
RICHARDSON, Anne d/o Robert Richardson bap 26 Sep
1708; SPPR
RICHARDSON, Charles & **PLANT**, Elizabeth; DOM 31 Aug
1709; SPPR
RICHARDSON Charles s/o Charles Richardson b.d 20
May 1714; SPPR
RICHARDSON, Edmund s/o Robert Richardson bap 1 Jun
1712; SPPR
RICHARDSON, Elisabeth d/o Robert Richardson b.d. 2
Aug 1713; SPPR
RICHARDSON, Henry s/o Robert Richardson b.d. 3 Jun
1715; SPPR
RICHARDSON, John col. d.d. between 12 Nov 1762 and
13 Jun 1763; BP
RICHARDSON, Mary buried by 9 Oct 1753; BP
RICHARDSON, Richard d.d. between 17 Dec 1742 and
15 Oct 1744; BP
RICHARDSON, Robert & **GREEN**, Jane; DOM 22 Feb
1710/11; SPPR
RICHARDSON, William s/o Robert Richardson b.d. 28
Apr 1706; SPPR
RICHARDSON, William S. s/o William Richardson age
21 S carpenter POB King William POR King &
Queen & **ROUSE**, Nancy S. d/o Nathanel Trinyer
age 22 W POB POR King & Queen; DOM 12 Jan
1858 POM King & Queen by Isaac Digges; KQMR
RICHARDSON, William T. s/o William Richardson age
21 S carpenter POB King William POR King &
Queen & **ROUSE**, Nancy S. d/o Nathaniel Trenyen
age 22 W POB POR King & Queen; DOM 12 Jan
1858 POM King & Queen by R.H.Bagby; KQMR
RICK, Richard & **SHEPHERD**, Faneyl DOM Aug 1816; VCA
RICKMAN, Elizabeth d/o Thomas Rickman bap 22 Feb
1690/1; SPPR
ROADES, Mary d/o Charles Roades bap 7 Feb 1702/3;
SPPR
ROANE, Agnes d/o William Frazer (dec) of King
William killed by her husband, John Roane Jr.
d.d. 18 Jan 1810, having been married 2
months & 2 days. POD Newington, King & Queen;
VH
ROANE, John Jr. d.d. 15 Apr 1810 POD King & Queen
jail while awaiting trial for killing his
wife; VH
ROANE, Newman B. POR King William & **HANKIN**, Maria
G. d/o William **HANKIN** POR Williamsburg; DOM
20 May 1817 POM Williamsburg; VG
ROANE, Newman B. POR King William & **HANKIN**, Maria
G. eldest d/o William Hankin POR

101

Williamsburg; DOM 20 May 1817 POM
Williamsburg by Rev. Mr. Dennis; KWC

ROANE, Newman B. POR King William & **HANKINS**, Maria
G. eldest d/o William Hankins s POR King
William; DOM 20 May 1817 POM Williamsburg by
Rev. Dennis; RE

ROBBIN, Lumpkins bap 14 Feb 1789; VBHS

ROBERSON, Archa (?) s/o Lorenzo & Betty Roberson
age 21 S farmer POB POR King & Queen &
HUDGINS, Maria d/o John & Mary Hudgins age 21
S POR King & Queen; DOM 24 Dec 1857 POM King
& Queen by Isaac Digges; KQMR

ROBERTS, Mary d/o John Roberts bap 1 Apr 1688;
SPPR

ROBINEAU, William T. s/o Dr. George W. & Susan
Robineau b.d. 1830 POB Hanover POR New Kent &
BATKINS, Harriet "Henrietta E." d/o Boling &
Emily Batkins b.d. 1838 POB Hanover; DOM 31
Mar 1859 POM New Kent by James Fendall
Parkinson; KK2

ROBINSON, A.L. POR King William & **HALL**, Betsy POR
King William S; DOM 2 Apr 1806; VG

ROBINSON, A.L. POR King William & **HALL**, Betsy s
POR King William; DOM issue date 13 Apr 1806;
KWC

ROBINSON, A.L. POR King William & **HALL**, Betsy s
POR King William; DOM 2 Apr 1807; RE

ROBINSON, George POR King William & **HILL**, Louisa
POR King & Queen S; DOM 5 Dec 1816; VG

ROBINSON, Gregory POR King William & **HILL**, Louisa
s POR King & Queen; DOM 5 Dec 1816 by Rev.
Ro.B. Semple; KWC

ROBINSON, Gregory POR King William & **HILLS**, Louisa
s POR Essex; DOM 5 Dec 1816 by Robert B.
Semple; RE

ROBINSON, Harry attorney POR King William d.d.
issue dated 3 Oct 1771; KWC

ROBINSON, Harry s/o William Robinson POR King
William d.d.Oct 1771; VCA

ROBINSON, James C. d.d. 26 Aug 1821 age 21 POD
Lanesville, King & Queen; VCA

ROBINSON, John (the Honorable) & **BATHURST**, Mary
d/o Lancelot Bathurst (Robinson is her third
husband); DOM 1731; KK2

ROBINSON, John d.d. 11 May 1766; VMHB

ROBINSON, John d.d. between 4 Dec 1765 and 25 Aug
1766; SMP

ROBINSON, John member of the General Assembly POR
King & Queen d.d. issue dated 16 May 1766;
VCA

ROBINSON, P.B. Dr. POR King & Queen & **SPINDE**,
Virginia M. POR Essex S; DOM 13 Apr 1853; WA

ROBINSON, William minister of Stratton Major
    Parish d.d. between 3 Dec 1767 and 8 Nov
    1768; SMP
ROBINSON, William POR King & Queen b.d.1717 in VA;
    CVR
ROBINSON, William Rev. POR King & Queen d.d.1767
    in VA; CVR
ROE (or ROC), Thomas s/o Joseph Roe or Roc b.d. 1
    Jul 1714; SPPR
ROLLENS, Elizabeth POR King & Queen d.d.between 10
    Oct 1741 and 11 Oct 1742; SMP
ROOPER, Joseph s/o John Rooper b.d. 18 Oct bap 6
    Jan 1711/12; SPPR
ROOTES, Philip d.d. between 26 Sep 1755 and 19 Nov
    1756; SMP
ROOTES, Thomas Reade d.d. between 4 Dec 1765 and
    25 Aug 1766; SMP
ROOTES, Thomas Reade POR King & Queen & SMITH,
    Martha Jaquelin d/o John Smith; DOM 8 Feb
    1763; Middlesex Marriage Register
ROOTES, Thomas Rease & SMITH, Martha Jaquelin; DOM
    8 Feb 1763 POM King & Queen; VM
ROPER, Anne d/o John Roper bap 18 Feb 1699; SPPR
ROPER, Jane d/o John Roper bap 1 Dec 1700; SPPR
ROPER, Mary d/o John Jr. & Susan Roper bap 3 Mar
    1685/6; SPPR
ROPER, Mary d/o John Roper Sr. bap 25 Aug 1687;
    SPPR
ROPER, Rebecca d/o John Roper bap 26 Jul 1702;
    SPPR
ROPER, William s/o John Roper bap 2 Apr 1708; SPPR
ROSS, Anne d/o Richard Ross b.d. 25 Jan 171_; SPPR
ROSS, Elisabeth d/o Richard Ross bap 17 Dec 1710;
    SPPR
ROSS, Lydia d/o William Ross bap 11 Nov 1694; SPPR
ROSS, Phillis d/o Will & Elizabeth Ross bap 24 Jan
    1685/6; SPPR
ROSS, Rich s/o Will Ross bap 3 Mar 1687/8; SPPR
ROSS, Ruth d/o William Ross bap 6 Nov 1698; SPPR
ROSS, William s/o Richard Ross bap 12 Oct 1712;
    SPPR
ROSS, William s/o William Ross bap 15 Jun 1701;
    SPPR
ROW, Francis d.d. 1838 age 49 years 9 mo POR King
    & Queen; ONKH
ROW, Francis POR King & Queen & BUTLER, Lucy Ann
    POR King William S; DOM 13 May 1817; VG
ROW, Francis POR King & Queen & BUTLER, Lucy Ann s
    POR King William; DOM 13 May 1817 by Rev.
    John Mill; KWC
ROW, Francis POR King & Queen & BUTLER, Lucy Ann s
    POR King William; DOM 13 May 1817 by John
    Mills; RE

103

ROW, Jane Maria d/o Charles & Sarah ROW b.d.10 Aug
    1788; BF
ROW, Mary buried by 21 Oct 1765; BP
ROWE, James G. major POR King & Queen & HAWKINS,
    Harriet s POR Richmond; DOM 24 Feb 1819 by
    Rev. Courtney; RE
ROY, Beverley D. Dr. POR King & Queen & JOHNSON,
    Lucy Ammon d/o Christopher Johnson S POR King
    William; POM "Old Town" DOM 5 Oct 1831; RW
ROY, Beverley D. physicain POR King & Queen &
    JOHNSON, Lucy Ammon d/o Christopher Johnson s
    POR King William; DOM 5 Oct 1831 POM Old
    Town, King William; KWC
RUFFIN, Robert s/o Col. Ruffin POR King William
    age 19 d.d. issue dated 15 Jul 1775 POD
    Williamsburg; KWC
RUFFIN, William age 18 POR King William & WINFREY,
    Peggy G. age 15 POR King William; DOM 4 Oct
    1816 by Rev. Mills; RE
RUSSEL, John d.d. by 10 Nov 1760; BP
RYLAND, Charles Hill s/o Samuel P. Ryland &
    Catherine G. Hill b.d. 22 Jan 1836 POR
    "Norwood" King & Queen; VCA
RYLAND, Elizabeth [nee Garlick] w/o William S.
    Ryland d.d. 17 Jun 1826 age 24 POD Floyd's,
    King William; KWC
RYLAND, Elizabeth Herndon d/o Samuel P. Ryland &
    Catherine G. Hill b.d. 20 May 1832 POR
    "Norwood", King & Queen; VCA
RYLAND, Josiah s/o Joseph & Elizabeth Ryland b.d.
    abt 1767 d.d.1850 POR King & Queen &
    ANDERSON, Elizabeth Baylor wi/o Churchill
    Anderson d/o John Semple POR "Rose Mount",
    King & Queen; DOM 1 Jan 1798; VCA
RYLAND, Josiah s/o Samuel P. Ryland & Catherine G.
    Hill b.d. 17 Jan 1830; VCA
RYLAND, Martha Fleming d/o Samuel P. Ryland &
    Catherine G. Hill b.d. 9 Feb 1834 d.d. 17 May
    1896 POR "Norwood", King & Queen; VCA
RYLAND, Mary Peachey d/o Samuel P. Ryland &
    Catherine G. Hill b.d. 28 Aug 1838 d.d. 21
    Jun 1880; VCA
RYLAND, Robert Hill s/o Samuel P. Ryland &
    Catherine G. Hill b.d. 14 Apr 1828 d.d.20 Aug
    1882; VCA
RYLAND, Samuel Peachy s/o Josiah Ryland &
    Katherine Peachy POR "Farmington", King &
    Queen & HILL, Catherine Gaines d/o Robert
    Baylor Hill & Martha Fleming Gaines POR King
    & Queen; DOM 12 Dec 1825; VCA
RYLAND, William S. POR King William & FLEET, Susan
    d/o Cap. William Fleet POR King & Queen; DOM
    11 Mar 1830 by Elder Robert Ryland; KWC

RYLAND, William S. POR King William & **FLEET**, Susan
d/o Capt. William Fleet S POR King & Queen;
DOM 11 Mar 1830; RH

RYLAND, William Semple POR King William & **FLEET**,
Susan d/o Capt. William Fleet POR King &
Queen; DOM 11 Mar 1830 by Robert Ryland; VCA

SALMON, Thomas buried by 10 Oct 1722; BP

SALTER, Mary d/o William & Mary Salter b.d. 10 Jul
1779 d.d. 25 Dec 1824 POD Surry; KK2

SAMPSON, Ann Bush d/o Jim Sampson & Martha Ann
Bresley FPOC (Jim is a farmer) POB POR King
William b.d. Sep 1853; ROBKW

SAMUEL, Winnefred bap 25 Nov 1788; VBHS

SANBIGE, Thomas & **CHAPPELL**, Frances; DOM 20 Feb
1712; SPPR

SANDERS, John & **WADDILL**, Elizabeth; DOM 7 Aug
1709; SPPR

SANDERS, Laney Jones s/o Susannah Sanders buried
by 28 Apr 1777; BP

SANDERS, Susannah d.d. by 28 Apr 1777; BP

SATTERWHITE, Thomas POR King William & **TALLEY**,
Martha T. POR Hanover; DOM 19 Mar 1812; RE

SAUNDERS, James s/o ___Upshar & Miss Saunders age
38 W no occupation POB open & **LANE**, Martha
d/o Horace & Lucy Lane age 41 S POB King &
Queen Co; DOM 25 Aug 1853 POM King & Queen by
J.W.Shackford; KQMR

SAVAGE, Thomas Littleton POR New Kent & **SAVAGE**,
Mary Burton d/o Col Littleton Savage POR
Northampton; DOM issue date 17 Jun 1789; VIC

SAVAGE, William POR New Kent & **WHITLOCK**, Sally s
POR Henrico; DOM 29 Nov 1794; VGRMA

SAVORY, Elizabeth d/o John Savory bap 17 Oct 1686;
SPPR

SAYRE, Samuel William & **BASSETT**, Virginia d/o John
Bassett & Elizabeth Carter Browne b.d. 20 Sep
1787 POB "Elsing Green" King William; DOM 20
Sep 1806 POM "Farmington" Hanover; KK2

SCHOOLS, Fanny w/o Thomas Schools d.d. 30 Dec
1858; FB VSA #34117

SCHOOLS, John b.d. 29 Dec 1809; FB VSA #34117

SCHOOLS, Solomon G. s/o Taliaferro Schools age 29
S mechanic POB Essex Co POR King & Queen &
SCHOOLS, Malvina A. d/o Solomon G. Schools
age 21 S POB Essex Co POR King & Queen; DOM
26 May 1860 POM King & Queen; KQMR

SCHOOLS, Tazwell s/o Uriah & Harriett Schools age
26 S farmer POB King & Queen & **ELLIOTT**,
Malinda d/o Sthreshly & Polly Elliott age 27
S POB King & Queen; DOM 21 Dec 1857 POM King
& Queen by Howard W. Montague; KQMR

SCHOOLS, Thomas b.d. 28 Apr 1778; FB VSA #34117

SCHOOLS, Thomas d.d. 8 Jan 1850; FB VSA #34117

SCLATER, John d.d. between 1 Feb 1733 and 17 Oct
    1734; BP
SCRUGGS, Henry & GROSE, Anne; DOM 25 Jan 1685/6;
    SPPR
SCRUGGS, John & PORTER, Judith; DOM 4 Aug 1709;
    SPPR
SELDON, Miles Jr. & ARMISTEAD, Betty d/o Gill
    Armistead & Betty Allen of New Kent b.d. 9
    Mar 1752; DOM 27 Mar 1774; KK1
SEMPLE John Walker s/o John Semple & ROBERTSON,
    Lucy d/o Donald Robertson POR Drysdale
    Parish; DOM 23 Mar 1797; VCA
SEMPLE, Eliza d/o James Semple & Sarah Harwood
    b.d. 1795; VCA
SEMPLE, Elizabeth Baylor d/o John Semple POR "Rose
    Mount", King & Queen b.d. 19 Dec 1763; VCA
SEMPLE, Elizabeth wi/o John Semple d.d. 1790; VCA
SEMPLE, James POR Essex & GARLICK, Mary P. POR
    King William s DOM 8 Aug 1828; VG
SEMPLE, James POR Essex & GARLICK, Mary P. s POR
    King William; DOM 8 Aug 1828 by Rev.
    Ro.B.Semple; KWC
SEMPLE, James s/o John Semple POR "Rose Mount",
    King & Queen b.d. 10 Feb 1765 d.d. 4 Mar
    1806; VCA
SEMPLE, John s/o James Semple d.d. Feb 1770; VCA
SEMPLE, John s/o James Semple of "Dreghorn" b.d.
    1727 POR "Rose Mount" King & Queen & WALKER,
    Elizabeth; DOM 17 Jan 1761; VCA
SEMPLE, John Walker s/o John Semple of "Rose
    Mount", King & Queen b.d. 18 Nov 1761; VCA
SEMPLE, Robert Baylor s/o John Semple & LOWRY, Ann
    d/o Col. Thomas Lowry si/o Frances Lowry; DOM
    1 Mar 1793; VCA
SEMPLE, Robert Baylor s/o John Semple POR "Rose
    Mount", King & Queen POR "Mordington", King &
    Queen b.d. 20 Jan 1769 d.d. 25 Dec 1831 POD
    Fredericksburg; VCA
SETON, Captain d.d. issue dated 14 Jul 1771 POD
    King William; KWC
SEWARD, George L. s/o Lewis & Sarah Seward age 22
    S farmer POB Middlesex Co & WALDEN, Mary d/o
    Richard & Elizabeth Walden age 16 S POB King
    & Queen Co; DOM 20 Dec 1853 POM King & Queen
    by R.A.Christian; KQMR
SEWARD, Mary d.d. 23 Jan 1772; SMP
SHACKELFORD, Arthur B. s/o Robert T. & Lucy
    Shackelford age 25 S farmer POB POR not
    stated & DUNN, Ella J. d/o Sthreshley & Mary
    A. Dunn age 16 S POR King & Queen; DOM 27 Dec
    1857 POM King & Queen by Alfred Bagby; KQMR
SHACKELFORD, George D. & LEWIS, Martha C.; DOM 13
    Oct 1817 POM King & Queen; VM

SHACKELFORD, John d.d. between 24 Aug 1756 and 21 Nov 1758; SMP

SHACKLEFORD, Richard d.d. between 10 May 1768 and 12 Jul 1774; SMP

SHELBOURN, Thomas buried by 15 Oct 1742. He probably died in March 1742; BP

SHELLER, John & **MUNK**, Johanna; DOM 20 Jan 1708/9; SPPR

SHEPPARD, James & **GENTRY**, Priscilla d/o John Gentry; ML 15 Apr 1785 King William ML; VCA

SHERMER, John d.d. between 19 Oct 1772 and 30 Oct 1775; BP

SHIELD, Samuel rector of Drysdale Parish & **HANSFORD**, Molly POR York S; DOM issue dated 7 Jul 1775; VG

SHIELDS, Chapman Simpson b.d. 30 May 1803 POB Hanover & **STEWART**, Sarah Smith b.d. 9 May 1807 POB King & Queen; DOM 15 or 18 Jul 1830 by John Byrd; IR Flores

SHOEMAKER, Francis d.d. between 5 Oct 1724 and 13 Oct 1725. His death date is probably Feb 1724; BP

SIMES, Matthew & **MITCHELL**, Hannah; DOM 3 Mar 1708/9; SPPR

SIMONS, Thomas & **MOORE**, Johana; DOM 26 Jun 1699; SPPR

SIMPKINS, William C. & **STEWART**, Eliza d/o James Stewart & Jane Nunn; DOM 4 Mar 1824; IR Flores

SIMSON, John & **SPURLOCK**, Sarah; DOM 24 Jul 1712; SPPR

SIZER, Augustus POR "Millwood", King William & **RYLAND**, Elizabeth Herndon d/o Samuel Ryland & Catherine Hill POR King & Queen; DOM 18 Nov 1858; VCA

SKAIFE, John minister of Stratton Major Parish POR King & Queen d.d. 4 Nov 1736; VG

SKAIFE, Susanna w/o Rev. John Skaife POR King & Queen POD Williamsburg d.d. 1 Nov 1736; VG

SLATER, Overton G. & **BLAYTON**, Mary T.; DOM issue dated 11 Dec 1851 by Thomas S. Morris; RH

SLAUGHTER, Elizabeth Anne b.d. 1760 d.d. 16 Jul 1829; KWH

SMITH, Elizabeth d/o George & Mary Smith bap 29 Oct 1673; SPPR

SMITH, Elizabeth d/o Thomas & Barbara Smith imported to New Kent by Thomas Scott and John Drummond before 29 Oct 1696; C&P3

SMITH, George William governor of VA & **ADAMS**, Sarah d/o Richard Adams & Elizabeth Griffin POR New Kent; DOM 7 Feb 1793; KK1

SMITH, Henry L. POR King & Queen & **PHILPOTTS**, Nancy p.m. POR King & Queen DOM 8 Feb 1848 by Elder John Spencer; RCA

SMITH, Horace s/o Jamison & Nancy Smith age 30 W
    shoemaker POB POR King & Queen & CARLTON,
    Miss d/o Isaac Carlton age 20 S POB Essex POR
    King & Queen; DOM Mar 1854 POM King & Queen
    by William B. Todd; KQMR
SMITH, Ida Carlton b.d. 9 Sep 1854 d.d. 7 Sep
    1909; MBC
SMITH, John POR Henrico & AMOSS, Cicely; DOM 22
    Sep 1709; SPPR
SMITH, John s/o David & Elizabeth Smith bap 24 Oct
    1686; SPPR
SMITH, Rebeckah buried by 10 Oct 1737; BP
SMITH, Thomas & Barbara his wife imported to New
    Kent by Thomas Scott & John Drummond before
    29 Oct 1696; C&P3
SMITH, Thomas d.d. by 30 Oct 1775, possibly 4 Apr
    1775; BP
SMITH, Thomas s/o Thomas & Barbara Smith imported
    to new Kent by Thomas Scott and John Drummond
    before 29 Oct 1696; C&P3
SMITH, Thomas s/o Thomas Smith (dec) buried by 23
    Feb 1779 (probably May 1778); BP
SMITHE, George N. s/o John & Lucy Smith age 28 S
    POB POR New Kent & ALLEN, Sarah A. aka Sallie
    d/o Dr. Ed W. & Eliza Allen age 18 S POB
    Henrico POR New Kent; DOM 9 Feb 1860 POM New
    Kent by James F. Parkinson; NKMR
SMITHEY. Gouldman S. & BROADDUS, Mary s POR King &
    Queen; DOM 23 Jan 1831 by Rev. Mr. Clark; VCA
SNOWE, Rebecca d/o Richard & Mary Snowe bap 1 Aug
    1686; SPPR
SNOWE, Richard & BANKS, Mary; DOM 30 Dec 1685;
    SPPR
SORRELL, Joseph POR Caroline & MAHON, Catherine
    POR King William; DOM 21 Dec 1837; RW
SORRELL, Joseph POR Caroline & MAHON, Catherine
    POR King William s ; DOM 21 Dec 1837 by Rev.
    George W. Trice; KWC
SOUTH, Robert s/o Harry & Polly South age 32 W
    farmer POB King & Queeen Co & TURNER, Susan
    d/o Meador Turner & Nancy Jeffries age 17 S
    POB King & Queen Co; DOM 19 Jun 1853 POM King
    & Queen by William B. Todd; KQMR
SOUTHERLAND, George POR King William d.d.before 28
    Oct 1702; C&P3
SOUTHERLAND, George, s/o George Southerland POR
    King William by 28 Oct 1702; C&P3
SOUTHERLAND, Phillip s/o George Southerland POR
    King WIlliam 28 Oct 1702; C&P3
SOWARD, Thomas d.d. between 25 Aug 1766 and 29 Sep
    1766; SMP
SPAINE, Mary d/o Ann Spaine bap 23 Jan 1687/8;
    SPPR

SPEARS, John & **AUSTIN**, Margaret; DOM 7 Dec 1708; SPPR

SPENCER, Gideon & **CLAYBROOK**, A.H.; DOM 21 Oct 1828 POM King & Queen; VM

SPENCER, Robert M. merchant POR King & Queen & **SOUTHGATE**, Louisa eldest d/o John Southgate POR King & Queen; DOM 26 Feb 1820 by William Todd; RE

SPENCER, Susannah d/o Thomas & Ann Spencer bap 3 Nov 1686; SPPR

SPERILL, Mary d/o Robert Sperill & Ann Butterfield bap 20 Sep 1686 being aged 4 years the 5th of Oct; SPPR

SPILLER, Benjamin C. attorney d.d. 20 Sep 1827 POR POD King William; KWC

SPOTSWOOD, John eldest s/o Alexander Spotswood, (dec) & **DANDRIDGE**, Mary d/o Hon.William Dandridge (dec); DOM 24 Oct 1745 POM King William; KWC

SPOTSWOOD, John s/o Alexander Spotswood & **DANDRIDGE**, Mary d/o William Dandridge; POM King William 24 Oct 1745; VG

SPURLOCK, William & **TONEY**, Anne; DOM 15 Jun 1709; SPPR

STANHOPE, Jeremiah d.d. between 15 Oct 1744 and 23 Sep 1745; BP

STANUP, John d.d. before 1721; BP

STARLING, Jane G. d/o Captain Roderick Starling d.d. 22 Dec 1824 age 20; KWC

STARLING, Roderick captain d.d. 10 Apr 1828 age 68; KWC

STEED, Goerge W. s/o Robert E. & Fanny R. Steed age 38 S steam boat captain POB Norfolk & **BRUMBRY**, Josephine d/o Robert & Mary M. Brumbry age 19 POB King & Queen Co; DOM 4 Sep 1853 by William B. Todd; KQMR

STEWARD, Daniel d.d. by 12 Nov 1762; BP

STEWART, Benjamin Holmes s/o James Stewart & Jane Q. Nunn b.d. 1 Jul 1804 d.d. 13 Feb 1843 & **SONGEST** or Longest, Elizabeth; DOM 30 Mar 1825; IR Flores

STEWART, Eliza d/o James Stewart & Jane Q. Nunn b.d. 30 Aug 1800 d.d. 21 Dec 1824; IR Flores

STEWART, James b.d. 29 Aug 1776 POB near Pamunkey River d.d. 6 Oct 1820 & **NUNN**, Jane Quarles d/o Thomas Nunn & Sarah Smith; DOM 14 Jan 1798; IR Flores

STEWART, James s/o James Stewart & Jane Q. Nunn b.d. 30 May 1810 POB King & Queen & **SHIELDS**, Mary Cary (sister of Chapman Simpson Shields); POM TN; IR Flores

STEWART, Jane Quarles d/o James Stewart & Jane Q. Nunn b.d. 7 Mar 1809 POB King & Queen d.d. 26 Jul 1816; IR Flores

STEWART, John Nunn s/o James Stewart & Jane Q. Nunn b.d. 19 Nov 1802 & **HOSKINS**, Isabella J.; DOM 20 Dec 1825; IR Flores

STEWART, Martha d/o James Stewart & Jane Q. Nunn b.d. 2 Dec 1816 POB King & Queen d.d. 2 Mar 1817; IR Flores

STEWART, Mary Virginia d/o William Robert Stewart & Mary Ellen Chandler b.d.17 Nov 1843 POB New Kent; FB #30754

STEWART, Nancy Holmes d/o James Stewart & Jane Q. Nunn b.d. 15 Nov 1811 POB King & Queen d.d. 21 Sep 1812; IR Flores

STEWART, Sarah Smith d/o James Stewart & Jane Q. Nunn b.d. 9 May 1807 POB King & Queen d.d. 21 Apr 1860; IR Flores

STEWART, Thomas Nunn s/o James Stewart & Jane Q. Nunn b.d. 30 Jul 1815 POB King & Queen d.d. 13 Feb 1817; IR Flores

STEWART, Thomas s/o James Stewart & Jane Q. Nunn b.d. 13 Apr 1799 d.d. 21 Sep 1804; IR Flores

STEWART, William s/o James Stewart & Jane Q. Nunn b.d. 5 Oct 1805 d.d.15 Jan 1807; IR Flores

STOKES, SthreshlY & **SKELTON**, Virginia; DOM 1857 POM King & Queen; KQMR

STONE, John & **AMOSS**, Rebecca; DOM 21 Jan 1704/5; SPPR

STONE, John s/o Will & Mary Stone bap 15 Jan 1685; SPPR

STONE, William & **DENNETT**, Elizabeth; DOM 20 Jan 1709/10; SPPR

STONE, Will s/o Will & Mary Stone bap 15 Jan 1682; SPPR

STOUT, Samuel POR Orange & **BOYD**, Mary E. s POR King William; DOM 21 Feb 1828 by Rev. Dudley Atkinson; KWC

STOUT, Samuel POR Orange Co & **BOYD**, Mary E. POR King William s DOM 21 Feb 1828; VG

STRACHEY, john d.d. between 26 Sep 1755 and 19 Nov 1756; SMP

STREET, George W. s/o Henry Street & Roberta Gresham age 25 S farmer POB Hanover Co & **GRESHAM**, Lucy J. d/o Henry Gresham & Maria Cartney age 27 S POB King & Queen Co; DOM 19 Nov 1853 POM King & Queen by R.W.Cole; KQMR

SUTER, Sarah d/o Simon & Sarah Suter imported to King & Queen by Barth Fowler before 26 Apr 1698; C&P3

SUTER, Simon & Sarah his wife imported by Barth.Fowler to King & Queen Co before 26 Apr 1698; C&P3

SUTER, Simon s/o Simon & Sarah Suter imported by Barth.Fowler to King & Queen before 26 Apr 1698; C&P3

SUTER, Thomas s/o Simon & Sarah Suter imported by
   Barth Fowler to King & Queen Co before 26 Apr
   1698; C&P3

SUTER, William s/o Simon & Sarah Suter imported by
   Barth.Fowler to King & Queen before 26 Apr
   1698; C&P3

SWEENEY, Francis [sic] w/o William T. Sweeney POR
   New Kent age 61 d.d. 27 Oct 1847 POD New
   Kent; RCA

TALIAFERRO, Elizabeth wi/o Christopher Taliaferro
   age 86 d.d. 7 Dec 1836 POD residence of Miss
   Ann Taliaferro King William; RCA

TALIAFERRO, Walker & **COLE**, Mildred; DOM before 24
   Jul 1811; KWD 6 pg 234

TALIAFERRO, William d.d. between 30 Nov 1759 and
   24 Nov 1760; SMP

TAYLOR, Ann Randolph d/o George & Catherine Taylor
   bap. 22 Apr 1830 POR King William; SMPR

TAYLOR, Benjamin T. s/o Richard & Elenor Taylor
   age 33 S "shff" & farmer POB King William &
   FAULKNER, Ethline d/o John & Francis Motley
   age 29 W POB King & Queen; DOM 30 Mar 1854
   POM King & Queen by William B. Todd; KQMR

TAYLOR, George d.d.Oct 1841 age 6 POR King
   William; SMPR

TAYLOR, George s/o George & Catherine Taylor bap.
   4 Mar 1838 POR King William; SMPR

TAYLOR, James POB King & Queen & **THOMPSON**, Martha
   d/o Col.Roger Thompson of St.Peter's Parish,
   New Kent; DOM 1699; ONKH

TAYLOR, James POB St Stephen's Parish, King &
   Queen b.d. 1675 d.d. 1729 POD Drysdale
   Parish; ONKH

TAYLOR, James POR King & Queen & **GREGORY**, Mary d/o
   John Gregory POR Old Rappahannock Co.; DOM 10
   Aug 1682; SAR

TAYLOR, James POR King & Queen d.d. 30 Apr 1698;
   SAR

TAYLOR, John d.d. by 10 Nov 1760; BP

TAYLOR, John S. POR New Kent & **AUSTIN**, Mary d/o
   Herbert & Betsey Austin; DOM issue dated 21
   Jun 1849 POM New Kent by Thomas S. Morris;
   KK1

TAYLOR, John s/o James Taylor & Mary Gregory POR
   King & Queen b.d. 1696 d.d. 1780; SAR

TAYLOR, Richard POR New Kent & **GREGORY**, Lucy w;
   DOM 13 Oct 1773; taken from Charles City
   County Marriage Register

TAYLOR, Richard s/o Richard Squire Taylor POR
   Hanover & **TEMPLE**, Elizabeth d/o Benjamin
   Temple POR Presque Isle King William; DOM
   before 24 Jun 1817; KWD 5 pg.40

TAYLOR, Sarah buried by 15 Oct 1741; BP

TAYLOR, Sarah d.d. between 6 Oct 1757 and 16 Oct 1758; BP

TAYLOR, Temple s/o Brooking Taylor & Lucy A. Taylor age 29 S farmer POB open & SCHOOLS, Roberta d/o Waller Schools & Rebecca Schools age 17 S POB King & Queen Co; DOM 29 Nov 1853 POM King & Queen by Ro.W. Cole; KQMR

TAYLOR, William Randolph d.d. May 1840 age 6 POR King William; SMPR

TEMPLE wi/o Jack Temple d.d. 30 Apr 1822 POD King William; KWC

TEMPLE, Joseph & ARNOLD, Ann d/o Benjamin Arnold DOM pre 10 Feb 1737 (newspaper issue date); VG

TEMPLE, Lucy w/o Baylor Temple age 19 POR Walkerton, King 7 Queen; VCA

TEMPLE, Molly [nee Mollie Brooke Baylor] wi/o Col. Benjamin Temple POR King William d.d.7 Aug 1820 age 72; KWC

TERRELL, Anne d/o William Terrell & Susannah Waters POR New Kent married David LEWIS; VSA#34209

TERRELL, David s/o William Terrell & Susannah Waters d.d. 1759 POD Caroline Co; VSA#34209

TERRELL, Edward A. s/o Richmond & Elizabeth Terrell tailor POB New Kent POD Fluvanna d.d. 30 Mar 1853 age 32; taken from the death register of Fluvanna County,VA

TERRELL, Henry s/o William Terrell & Susannah Waters POB New Kent d.d. 1760 POD Caroline Co; VSA#34209

TERRELL, James s/o William Terrell & Susannah Waters POB New Kent d.d. abt 1772 POD Caroline Co; VSA#34209

TERRELL, Joel s/o William Terrell & Susannah Waters POB New Kent d.d. abt 1758 POD Hanover Co; VSA#34209

TERRELL, John s/o William Terrell & Susannah Waters POB New Kent d.d.1785 POD Franklin Co, NC; VSA#34209

TERRELL, Richmond Jr. s/o Richmond Terrell POR New Kent b.d. abt 1656; VSA#34209

TERRELL, Timothy s/o Richmond Terrell POR New Kent b.d.1658; VSA#34209

TERRELL, Timothy s/o William Terrell & Susannah Waters POB New Kent d.d. 1763 POD Orange Co; VSA#34209

TERRELL, William s/o Richmond Terrell POR New Kent b.d. abt 1660; VSA#34209

TERRELL, William s/o William Terrell & Susannah Waters POB New Kent d.d.1755 POD Caroline Co; VSA#34209

TERRY, S.Q. s/o Mrs. Ann Rains POR King William age 25 d.d. issue dated 12 May 1809; KWC

THOMSON, John & Alice his wife imported to King & Queen by 25 Apr 1701; C&P3

THOMSON, Mary buried by 23 Feb 1784; BP

THOPSON, James POR New Kent & **JONES**, Sarah POR New Kent ML New Kent DOM 21 Dec 1825; CTR

THORNTON, Elizabeth R. d/o James R. Thornton & Judith C. Pemberton b.d. 27 Aug 1807 d.d. 21 Jul 1831; KWH

THORNTON, Francis s/o James R. Thornton & Judith Coleman Pemberton b.d. 6 Sep 1805; KWH

THORNTON, James R. POR Gloucester (d.d. Feb 1834) & **PEMBERTON**, Judith Coleman d/o Wilson C. & Wealthean Pemberton; DOM 1804; KWH

THORNTON, James R. s/o James R. Thornton & Judith Coleman Pemberton b.d. 21 Feb 1812 d.d. 1 Nov 1849 at "Clifton"; KWH

THORNTON, Jane Pemberton d/o James R. Thornton & Judith Coleman Pemberton b.d. 31 Aug 1817 d.d. Aug 1848; KWH

THORNTON, John Anthony s/o James R. Thornton & Judith Coleman Pemberton b.d. 29 Oct 1826; KWH

THORNTON, John d.d. between 27 Oct 1729 and 13 Mar 1730; BP

THORNTON, John Wilson s/o James R. Thornton & Judith Coleman Pemberton b.d. 1 Jun 1814; KWH

THORNTON, Maria Susan d/o James R. Thornton & Judith Coleman Pemberton b.d. 28 Dec 1809; KWH

THORNTON, Sterling S. s/o James R. Thornton & Judith Coleman Pemberton b.d.6 Nov 1819; KWH

THORNTON, Wealthean d/o James R. Thornton & Judith Coleman Pemberton b.d. 11 Jan 1822; KWH

THORNTON, William A. s/o Jame R. Thornton & Judith Coleman Pemberton b.d. 6 Dec 1824; KWH

THORPE, Thomas d.d. between 21 Nov 1758 and 30 Nov 1759; SMP

THURSTON, Hesikiah W. s/o Benjamin & Julia Thurston age 23 S farmer POB POR King & Queen & **BEW**, Martha E. d/o Thomas Bew & Caty Brey age 23 S POB POR King & Queen; DOM 16 Apr 1856 POM King & Queen by Thomas B. Evans; KQMR

THURSTON, William s/o Benjamin Thurston age 22 S farmer POB POR King & Queen & **MILBY**, Elizabeth F. d/o Ro. & Mary Milby age 15 S POB POR King & Queen; DOM 2 Mar 1858 POM King & Queen by James C. Crittenden; KQMR

TIMBERLAKE, Elizabeth R. wi/o Henry Timberlake age 64 d.d. issue dated 29 Jul 1836 POD Pleasant Grove, King William; RCA

TIMBERLAKE, Mary Ann w/o Thomas N. Timberlake d.d. 17 Jan 1847 POD Barhamsville, New Kent; RCA

TIMBERLAKE, Thomas N. POR New Kent & **GRESHAM**, Mary T. S POR James City; POM James City DOM 21 Feb 1848 by Rev.J.S.R.Clarke; RCA

TIMPSON, Jude & Jane his wife imported to King & Queen Co by Barth. Fowler before 26 Apr 1698; C&P3

TODD, Frances B. w/o Rev. William Todd POR King & Queen eldest d/o Major Joseph Gwathmey POR King William d.d. 9 Jun 1820; KWC

TODD, Francis s/o William Todd POR King & Queen b.d.before 1693; C&P3

TODD, Margaret d/o William Todd POR King & Queen b.d.before 1693; C&P3

TODD, Marius P. s/o William B. Todd & M.C.Todd age 22 S farmer POB King & Queen & **BOYD**, Mary P. d/o Robert B. & Mary Boyd age 19 S POB King & Queen; DOM 27 Apr 1854 POM King & Queen by William B. Todd; KQMR

TODD, Thomas Waring d.d. 19 Dec 1828 POR POD Millbrook, King William; KWC

TODD, William minister POR King & Queen & **HILL**, Harriett s POR King William; DOM 10 Jan 1822; KWC

TODD, William POR King & Queen & **HILL**, Harriet POR King William S; DOM 10 Jan 1822; VG

TODD, William POR King & Queen d.d. between 29 Apr 1693 & 25 Oct 1695; C&P3

TOLER, Thomas U. POR King William & **HUNTON**, Catherine s POR King William; DOM 26 Dec 1826 POM Bear Garden by Rev. D. Atkinson; KWC

TOLER, Thomas V. POR King William & **HUNTON**, Catherine POR King William S; POM Bear Garden DOM 26 Dec 1826; VG

TOMPKINS, William Fleet b.d. 27 Sep 1781 d.d. 19 Apr 1829 s/o Christopher & Ann (Fleet) Tompkins; KWC

TOWNLEY, Robert & **ANDERSON**, Jane POR King & Queen DOM 29 Dec 1781; CCPR

TRANT, George attorney POR King William & **WALKER**, Mary E. d/o Thomas Walker POR King William; DOM 16 Dec 1806; KWC

TRANT, George attorney POR King William & **WALKER**, Mary E. s POR King William; DOM 15 Dec 1809; RE

TRANT, George POR King William & **WALKER**, Mary E. d/o Thomas Walker POR King William; DOM 16 Dec 1809; VG

TRANT, Lawrence & **HILL**, Fannie B. d/o Baylor Hill POR King William; DOM 10 Nov 1831 by Rev. Mr. Hatchett; KWC

TRANT, Lawrence & **HILL**, Fanny B. d/o Baylor Hill POR King William; DOM 10 Nov 1831; RW

TRAVERS, Elizabeth Teagle d/o Raleigh Travers &
Elizabeth S. Daniel b.d. 23 Jul 1836 d.d. 13
Sep 1837; MBC

TRENT, Joseph POR Richmond & **REYNOLDS**, Nancy s POR
New Kent; DOM issue date 26 May 1809 RE

TUCKER, Adolphus captain POR Brunswick & **RUFFIN**,
Mary E. d/o William Ruffin S late POR King
William; POM LaGrange, TN DOM 29 May 1834; RW

TUCKER, James Henry s/o John P. & Susan E.C.
Tucker age 25 d.d. 16 Jan 1847; RCA

TUCKER, John & **PIGG**, Frances POR King & Queen; DOM
18 Jul 1782; CCPR

TUNSTALL, Miles C. POR New Kent & **BURTON**, Eliza A.
POR New Kent S; ML Hanover Co DOM 4 Nov 1830;
CTR

TUNSTALL, Robert POR King & Queen & **SMITH**, Ann d/o
John Smith POR Richmond Co; DOM 7 Jan 1795;
taken from MARRIAGES OF RICHMOND COUNTY, VA
by George H.S.King

TUREMAN, John s/o George Tureman had tobacco
levied for his benefit 10 Oct 1743; SMP

TURNER, Charles & **COX**, Mary ; DOM 12 Aug 1695;
SPPR

TURNER, Henry & **BAKER**, Mary; DOM 6 Jan 1708/9;
SPPR

TURNER, James POR King William (Visitor newspaper
says he is from Bath) & **KING**, Mary p.m. POR
King William; DOM 6 Mar 1810; RE

TURNER, Jane Columbia w/o Benjamin Turner b.d. 11
May 1820 d.d. 17 Jul 1850 POR Locust Grove,
King William; VCA

TURNER, William & **WHITLOCK**, Dorthy; DOM 20 Apr
1726; SPPR

TYLER, John attorney POR Charles City Co &
CHRISTIAN, Letitia 3rd d/o Robert Christian
POR New Kent; DOM 29 Mar 1813; RE

TYLER, Kate Gresham w/o L.A.Tyler d/o E. & I.
Gresham b.d. 22 Jul 1849 d.d. 2 Mar 1893; MBC

TYREE, Lucy buried by 19 Oct 1772; BP

TYREE, Roger d.d. by 10 Oct 1761; BP

VAIDEN, Albert Henry s/o Melville Vaiden b.d.Jan
1847; KWH

VAIDEN, Ida d/o Melville Vaiden b.d.Apr 1851; KWH

VAIDEN, Mary Aspasia d/o Melville Vaiden b.d. 27
Sep 1845; KWH

VAIDEN, Mary Melville d/o Melville Vaiden b.d.7
May 1859; KWH

VAIDEN, Melville s/o Isaac & Judith Vaiden POR
"Lofty Retreat" New Kent & **STUBBLEFIELD**, Mary
Lucy; DOM 10 Mar 1840; KWH

VAIDEN, Melville s/o Isaac & Judith Vaiden POR New
Kent & **MEANLEY**, Maria L.; DOM 29 Jul 1859;
KWH

VAIDEN, Nancy d/o Ambrose Edwards POB King William
w/o Micajah Vaiden POR New Kent d.d.25 May
1835; KWH
VAIDEN, Olivia Anne d/o Melville Vaiden b.d.4 Mar
1853; KWH
VAIDEN, Sallie Anne d/o Isaac & Judith Vaiden
b.d.Oct 1821 POB New Kent; KWH
VAUGHAN, Alice J. d/o Ludford A. & Jane F. Vaughan
b.d. 13 Jun 1853; KQBR
VAUGHAN, John & POINDEXTER, Sara; DOM 5 Nov 1686;
SPPR
VENABLES, Abraham s/o Abraham Venables POR
St.Peter's Parish, New Kent b.d. 1700 d.d.
1769; SAR
VENN, John POR New Kent d.d. before 6 Jun 1699;
C&P3
VSA #34267
WADDILL, Anne d/o William Waddill Jr. bap 24 Jan
1713; SPPR
WADDILL, Elizabeth d/o Charles Waddill b.d. 31 Mar
1715; SPPR
WADDILL, Mary d/o John Waddill bap 27 Sep 1713;
SPPR
WADDY, Anthony s/o Anthony & Sarah Waddy b.d. 14
Dec 1714; SPPR
WADE, Grandison POR New Kent & BURNETT, Dicey POR
Hanover; ML Hanover DOM 2 Feb 1826; CTR
WADE, Granville POR New Kent & HIGGINS, Lucy POR
New Kent; ML New Kent DOM 18 Nov 1830; CTR
WAIDE, Edmund POR Hanover Co & ATKINSON, Delthy
Ann POR King William; ML King William DOM
16 Jan 1838; CTR
WALDEN, Benjamin & DUDLEY, Mary POR King & Queen;
DOM 29 Jan 1791; CCPR
WALDEN, Charles & ISON, Mary POR King & Queen; DOM
29 Dec 1791; CCPR
WALDEN, John & CRITTENDON, Frances POR King &
Queen; DOM 24 Mar 1792; CCPR
WALDEN, Richard & DUDLEY, Hannah POR King & Queen;
DOM 25 Oct 1792; CCPR
WALDEN, Richard s/o Richard & Catherine Walden age
50 W farmer POB POR King & Queen & GARRETT,
Mary d/o James & Joana Baker age 50 W POB
Middlesex POR King & Queen; DOM 27 May 1856
POM King & Queen by Isaac Digges; KQMR
WALDEN, Warner & WALDEN, Elizabeth POR King &
Queen; DOM 27 Oct 1787; CCPR
WALKER, Anne d/o William & Elizabeth Walker b.d.
26 Sep 1714; SPPR
WALKER, Baylor s/o John Walker & Elizabeth Baylor
& HILL, Frances d/o Humphrey Hill & Frances
Baylor POR Locust Grove; DOM 25 May 1759; FB
WALKER, Baylor s/o John Walker & Elizabeth Baylor
b.d. 28 Jan 1737; FB

WALKER, Elizabeth d/o John Walker & Elizabeth
Baylor b.d. 19 May 1741; FB

WALKER, Elizabeth d/o William Walker bap 28 Aug
1715; SPPR

WALKER, Frances A. d/o Major Humphrey Walker POR
King & Queen w/o John H. Walker of King
William age 63 d.d. 1854; VCA

WALKER, John & **BAYLOR**, Elizabeth DOM 9 Nov 1735;
FB

WALKER, John b.d. 7 Apr 1711; FB

WALKER, John s/o Humphrey Walker (s/o Baylor
Walker) & Frances Temple & **SHEPHERD**, Margaret
Watkins d/o William & Eliza Shepherd DOM 29
Jan 1829 POM Methodist Episcopal Ch,
Gloucester Circuit; Diary of John Walker

WALKER, Mary Peachy d/o Thomas & Susannah Walker
DOM 1732; Walker FB

WALKER, Robert POR King & Queen & **POWELL**, Nancy F.
PPOR Amherst; DOM 1 May 1792; VGGA

WALKER, Susannah d/o John Walker & Elizabeth
Baylor b.d. 28 Nov 1736; FB

WALKER, Tandy s/o Solomon Walker b.d. 13 [probably
Dec] 1714; SPPR

WALKER, Temple POR King & Queen & **TALIAFERRO**, Lucy
s POR King William; DOM 9 Aug 1821 by Rev.
Ro.B.Semple; KWC & VG

WALKER, Thomas s/o Thomas & Susannah Walker &
THORNTON, Mildred w/o Meriwether Thornton;
DOM 1741;   Walker FB

WALKER, Thomas s/o Thomas & Susannah Walker b.d.25
Jan 1715 POB King & Queen d.d.9 Nov 179_ POD
Albemarle; Walker FB

WALKER, Watson POR King & Queen & **TEMPLE**, Lucy
Waring; DOM 2 Dec 1858 POM Essex; Essex Co.
Marriage Register

WALKER, William & **CLOPTON**, Elizabeth; DOM 19 Jan
1713; SPPR

WALL, John d.d. 29 Nov 1773; BP

WALLER, John Walker d.d. 22 May 1815 POD King
William; KWC

WALLS, William s/o William Walls & Elizabeth Walls
age 26 S POB Middlesex Co carpenter & **BROWN**,
Sarah d/o Mandy Brown & Frances Brown; DOM 3
Dec 1852 POM King & Queen by W.S.Baynham;
KQMR

WALTON, Ann d/o George Walton bap or b.d. 13 Sep
1713; SPPR

WALTON, George & **ROPER**, Sarah; DOM Feb 1710/11;
SPPR

WALTON, Jane d/o George Walton b.d. 1715; SPPR

WALTON, Thomas Streshly b.d. 9 Oct 1853 d.d. 22
Jan 1923; MBC

WALTON, William M. s/o E.P. & Jennetta C. Walton
(E.P. was a preacher & teacher) b.d. 25 Sep
1853; KQBR

WARE, Jacob & **ADAMS**, Susanna; DOM 3 Feb 1790/1;
SPPR

WARE, John & **GREEN**, Susan POR King & Queen; DOM 8
Nov 1788; CCPR

WARE, Robert d.d. 1804 pastor of Lower King &
Queen Church; ONKH

WARING, John d.d. 11 Sep 1857 POD New Kent issue
date 19 Sep 1857; WA

WARREN, Robert d.d. 7 Oct 1822 POD Williams Ferry,
King William; KWC

WARRIN, John POR Wayinoak & **SPURLOCK**, Susanna; DOM
13 Oct 1709; SPPR

WASHINGTON, Cornelius age 25 S free POC POR King &
Queen & **GILMORE**, Julia age 20 S free POC POR
King & Queen; DOM 3 Jan 1860 POM King &
Queen; KQMR

WASHINGTON, John s/o John & Ann Washington age 27
S lawyer POB Caroline Co & **BOYD**, Roberta B.
d/o Robert & Mary A. Boyd age 17 S POB King &
Queen Co; DOM 7 Aug 1853 POM King & Queen by
William B. Todd; KQMR

WASHINGTON, W. & **VASS**, Ann eldest d/o Mordecai
Abrahams p.m. POR King William; DOM 11 Mar
1831 by Rev. Mr. Hatchett; RH

WATERS, James POR King William & **TOOMBS**, Judy POR
Hanover Co ML Hanover Co DOM 9 Jan 1834; CTR

WATERS, John POR King William & **TOOMBS**, Jane POR
Hanover; ML Hanover 4 Feb 1823; CTR

WATKINS, Edward s/o Lewis Watkins b.d. 3 Jan 1714;
SPPR

WATKINS, Elliza A. d/o Christopher & Sophia J.
Watkins b.d. 25 Aug 1853: KQBR

WATKINS, John Henry s/o John Wood Watkins and Lucy
Dix age 38 W farmer POB King & Queen &
DURHAM, Ann E. d/o George Durham & Frances
Dickison age 26 S POB King & Queen Co; DOM 1
Aug 1853 POB King & Queen by R.Y.Henly; KQMR

WATKINS, John s/o Lewis Watkins b.d. 27 Oct 1714;
SPPR

WATKINS, Lewis & **STONE**, Margaret; DOM 6 Jan
1711/12; SPPR

WATTS, Edward & **GARRETT**, Ann POR King & Queen; DOM
21 Dec 1787; CCPR

WATTS, Hugh & **MARYE**, Joanna POR New Kent DOM 29
Jan 1683/4; CCPR

WEAVER, Thomas & **STRANGE**, Judith; DOM 29 Jun 1715;
SPPR

WEBB, Dorothy w/o James Webb d/o Gabriel
Throckmorton d.d 7 Jan 1829 age 60; VCA

WEBB, Henry POR New Kent & **GORDON,** Susan E. d/o
Dr. Thomas C. Gordon POR Tappahannock, Essex;
DOM 1 Mar 1854; WA

WEBB, James s/o James Webb & Mary Smith d.d. 19
Feb 1832 age 69; VCA

WEBB, John & **MARTIN,** Mary; DOM 12 Feb 1712; SPPR

WEBBER, Augustin s/o Philip Webber b.d. 14 Sep
1713; SPPR

WEBSTER, Edward & **NEWMAN,** Judith aka Judith Jones;
DOM 27 Oct 1743; SPPR

WEBSTER, Joseph & **BAUGHAN,** Rebecca; DOM 18 Jul
1686; SPPR

WEST, John s/o John West & Unity Croshaw POR New
Kent & **ARMISTEAD,** Judith d/o Col. Anthony
Armistead POR Elizabeth City Co; DOM 15 Oct
1695; EHR

WEST, Nathaniel s/o John West POR King William &
MACON, Martha Woodard d/o William Woodard
wi/o Gideon Macon; DOM 1699; EHR

WEST, Robert s/o John West age 32 S sailor POB
King & Queen & **COOPER,** Emily d/o Qubar?
Cooper age 21 S POB King & Queen; DOM 29 Apr
1854 POM King & Queen by Isaac Diggs; KQMR

WESTMORE, William B. Dr. POR King William & **ROANE,**
Anna Maria d/o Thomas Roane; DOM 16 Aug 1820;
KWC

WHALE, John POR New Kent d.d.before 28 Oct 1697;
C&P3

WHITE, Alexander rector of St. David's Parish POR
King William d.d. 18 Oct 1776; KWC

WHITE, Oliver will dated Oct 1863 brother David
daughter Lucy; BKQCHS

WHITING, John d.d. between 1767 and 1771; SMP

WHORTON, Thomas Jr. & **HARRIS,** Honor; DOM 29 Sep
1709; SPPR

WIATT, Pitman & **FULLER,** Martha POR King & Queen;
DOM 1 Jun 1782; CCPR

WILK, Richard POR New Kent & **WOODWARD,** Sarah s POR
New Kent; married on the Thur.following 21
Apr 1836 by Rev. S.W.Jones; VCS

WILKINSON, James H. POR New Kent & **ARMISTEAD,**
Maria B. POR New Kent; DOM 26 Aug 1819 by
William Ratcliff; RCC

WILLAROY, Abraham POR St. John's Parish, King
William & **LIPSCOMB,** Dorothy d/o Ambrose
Lipscomb ((dec)) in King William by 2 May
1705; C&P3

WILLERY, John POR King William & **FAUKNER,** Mary
Jane POR Hanover Co S ML Hanover Co DOM 24
Jan 1835; CTR

WILLETT, James & **CROUCH,** Mary B. 3rd d/o James R.
Crouch POR King William; DOM 6 Apr 1820 by
John D. Blair; RCC

WILLFORD, Charles & ELLIS, Sara; DOM 15 May 1686;
SPPR
WILLIAMS, Adomiram & LUMPKIN, Syvelia d/o Robert
Lumpkin POR King & Queen; DOM 14 Sep 1848; VA
MARRIAGE BONDS OF RICHMOND CITY by Reddy &
Riffe
WILLIAMS, Bartlett attorney & CLOUGH, Sally s POR
New Kent; DOM 21 Dec 1781; VG
WILLIAMS, Beverley Julius POR New Kent d.d. 5 Aug
2838 POD New Kent; RW
WILLIAMS, Christopher b.d. 1763 POR King William;
VCA
WILLIAMS, David d.d. between 15 Oct 1744 and 23
Sep 1745; BP
WILLIAMS, Dumpen illigetimate s/o Mary Williams
FPOC b.d. 1 Nov 1853; KQBR
WILLIAMS, Elizabeth buried by 1 Oct 1767; BP
WILLIAMS, James b.d. 1763 POB POR New Kent d.d. 29
Sep 1840 & ____, Pattey b.d. 3 Aug 1765; DOM
7 Mar 1784; Rev Pension File 6506
WILLIAMS, James E. Dr. POR Newtown, King & Queen &
HARRISON, Mary F. d/o Robert H. Harrison
(dec) POR Caroline; DOM 18 May 1853; WA
WILLIAMS, James s/o James Williams POR New Kent &
RUTHERFOORD, Ann Maria d/o James B.
Rutherfoord; DOM 12 Nov 1816; VP
WILLIAMS, James s/o James Williams POR New Kent &
BROTHERHOOD, Ann Maria d/o Joshua Brotherhood
POR Richmond; DOM 12 Nov 1816 by John D.
Blair; RE
WILLIAMS, John s/o Randal Williams bound out 15
Oct 1742; BP
WILLIAMS, Montague merchant POR King William d.d.
7 Aug 1812; KWC
WILLIAMS, Randal d.d. by 15 Oct 1742; BP
WILLIAMS, Reuben E.W. s/o Isaac & Harriet Waller
age 22 S POB King & Queen farmer & EUBANK,
Dicey d/o Thomas & Lucy Eubank age 23 S POB
King & Queen Co; DOM 2 Jan 1853 POM King &
Queen by R.H.Bagby KQMR
WILLIAMS, Thomas d.d. between 21 Jun 1736 and 10
Oct 1737; BP
WILLIAMSON, Benjamin Temple age 28 POR King
William d.d. 20 Dec 1831; RE
WILLIAMSON, Elizabeth d/o John Williamson b.d. 24
Jan 1714; SPPR
WILLIAMSON, John POR Richmond & DUDLEY, Fanny s
POR New Kent; DOM 21 Feb 1807 by Rev.
McBlair; RE
WILLIAMSON, Robert C. merchant & CHAMBERLAYNE,
Lucy P. s POR King William; DOM issue date 2
Jun 1818 by Rev. John D. Blair; KWC

WILLIAMSON, Robert C. POR Richmond merchant &
CHAMBERLAYNE, Lucy P. s POR King William; DOM
26 May 1818 by John D. Blair; RE
WILLIAMSON, Robert C. POR Williamsburg &
CHAMBERLAYNE, Lucy P. POR King William S DOM
either 2 Jun 1818 or 26 May 1818; VG
WILLIS, Richard A. s/o John Willis age 37 W
waterman POB POR King & Queen & BRAY, Mary C.
d/o Thomas Bray age 28 S POB POR King &
Queen; DOM 11 Jul 1860 POM King & Queen KQMR
WILSON, John W. s/o Robert Wilson & Bouthy(?)
Meggs age 28 S free POC shoemaker POB
Gloucester POR King & Queen & WILLIAMS, Mary
E. d/o George Anson & Elizabeth Williams age
18 S free POC POB POR King & Queen; DOM 12
Jun 1856 POM Middlesex by Archer Bland KQMR
WILSON, Ruben B. s/o George Wilson & Frances Row
age 23 S farmer POB POR King & Queen & MINOR,
Eliza Ann d/o Ephraim Minor age 23 S POB
Bedford POR King & Queen; DOM 15 Dec 1859 POM
King & Queen by Howard W. Montague KQMR
WINCH, William POR New Kent & CUSTIS, Fanny Parke
d/o John Custis S; issue date 29 Jun 1739 VG
WINCH, William POR New Kent & CUSTIS, Fanny Parke
only d/o Hon. John Custis; issue date 29 Jun
1739; KWC
WINCHESTER, Arthur & BUTLER, Mary; DOM 21 Jan
1704/5; SPPR
WINFREY, Elinor d/o Jacob Winfrey & Elizabeth
Alford bap 6 Apt 1707 POB New Kent; SPPR
WINFREY, Elizabeth d/o Jacob Winfrey & Elizabeth
Alford bap 10 Apr 1709 POB New Kent d.d. 23
Aug 1709 POD New Kent; SPPR
WINFREY, Henry s/o Jacob Winfrey & Elizabeth
Alford bap 4 Feb 1710 POB New Kent; SPPR
WINFREY, Jacob POR New Kent & ALFORD, Elizabeth
d/o John Alford Sr.; DOM 3 Nov 1698 POM New
Kent; SPPR
WINFREY, Jacob s/o Jacob Winfrey & Elizabeth
Alford bap 14 May 1704 POB New Kent; SPPR
WINFREY, Jane d/o Jacob Winfrey & Elizabeth Alford
bap 25 Dec 1701 POB New Kent; SPPR
WINFREY, John s/o Jacob Winfrey & Elizabeth Alford
bap 24 Sep 1699 POB New Kent; SPPR
WINSTON, Anthony s/o Isaac Winston (prob.s/o
Anthony Wonston of New Kent) & Mary Dabney
b.d. 29 Sep 1723 d.d. 29 Feb 1747/8; SAR
WISE, Mahalah A. w/o John D. Wise d/o Thomas Lewis
(POR Accomack) age 36 POR POD King & Queen
d.d. 15 Feb 1847 RCA
WOOD, James POR King & Queen will dated 7 Jan
1722; VCA
WOOD, Robert & ALFORD, Mary; DOM 21 Oct 1711; SPPR

WOODWARD, Lancelot d.d. between 14 Oct 1748 and 18
    May 1750; BP
WOODWARD, P.T. b.d. 6 Apr 1821 d.d. 3 Jan 1892
    clerk of Middlesex Court; MBC
WOODWARD, R.H. Dr. b.d. 11 Sep 1825 d.d. 31 Oct
    1864; MBC
WOODWARD, Richard H. s/o Philomen & Elizabeth R.
    Woodward age 31 S Dr. POB POR Middlesex &
    POLLARD, Susan C. d/o John & Julia Pollard S
    POB POR King & Queen; DOM 6 Nov 1856 POM King
    & Queen KQMR
WOOLAMS, John & HENDERSON, Sarah; DOM Dec 1711;
    SPPR
WORMELEY, Carter W. POR Fredericksburg Dr. &
    LIGHTFOOT, Ellen B. d/o Philip Lightfoot s;
    DOM 10 Oct 1836 POM Port Royal by Rev.
    Friend; KWC
WORMELEY, John Taloe d.d. 16 Apr 1857 POD King
    William age 48 issue date 2 May 1857; WA
WORMELEY, John Tayloe age 48 d.d. 16 Apr 1857 POD
    Presque Isle, King William WA
WORMLEY, Carter W. Dr. POR Fredericksburg &
    LIGHTFOOT, Ellen B. d/o Philip Lightfoot S;
    POM Port Royal,Caroline issue date 11 Oct
    1836 RW
WRIGHT, John W. s/o Richard Wright age 24 S
    carpenter POB POR King & Queen & COSBY, Sarah
    E. d/o Leland Cosby age 21 S POB POR King &
    Queen; DOM 15 Dec 1859 POM King & Queen by
    Richard H. Bagby KQMR
WRIGHT, Mary L. w/o William G. Wright b.d. 27 Feb
    1834 POB Essex d.d. 16 Sep 1880; MBC
WRIGHT, Philip POR King & Queen & GARRETT, Frances
    s POR King & Queen; DOM 17 Dec 1818 by Mr.
    Todd RCC
WRIGHT, W.G. b.d. 28 Dec 1819 POB King & Queen
    d.d. 7 Dec 1897; MBC
WRIGHT, Wesley s/o William Wright & Catherine
    Garrett age 34 W Dr. POB King & Queen POR
    Middlesex & MOORE, Martha Ellen d/o Richard
    Moore & Louisa Watts age 23 S POB POR King &
    Queen; DOM 18 Jun 1856 POM King & Queen by
    Thomas B. Evans KQMR
WRIGHT, William H. s/o Robert G. Howerton &
    Elizabeth Howerton age 37 s POB Caroline
    house joiner & HOWERTON, Ellen V. d/o Beverly
    & Mary B. Wright age 21 s POB King & Queen
    Co; DOM 20 Feb 1853 POM King & Queen by Gi___
    Price The parents of the bride and groom seem
    to be reversed in the marriage register. I
    listed them the way they appeared in the
    register. KQMR
WYATT, Levi s/o Thomas & Caty Wyatt age 28 S
    farmer POB King & Queen & RICHISON, Catherine

d/o John & Sarah Richeson age 18 S POB King & Queen; DOM 4 Dec 1856 POM King & Queen by Isaac Digges KQMR

WYATT, Richard s/o Richard Wyatt d.d. 1768 POD King & Queen ONKH

WYNNE, Thomas H. s/o H.H.Wynne age 21 S farmer POB York POR Warwick & **HOWERTON**, Henrietta d/o Robert Howerton age 20 S POB POR King & Queen; DOM 5 Dec 1860 POM King & Queen KQMR

AARON 6
ABBOTT 9
ABRAHAMS 6
ABRAMS 6
ACRE 6
ACREE
6,32,45,54,57,98
ADAMS
1,6,7,8,28,54,81,96,10
7,118
ADDISON 8
ALDRIDGE 3,5,8
ALEXANDER 8
ALFORD 8,61,121
ALKINSON 18
ALLEN
1,2,9,10,11,13,25,38,6
9,106,108
ALLIN 4,9,67
AMESON 9
AMETE 9
AMMON 9,71
AMMONS 9,71
AMOS 9
AMOSS 9,108,110
ANDERSON
5,6,9,10,35,37,64,74,1
04,114
ANDREWSON 10
ANSON 121
APERSON 10
APPERSON 1,10,13
ARMISTEAD
10,11,90,106,119
ARMSTRONG 11,45
ARNOLD 11,14,42,112
ARNOTT 11
ASHCRAFT 11
ASHCROFT 11
ASHLING 11
ASKEW 11
ATKINS 11
ATKINSON
11,38,40,47,82,83,84,9
7,98,114,116
AUSTIN 11,12,109,111
AXFORD 12
AYLETT 12,42,47
BACON
1,2,12,13,24,32,47
BAGBY
13,14,22,32,46,53,54,5
8,64,69,100,106,120,12
2

BAGLEY 32,94
BAGWELL 14
BAILEY 14,21,64
BAITLE 28
BAITUP 28
BAIZEY 14
BAKER 115,116
BALL 14,75
BANKHEAD 53
BANKS 14,53,108
BAPIST 80
BARDRICK 14
BAREFOOT 14
BARKER 8,14,15,41
BARNETT 14
BARNS 15
BARRAM 15
BARRETT 15
BARRICK 15
BASSETT
1,15,16,17,18,33,38,40
,53,68,105
BATES 18,30,54,96
BATHURST 18,38,102
BATKINS 99,102
BAUGHAN 18,119
BAYLEY 34
BAYLOR
18,60,61,65,66,116,117
BAYLY 18
BAYNHAM 117
BELL 18,65,81
BEN 18
BERKELEY 18,74
BERRELL 18
BERTRAND 59
BETTES 18
BEVERLEY 100
BEW 113
BIBEY 19
BIDJEST 9
BIGGER 19
BINFORD 10
BINGHAM 19
BINNS 19,20,92
BIRD 5,20,54,73
BIVENS 77
BLACKBURNE 20
BLACKWELL 20
BLAND
5,6,20,28,41,60,121
BLAIR
20,30,64,97,119,120,12
1

124

BLAYTON   107
BLUEFORD   77
BOHANNON   20
BON   20
BOND   61
BOOKER   27
BOOTHE   23
BORER   21
BOSHER   21,38
BOSTICK   36
BOUGHTON   21,90
BOULES   21
BOULWARE
3,4,6,18,35,53
BOURN   21
BOWDEN   6,95
BOWERY   21
BOWLES   21
BOYD
11,21,110,114,118
BOYDE   21
BOZE   29
BRADGER   21
BRADLEY   69
BRAXTON   21,22,52,92
BRAY   22,113,121
BRAYS   4,5
BREEDEN   22,96
BRESLEY   105
BRIGGS   74
BRISTOW   9,22
BROACH   22
BROACHE   39
BROADDUS
35,79,96,100,108
BROCK   23
BROCOW   20
BROGMAN   23
BROKENBOROUGH   12,23
BROOK   23
BROOKE   23,53
BROOKER   23
BROOKING   23
BROOKS   23,58
BROTHERHOOD   120
BROTHERS   23
BROWN
6,10,23,24,35,46,61,76
,91,95,117
BROWNE
15,16,17,24,40,49,53,1
05
BRUMBRY   76,109
BRYAN   24

BRYCE   35,65
BUGG   24
BULLINGTON   45
BULLOCK   24,26,27
BURBIDGE   24
BURCH   25
BURCHELL   25
BURDETT   25
BURGESS   25,91
BURKE   25
BURNET   25,116
BURRUS   25
BURTON   25,35,50,115
BURWELL
16,17,18,26,33
BUTLER
26,43,44,103,121
BUTMAN   26
BUTTERFIELD   109
BUTTLER   26
BUTTS   1,4,6,26
BYRD   107
CADE   26,63
CAMBO   26
CAMM   26,27
CAMPBELL   27,35,58
CARLTON
5,27,34,46,108
CARPENTER   28
CARR   20,28
CARRINGTON   28
CARTER
9,17,22,28,53,79
CARTNEY   110
CARY   17
CASE   28
CATLETT   28
CAUL   12
CAUTHORN   41
CAVE   98
CHADICK   15,28
CHAFORD   28
CHAMBERLAYNE
15,16,28,29,57,97,120,
121
CHAMBERS   29
CHANDLER   29,33,110
CHAPELL   29
CHAPMAN   20
CHAPPELL   100,105
CHAPPILL   29
CHARLES   29
CHARLTON   29
CHASLIN   29

DIGGS
26,28,33,34,35,41,46,5
1,55,62,66,70,82,84,88
,93,96,101,102,119,123
DIKE   41
DILLAN   41
DILLARD   47,84
DINSMORE   41
DIX   41,118
DIXON   41
DOBSON   41
DOE   41
DOGGETT   101
DOLLARD   41
DOLLER   41
DORAN   41
DORMER   41
DOSWELL   42
DOUGLAS   42
DOUGLASS   42
DOWE   42
DOWNEY   85
DREWRY   42
DRUMMAND
47,49,50,51,91,107,108
DUDLEY
5,34,39,42,92,120
DUGAR   26,42
DULING   42
DUMAS   42
DUNCAN   42
DUNGEE   42,43
DUNGY   43
DUNKERTON   43
DUNN   53,106
DURBRIDGE   3
DURHAM   43,72,118
DUVAL   43,79,92
EACHO   43
EARNEST   43
EASLEY   80
EASTHAM   43
EASTWOOD   34,43,55,78
EDLOE   32
EDWARDS
14,25,36,43,44,45,58,7
9,94,116
ELLETT   44,45
ELLIOTT   45,105
ELLIS   45,120
ELLISON   45
ELLYSON   45
ELMOR   45
ELMORE   45

ENGLAND   46
EPECEN   46
EPERSON   46
EPPERSON   46
EPPES   9,46
EPPESON   46
ESROTT   46
EUBANK
3,25,27,46,59,80,120
EVANS
4,18.35,46,47,56,63,84
,122
FAIRFAX   47
FAKIRE   47
FALL   47
FARINHOLT   3,47
FARINHOLTZ   47
FARRAR   47
FARY   47
FAUKNER   119
FAULKNER   47,111
FAUNTELROY   33,47,48
FEARE   48
FENNELL   48
FERGISON   48
FIELD   1,2,5,6
FINALL   48
FINCH   43,48
FLEET
13,14,35,46,48,49,88,8
9,104,105
FLEMING   1,2,4,49,99
FLOYD   49,100
FOGG   49,50
FORD   30,32,50
FORGESON   50
FORTUNE   50
FOSTER   1,2,3,50
FOWLER   110,111,114
FOX
5,11,20,30,46,50,52
FRANCIS   75
FRANSES   50,51
FRAYSER   37,75
FRAZER   77,101
FREEMAN   51
FRIEND   122
FRITER   35
FULLER   119
FULLILOE   51
FURTIN   51
FUSSELL   15,20
FUZELL   51
FUZZELL   51

GADBERRY 51
GADDEY 51
GAINES
3,28,51,64,65,66,85,10
4
GALING 52
GARDNER 5,6,52,54
GARLAND 52
GARLICK
27,52,53,57,65,66,106
GARNETT
4,5,24,53,68,88
GARRARD 53
GARRAT 53
GARRETSON 53
GARRETT
6,24,27,44,53,54,78,11
6,118,122
GARROTT 58
GARY 44,47,54
GATEWOOD
21,40,54,62,80,93,94,9
5
GATHWRIGHT 68
GAUTERIE 54
GAYLE 54
GEDDY 55
GENTRY 55,107
GEROW 55
GIBSON 55
GILL 55
GILLAM 55
GILLIAM 12
GILLUM 55
GILMAN 55
GILMORE 51,118
GLASEBROOK 55
GLASS 55
GLEN 20
GLENN 20
GOALDER 55
GODDIN 55,56
GOING 56
GOLDMAN 4,56
GOODIN 56
GOODING 56
GOODINGS 56
GOODMAN 56
GOODWIN 56
GOOGER 2,3,56
GORDON 56,119
GOUGH 56
GOULDMAN 56,57,82,93
GOVAN 57,65

GRAHAM 70
GRAMSHILL 59
GRANGER 57
GRANTLAND 57
GRAVES 31,57,92
GRAY 57
GREADMAN 53
GREEN 57,58,101,118
GREENE 58
GREENWOOD 43
GREGORY 44,58,62,111
GRESHAM
1,4,5,58,59,110
GRESHEM 59,114
GREY 4,10
GRIFFIN
6,7,8,28,59,81,107
GRIFFITH 59
GRIGGS 59
GRINDLEY 59
GRISLEY 59
GROOM 59
GROSE 106
GUILLAM 59
GUNN 59
GUNNELL 59
GUTHERIE 59
GUTHRIE 5,27,55,60
GWATHMEY
4,37,42,51,52,53,60,61
,114
GWYN 61,99
HACHER 34
HAGGIN 12
HAGERTY
HALL 51,52,54,61,102
HALLYBURTON 61
HANFORD 39
HANKIN 101
HANKINS 102
HANNA 61
HANSFORD 107
HARDCASTLE 61
HARDDEN 61
HARFIELD 61
HARGROVE 61
HARMAN 19,61
HARPEN 42
HARPER 61
HARRIS 61,62,119
HARRISON 62,120
HART
2,4,27,41,55,62,74,88
HARTWELL 80

PARRISH 93
PARSONS 32,93
PASLEY 93
PATISON 94
PATTESON 13,93
PATTISON 93,94
PAUL 94
PEACE 94
PEACOCK 94
PEAKE 74
PEARCE 34
PEARSON 19,20,94
PEASLEY 94
PEAY 11
PEDLEY 94
PEEKE 94
PEIRCE 47
PEIRSON 94
PEMBERTON
44,45,58,94,97,113
PENDLETON
31,43,46,54,78,91,94,9
5
PENICK 95
PENNINGTON 95
PERKINS 95
PERRY 95
PERSON 95
PETERS 95
PETHWOOD 95
PEYTON 13
PHILLIPS 90,95
PHILPOTTS 107
PICKRING 95
PIERCE 49,95,96
PIGG 115
PILLSBERRY 42
PILSBERRY 78
PILSBURY 96
PINES 96
PINICK 96
PIRAM 96
PIRANT 96
PIRSON 96
PIRTLE 87
PITMAN 96
PITTS 42,96
PLANT 96,101
PLANTINE 96
PLEASANTS 30
PLUMER 84,92
POINDEXTER
32,69,96,97,116
POINTER 88

POLLARD
5,49,52,65,66,67,97,12
2
POMFREY 97
PONTIN 98
PONTON 98
PORTER 98,106
POSLY 12
POWEL 49
POWELL
37,42,49,58,98,117
PRICE 20,76
PRIOR 98
PRITCHET 18
PROSSER 98
PRYER 98
PULLAM 98
PULLER 98
PULLUM 98
PURDE 98
PURDEY 98
PURDIE 98
PYNES 66
PYRANT 98
QUARLES 32,98,99
RABINEAU 99
RAGLIN 99
RAGLING 99
RAMSEY 99
RANDELL 99
RANDOLPH 99
RAPIER 99
RATCLIFFE 84,99,119
RAWLEIGH 65,99
RAXFORD 99
RAYLE 99
RAYLEE 99
RAYMOND 99
REABY 99
READE 99
REAMY 100
REDD 100
REDDCOCK 100
REID 100
RENALL 100
RENALLS 100
RENN 89,100
REYNOLDS 34,100,115
RHODES 100
RICE 85,100
RICH 18,100
RICHARDS 101
RICHARDSON 9,29,101
RICHASON 25

WILLIAMS
64,75,120,121
WILLIAMSON 89,120,121
WILLIS 35,37,121
WILSON 9,121
WINCH 121
WINCHESTER 121
WINFREY 2,3,104,121
WINSTON 121
WISE 121
WOOD 121
WOODE 100
WOODWARD 26,80,122
WOOLAMS 122
WORMELEY 122
WORMLEY 122
WORTHAIN 72
WRIGHT
3,4,14,43,66,122
WYATT 55,122,123
WYNNE 123
YARRINGTON 5
YATES 64,99
YORRINGTON 35
YOUNG 4,5

Other books by the author:

CD: Heritage Books Archives: Virginia Marriage Records

Marriage Records of the City of Fredericksburg, and of Orange, Spotsylvania, and Stafford Counties, Virginia, 1722-1850

Marriage Records of the City of Fredericksburg, and the County of Stafford, Virginia, 1851-1900

Marriages in the New River Valley, Virginia: Montgomery, Floyd, Pulaski, and Giles Counties

Marriages in Virginia: Spotsylvania County, 1851-1900 and Orange County, 1851-1867

Marriages of Caroline County, Virginia, 1777-1853

Marriages of Orange County, Virginia, 1747-1880

Marriages of Orange County, Virginia, 1757-1880

Skeletons in the Closet: 200 Years of Murders in Old Virginia

Made in the USA
Middletown, DE
21 December 2019

81677063R00086